Steven Primrose-Smith was born in Darwen, near Blackburn, in 1970. He has a BA in English Language and Philosophy, a BSc in Mathematics and an MA in Philosophy. His first book, *No Place Like Home, Thank God*, an Amazon International bestseller, described his three-year, 22,000-mile bicycle ride around Europe during which he ate various unsavoury items including a brain, a handful of maggots and a marmot. He followed this with more bestsellers: *Route Britannia* tells of his 5,000-mile bicycle ride through every county in Britain; *Biking Broken Europe* visits dozens of odd and wonderful independence-seeking regions of Europe including three frozen conflict zones; *George Pearly is a Miserable Old Sod* is a comic novel about the most hated man on the Costa del Sol. *The Quest for the Holy Quail* is his ninth book.

Also by Steven Primrose-Smith

FICTION

George Pearly is a Miserable Old Sod

Love and Other Complete Wastes of Time

How Not To Be a Unicorn

TRAVEL

No Place Like Home, Thank God

Hungry for Miles

Route Britannia, The Journey South

Route Britannia, The Journey North

Biking Broken Europe

THE QUEST FOR THE HOLY QUAIL

A 3,000 Mile Plague-Time Bicycle Ride through Morocco and Its Freakiest Food

Steven Primrose-Smith

First published in 2020 by Rosebery Publications
1 Perwick Rise, Port St Mary, Isle of Man

Copyright © 2020 Steven Primrose-Smith
All rights reserved.
steven@primrose-smith.com

ISBN: 9798666519202

Except in the United States of America,
this book is sold subject to the condition
that it shall not, by way of trade or otherwise,
be lent, re-sold, hired out, or otherwise circulated
without the publisher's prior consent in any form
of binding or cover other than that in which it is
published and without a similar condition including
this condition being imposed on the subsequent purchaser.

Names have been changed where appropriate.

Photographs and maps related to this book can be found at *primrose-smith.com*.

Table of Contents

Chapter 1: Sleeping with a Policeman..7

Chapter 2: Mountains of Drugs..26

Chapter 3: A Tale of Two Cities..52

Chapter 4: The Worst of Morocco...70

Chapter 5: A Camel in the Capital..88

Chapter 6: The Pearl of the Atlantic...107

Chapter 7: The Ghosts of Agadir..122

Chapter 8: Long Live King Steven..135

Chapter 9: Stains and Desert Lanes...150

Chapter 10: Digging for Dinosaurs..168

Chapter 11: Gorging on Gorges..178

Chapter 12: Moroccywood..191

Chapter 13: An Infector Calls...201

Chapter 14: Dream Sequence...217

Chapter 15: No Way Out..228

Chapter 16: Run For Your Life..239

Chapter 17: A New Home..264

Epilogue..279

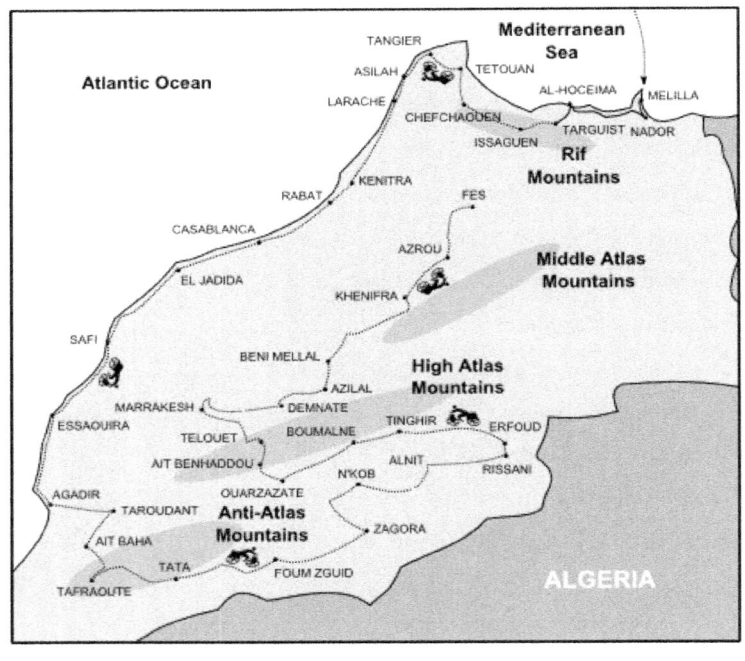

Fig.1: Steven's route through Morocco

Chapter 1: Sleeping with a Policeman

Melilla and Al-Hoceima

We crept along the dark alleyways of the medina, nervously peering into every recess we passed.

"He could be hiding in any one of these," I said, "ready to pounce."

Following behind us, Damian and his girlfriend Jo remained silently stoic but looked uncomfortable.

"He'll know these lanes like the back of his hand." We shared dark glances. "And he'll have friends here. Lots of friends."

"Maybe we should go back to the hotel."

"Maybe we should just go home in the morning."

"Yeah."

"Absolutely."

For a fun weekend mini-break, it'd be fair to say we'd got ourselves into a right old tizzy.

It had started pleasantly enough. We'd sailed a windless Mediterranean from Spain to Morocco's Tangier across the Strait of Gibraltar, only nine miles wide at its narrowest. From the coast it looks easily swimmable, if you don't mind fast currents, 300 ships a day and the occasional killer whale.

And we were researched up to the eyeballs. We'd head straight to the port-side train station in Tangier and hop on a carriage to Fes and a preselected hotel. We were all suitably covered, especially the women, whose bare skin would otherwise so terrify and titillate local sensibilities. Nothing could go wrong.

"Where you from?"

A scruffily double-denimed middle-aged tout latched on to us as we marched confidently out of the port.

"Ignore him," one of us said.

"Ah, you're English. You need a hotel?"

"No."

We carried on moving.

"I know a cheap place," he continued. "Very clean."

He stuck to us as we headed towards the train station. Surely he wouldn't follow us all the way to Fes.

We smashed through the station's main doors, expecting hordes of people, ticket offices and a flashing destination board. The airplane hangar-sized room was entirely empty except for one sad-looking official sitting at a tiny desk. He looked up, bored, tapping a biro, and told us the main station had relocated miles away. Collectively, we came to the conclusion it was too far to walk and no one wanted to chance a taxi. We'd read warnings about those buggers.

"Tangier's a big city," I said. "Maybe we should just stay here."

There was a round of general nodding. I can't remember why we'd originally discounted Tangier when it was the most obvious place to visit. I think there'd been warnings about that too.

So this was how we ended up in a town for which we'd done zero research. These were the days before Google Maps. Finding your way around strange places unassisted wasn't as easy as it is now. Rather than by phone, you were more likely to see people navigating by sextant.

Our Moroccan Frank Gallagher was still shadowing us.

"You want a hotel?"

I glanced at my friends, and each of us silently nodded.

"OK then."

The place he took us to was fine. Maybe we'd misjudged this fella. As we'd walked there, the looks we received from locals lining the alleyways felt aggressive. It wasn't long after 9/11 and George Dubya's resulting "crusade", when our TV screens were full of angry Muslim crowds burning western flags. And despite their conservative outfits, our girlfriends were looked up and down lasciviously. Well, perhaps. In reality, it was hard to tell what was imagined behind those narrowed eyes. Were they being mentally undressed or ritualistically butchered? We were glad of our guide, his local knowledge and protective aura.

"It's easy to get lost in the medina," he said. "I can give you a tour."

I couldn't speak for the others, but I'd felt a little freaked out by our introduction to Morocco.

"Only five euro," he continued.

We all agreed immediately.

For half an hour he took us around town, down twisting, indifferentiable lanes that appeared to go nowhere, pointing out mosques and little holes in the street where bread was baked. The place felt simultaneously exotic and as seedy as a strip club's toilets.

He harrumphed when we refused to eat at his cousin's restaurant and took us instead to the obligatory carpet shop. Thrust into our hands were glasses of mint tea, served at a temperature beyond which water should have long since boiled away. Trapped by manners and the desire not to offend, we were subjected to the salesman's spiel, which, unlike his carpets, was well-worn.

Apparently, these rugs were made in the mountains by the most skilled artisans, the finest in the whole of Morocco. They'd even been selected by King Mohammed VI himself. Sorry, we explained, but we weren't in the market for a carpet. Before the tea had cooled sufficiently to sip, we'd already refused another 73 times. Sensing failure, he switched tactics and admitted sales weren't what they ought to be and that business was tough. I necked my tea, scalding my throat in the process, thanked them for the drink and announced I was leaving.

"Please, no. Don't leave."

Apparently, carpet sales were so scant his children were starving to death. And his wife couldn't look after them, not with her leg off like that. And gangrene in the other. Oh, and his old mum had only last week fallen into that threshing machine. I may have got the details of his misery wrong, but we'd definitely arrived in Pity City.

The door bell tinkled as I reached the alleyway. The others, however, were being too British about this. None of them wanted a carpet, but they endured the salesman's patter for another ten minutes, thereby prolonging his period of unwarranted hope.

Our guide announced he was taking us back to the hotel. He'd have received commission on any carpet sale and was angry we hadn't provided one. Once in the hotel lobby, I handed him our agreed five euro fee.

And that's when it kicked off.

"No, it's five euros *each*!" he demanded.

Of course it was.

What followed was an unpleasant argument. I'm generally a non-confrontational wuss, nodding a cheery "Yeah, it's great, thanks" to all sorts of awful service and terrible restaurant food – waiters pouring tureens of tomato soup over my head or serving up an omelette with "I hate you" spelled out in pubes, that kind of thing – but I despise being purposely conned.

The battle wore me down. Wouldn't it just be easier to give him the money? After all, I thought, it wasn't a fortune. But that's how this con functioned and, goddammit, there was a principle at stake, I think.

"OK. If you don't want my five euros, I'll put it back in my wallet then." I turned towards my room. "Come on, guys."

That did it. Our angry scammer stomped out of the hotel, breathing fire, but with his five euros and not a cent more.

It was a Pyrrhic victory. We all felt deeply uncomfortable. Afterwards, when we walked the alleys by ourselves, those piercing stares now harboured an injustice to be avenged, typical English bastards that we were. We braved it out for a short stroll, but obviously us cruel whities deserved the destruction of the World Trade Centre and everyone in it. It was only a matter of time before four more deaths would be added to the grim count of deceased and deserving infidels. Or, first thing in the morning, we could just check out of the hotel and head back to the port. So that's what we did.

Yes, I know. We over-reacted. We should've been cooler, but Morocco had been a shock we weren't anticipating. Given the short distance to get there, I'd expected it to be Spain in smiling turbans, but it definitely wasn't that.

The thought of returning to Morocco had mildly terrified me for years. But in the intervening two decades I'd grown up. My last ride, the one that included the frozen conflict zones of Transnistria, Abkhazia and Nagorno-Karabakh (*Biking Broken Europe*) had given me a taste for the world's dodgier corners. I now realised our guide's anger was an act. He planned to intimidate us until we took the easy way out and handed over the cash. And if we didn't, he'd move on to his next victim and not give us another moment's thought. He certainly wouldn't waste his time murdering us. After all, we'd receive our punishment in the afterlife.

Face your fears and do it anyway goes the coaching cliché. It was time to return to Morocco and confront that fear, exorcise the demons of my 2002 visit. But there was an uneasiness that still lingered. In the days before I was due to leave, I realised I wasn't looking forward to this trip. I was apprehensive, although about what I didn't know, and sometimes that can be the scariest fear of all.

*

Two days into 2020 I rolled down the hill from Cómpeta, the pretty, whitewashed mountain village where I'd spent winter. The sun shone as I freewheeled uninterrupted for a glorious half hour, descending to sea level. Three hours later, I arrived a little drippily at Malaga's sea terminal. I had a ticket for the 11pm boat to Spanish-held Melilla, an enclave in Morocco that, along with similarly owned Ceuta, undermines any Spanish claim that, morally speaking, the UK should return Gibraltar to Spain.

After clearing security, which involved more X-rays than an afternoon with Evel Knievel, I wheeled aboard and into a room where everyone had to leave their belongings – suitcases, holdalls and bicycles – entirely unsecured. If you fancy a trip to Africa and can't be arsed to pack a case, book yourself on this Balearia ferry. Just ensure you're first into the luggage room upon arrival and you can have your pick of the bags.

I'd made a new friend, another cyclist, an amiable young Canadian bloke called Jackson, a first name I'd only ever heard attached to Mr Pollack, that purveyor of toddler-quality paintings. But what did I know? "Jackson" apparently reached its peak for American newborns in 2012, and so his mum should be commended for being ahead of the curve in naming children after famous singing paedos.

Twenty-four-year-old Jackson had devised an exciting adventure. He planned to cycle as far down the west coast of Africa as he could. I mentioned Essaouira, a place I was looking forward to that seemed to be on his route too.

"Nah, I'm not going anywhere touristy," he said. "I want to avoid the hassle of people trying to sell me stuff."

He told me a story of how he'd been scammed in Cambodia. A young lad of about twelve had presented

Jackson with his little brother, a baby with a half-mangled face. Both his parents had died, the boy said, and he was doing the dutiful thing, bringing up his sibling alone.

"Please can you buy him some baby food?" he asked Jackson, who kindly agreed to go with him to the shop. "No, not that type. He's allergic to that. He can only have that one," the boy said, pointing to a particular brand, the most expensive in the shop.

Jackson thought it odd this poor lad would go for such a pricey product, but allergies were allergies. He made his purchase and gave the food to the grateful boy. Jackson later saw the same child, now minus his baby brother, down a backstreet, sniffing glue.

Once Jackson was out of the picture, the baby food was returned to the shop. The shopkeeper got a cut, as did the mother of the disfigured baby, and the child scammer spent what was left on Pritt Stick. It was a scheme worthy of Wile E. Coyote but, y'know, involving drugs and disabled kids.

He told me this story as we sat in the ferry's cafeteria, the only place we were allowed on board since neither of us had bought a cabin. Normally, ferry companies provide an airplane-style seat for us cheapskates to sleep in. Not this one. Our facilities were designed to be uncomfortable, our punishment for skimping on a room. All we had was a bench seat, individually divided to prevent lying down, that came up to the height of our lower backs. Signs told us we couldn't put our feet on the free-standing chairs and that we also weren't allowed to take off our shoes. There was probably a member of staff on hand whose duty, should we nod off, was to sprinkle broken glass into our mouths.

With the option of sleep removed, at least the ferry had food. Sort of. A weary ham panini, heated to just the right temperature to encourage maximum botulism, a coffee and a Fanta came to ten euros. I'm not saying Balearia is the worst possible option when crossing the Mediterranean, but, if you want a recommendation, perhaps first consider learning how to windsurf.

After my gourmet dinner I found a way to fold myself up like a hedgehog and catch a few minutes' sleep. The bright lights and refrigerated air pumped into the cafeteria all night long didn't help. Balearia had clearly taken sleep deprivation advice from the KGB.

Jackson had a better idea, one that didn't contravene any of the rules. He clambered over the seats and fell asleep in the gap between the cafeteria's curtains and its windows, an option not available to larger people. He believed himself to be invisible to the room, until his arse was slapped in the middle of the night by a young Moroccan fella. Perhaps he'd mistaken long-haired Jackson for a woman, but maybe he didn't care. After all, it's illegal to have sex outside of marriage in Morocco and the ensuing religiously-decreed sexual frustration might spill over into fondling any human at all, regardless of gender.

As the ferry slowed and an announcement to disembark was made, Jackson unfurled himself from his cosy nest.

"How did you sleep?" he asked.

"In the shape of a question mark."

*

At six in the morning, it was still dark when we arrived in Africa. We cycled out of the ancient port under Melilla's huge fortified walls and hunted for a café with little expectation of finding one open so early. But as we hit the town centre we stumbled upon one just setting up its outdoor plastic seating. Coffee was available and not at Balearia's stupid prices. And we could even take off our shoes if we wanted.

As we sat there, a Spanish bloke called Galvino kept bothering us. He spoke with a barely comprehensible accent and tried to give us tobacco, although we suspected it was something stronger. He left our table but then returned with a torch he also wanted to donate. Maybe he was just a nutter. This was confirmed when he came back again with a rain jacket for us. He got annoyed that we didn't want his crap, but we both had everything we needed. The bar manager eventually came out and gave him a telling off.

"Aren't you scared of cycling through Morocco?" Galvino asked us. He looked genuinely concerned. Should we be? The trepidation I'd felt in the days before the trip had subsided now I was here. OK, this wasn't Morocco yet, but the adventure had begun.

But why was this guy scared of a country just a mile or two up the road? Maybe there *was* a reason to fear it. Or perhaps it was that Balkan thing where each country's neighbour is full of thieves and murderers. That is, until you see it for yourself, and then you're told the land you've just left behind is the one with the terrifying criminals.

Originally, it'd been my plan to enter Morocco as soon as I could, but Melilla looked worthy of a longer viewing. Jackson disagreed. By eight o'clock it was properly light and time to continue on his way. I wished him well and off he cycled, leaving me alone with the idiot.

Within minutes, Galvino's dopey sister turned up. She ordered a large glass of juice and two toasts with paté, which she devoured noisily, not dissimilar to a warthog masticating a bucket of egg custard. Starting the day with a kick, Galvino was already on his fourth glass of anise. I got the feeling they were both going to stand up simultaneously, thank me for my generosity and then do a runner, leaving me with the bill. Pre-emptively, I quickly paid my share and said goodbye, still clueless as to why he'd attached himself to us.

It turned out I was wrong about Melilla, the old town being the only part worth seeing, reminiscent of Malta's Valletta. The rest of the place was a scruffy hole. And so I made the short, mile-long ride to the border, where I found chaos. On the Spanish side, hundreds of people sat around, waiting for something to happen. The place felt tense, as though if someone suddenly shouted "Boo!", everyone else would start screaming in horror.

I was a little concerned about my passport. Stored in jostling panniers for months on end, the gold embossed foil on its front cover, the text telling the customs official it was a passport at all, had been rubbed off. Maybe they wouldn't even let me in.

I came to a booth and showed my subpar paperwork. The guy inside spoke good English and asked me a few questions about my visit.

"Thank you," he finally said. "And welcome to Morocco!"

The world shifted, and not with any subtlety. Just over the border was Beni Ansar, the scruffy port town of larger Nador, nine miles up the road. It was instant Africa, or at least Africa as presented on TV from the busier and ropier parts of Nigeria. People, men mostly, were everywhere and the air smelled of burning tyres. Despite a bright, sunny day over the border in Melilla, here visibility was reduced by fumes and pollution. Dust was thick and hung in the air, crunching in my teeth. Every building was in the process of going up or falling down. If someone had told me the place was pulling itself back together after a recent earthquake, I wouldn't have been surprised. Indeed, there had been a 6.3 magnitude quake near here just four years before, although with only one death and fifteen injuries, I doubt it could be blamed for the current mess. It wasn't the best introduction to Morocco.

I kept moving and reached the city of Nador itself. The main road through this town of 160,000 didn't improve things aesthetically but added new features. Goats scavenged on patches of roadside wasteland. A head-scarfed woman sat nearby tending two sheep and a lamb. You don't see that in the centre of Blackburn.

My mind turned to practicalities. Legally speaking, you can't take more than a small amount of Moroccan currency in and out of the country. You'd have nothing to gain by doing so. The exchange rate outside Morocco is awful. I found an ATM and extracted as much as the machine would allow, 2000 *dirham* – about 200 euros – but I'd no idea how many days this would keep me fed and housed. Of the 132 countries listed on Numbeo's Cost of Living Index with rip-off Switzerland in first place, Morocco came in 104th. That was good news. Maybe my 200 euros would last the entire three-month trip.

I continued through Nador as the flat road turned hilly. With my post-Christmas blubberiness, it was going to take a week or two before I was comfortable again with climbing.

I stopped for a breather and a sleek, black car pulled up beside me. The driver, a well-groomed young fella, leaned over the passenger seat and offered to buy me a coffee. While this may have been a genuine act of kindness, I felt a little like a grubby urchin being picked up by a Moroccan Richard Gere. Our conversation was conducted in French, which perhaps added a frisson of sauciness. I'd been practising the language for the last few months and maybe it was my improved linguistic skills that enabled me to decline his offer politely rather than being railroaded into potentially lucrative but ultimately unwelcome bum sex.

In the early days of a new country, you notice unusual things that very quickly become the new normal. Here it was people, that they were *everywhere*, including the most unlikely places. Once I'd cleared town and was now out in what felt like a prolonged stretch of uninhabited wilderness, people – and when I say people I mean almost exclusively men – hung about at the side of the road, doing precisely nothing. While rolling, I like to play a game with myself that I call "Could I wild camp here?" However, every time I spied a potential location, a human would appear to render it compromised.

I was heading towards the Mediterranean coast road and a little way in front was another cyclist, a local. Nothing unusual about that, you might think. But the man suddenly swerved on to the opposite side of the road and stopped to examine a hunk of roadkill. After nudging the flattened creature with his sandal, he decided it unworthy of collection, or perhaps he was just leaving it to mature for a bit.

I hit the coast and trundled slowly westwards with low orange cliffs to my left and the blue Med beneath me to my right. Sadly, the beaches below were deep with cans and bottles and contained more plastic than Sharon Osbourne's face. There were few houses around here and fewer tourists. Either this pollution had accumulated slowly over years or had come from the sea. Whatever the reason, any modern Robinson Crusoe who popped a message into a bottle would have his rescue plea lost in the thousands washed up alongside it.

I was getting hungry and an opportunity presented itself. A roadside hawker was selling thirty-centimetre-diameter flatbreads.

"*Combien?*" I asked, enquiring how much the bread was.

He hopped from one foot to the other shiftily, claiming not to understand French. Although it's an official language of Morocco, along with Arabic, many people speak one of the Berber tongues instead. Even so, it seemed unlikely he didn't know the one French word most useful to a Moroccan salesman. It'd be like a Russian oligarch living in London and not understanding the words "tax evasion".

I was at a disadvantage, not having a clue how much the bread should cost. I also had no change, only the notes provided by the ATM. The bloke was more than happy with the twenty dirham, or two euros, I paid for two flatbreads. Of course he was. I later learned he'd overcharged me at least threefold. Still, a thing's true value is what it's worth to the buyer, and my hunger was definitely a two-euro one.

On the subject of money, throughout this book I'll list prices in *either* dirham *or* euro. To convert from the Moroccan currency to the European one, simply divide by ten. Sterling or US dollars are usually within 10% of the euro value these days. If you operate in Vietnamese dongs, I'm afraid you're on your own.

I was using the mapping app MAPS.ME. It informed me that no accommodation lay anywhere upon this road until the city of Al-Hoceima, too far for a chubster like me to reach today. Fortunately, in the early evening I saw an unlisted hotel. Unfortunately, it was closed.

As the day's light faded, I resigned myself to a night of wild camping. The land to my left was steep and rocky, offering nowhere to sleep. On my right was a cliff edge, although at times half a mile from the road, and I'd seen occasional tents pitched near to it. Maybe camping around here was not only allowed but popular. Or perhaps they were so far from the road that no one in authority could be arsed to give them a good talking to. Either way, it felt like permission of sorts.

I bumped my bike and bags over rocks and gravel to an ideal spot, close to the cliff edge but perhaps 300 metres from the road and mostly invisible to passing traffic. I tossed away any stones I didn't want sticking into my back all night long. I created a pitch as welcoming as a hug from Courtney Love, which is to say entirely inviting but still slightly rough.

I'd read that even official Moroccan campsites were generally dry and stony, and so I'd bought a new tent, one capable of standing without pegs, a requirement also for desert camping. Despite this being only the second time I'd built my little house, everything clipped into place with ease.

I stood back to admire my erection – oh, c'mon! – and was just about to take a photo of my first successful night's camp when I saw someone walking towards me from the road. Oh joy, it was a policeman.

"*Bonsoir!*" I said with the biggest smile I could muster. He didn't seem so happy. He muttered in what I took to be Arabic. I asked if he spoke French. He said he didn't but peppered whatever message he was trying to convey with frequent blasts of "*Interdit!*", the ineffectual French word for "forbidden". This wasn't good. Maybe my first night in Morocco was going to be spent in a prison cell.

In our basic French, we had a conversation.

"You need to leave and find a hotel," he said.

"The only hotel is closed."

"Then cycle to the next town."

"It's thirty miles away. It's dark. I have no lights."

He thought for a second.

"*Interdit!*" he barked uselessly.

There was something odd about this situation. Plod had appeared too quickly. Traffic around here was light. No one lived nearby. I doubted anyone would have reported me. Besides, what was the difference between my tent and all the others I'd seen on the clifftops?

He grew bored of me and paced about, kicking stones around. I suddenly realised what was happening. He'd found me *accidentally* and I was inconveniencing him. Yes, wild camping was illegal in Morocco, but he wanted me to move primarily because I'd nabbed the best spot around here. I later learned those clifftop tents were used by the authorities to keep a night-time eye on the Med, watching for illicit drug or people traffickers. It was basically a coast-wide stakeout operated by a team of middle-aged boy scouts.

By now I'd run out of French and so reverted to English.

"I tell you what. I'm not going – I *can't* go – but I'll just move my tent over there a little bit and leave you in peace here."

I cleared some stones from a slightly sloping patch of ground fifty metres away, carried the still-erect tent and climbed inside. The policeman disappeared for a moment, presumably back to a parked car, and returned with a tent of his own, a small, crappy, pop-up one full of large tears. If he'd known how defenceless I was to refuse, he should have requisitioned mine at gunpoint.

I slept as securely as I've ever done while wild camping. My first night in Morocco and the country had provided an armed guard.

*

A safe sleep it may have been, but it wasn't a comfortable one. A stray stone dug into my kidney every time I turned over. So I stopped moving and ended up stiffer than Jacob Rees-Mogg.

As I pushed my bike back to the road I stared through the holes of the policeman's tent. It looked empty. Maybe he'd rolled in the night and gone over the edge.

The scenery was more interesting today. Rather than lone houses there were small villages set back from the road and low but rugged, Trump-coloured mountains, folded into an alien landscape.

In total I passed through five police roadblocks, something that would become a daily feature of life in Morocco, but none was interested in me. This might change if they ever found that copper's body at the bottom of last night's cliff.

I moved sluggishly, desperate to stop for the day. I saw a sign saying I had just five miles to reach Al-Hoceima, my first explorable Moroccan town. Unfortunately, those five miles took me two sweaty hours. The town was built on a series of steep hills, and I climbed every one to reach its centre. There was a lot of pushing involved, but even this wasn't easy with deep roadside gravel on steep tarmac and pavements with foot-high kerbs to negotiate.

By the time I reached the centre I was ready to collapse. All I'd eaten all day was what remained of yesterday's now stale bread. I was so looking forward to my first proper Moroccan meal. And while we're on the subject of food, this is the right time to explain my objective. If you've read my other travel books, you'll know I'm a sucker for local dishes, the weirder the better, whether that's a marmot in Switzerland, an intestine sandwich in Turkey or poo-flavoured sausages in France. And Morocco has some *very* strange examples. I won't list them now – we'll meet them in time – but there were two of particular importance.

The first, probably because it sounded so disgusting, was stuffed camel spleen. Most people would balk at camel or spleen individually, let alone together, and then you have the additional mystery of what the hell it's stuffed with. I couldn't wait to try it. But such prizes weren't everywhere in Morocco, and for this tasty morsel I'd have to hang on until Fes, a city I planned to visit near the end of my ride.

Even more elusive was something I wasn't sure actually existed in the real world. One popular dish in Morocco is *pastilla*, a filo-like pastry traditionally stuffed with pigeon, although these days chicken is more common. But I found a web page that mentioned a special variety of this pie, one filled with a little bird that appears in the Torah, the Bible *and* the Koran. Could there be a more meaningful quest than one for the Holy Quail?

I arrived in Al-Hoceima, a town of 90,000 people or perhaps 280,000. My online and offline sources differed significantly. The true figure, whatever it was, lay somewhere nearer the higher number, given the hillsides densely encrusted in tower blocks.

Al-Hoceima wasn't a stunning city, but I'd nothing to

compare it to on this side of the Med. According to its entry on Wikipedia, it goes by the nickname "the Pearl of the Mediterranean", although if you search on that phrase alone, the internet seems to think this title rightfully belongs to Alexandria or Nice or Barcelona or Valencia, or in fact any sizeable coastal town that isn't Al-Hoceima.

For an ancient land like Morocco, this little city is almost Milton Keynesian in its modernity, having been built by the Spanish as recently as 1925. However, this was still long enough for a lot of it to look like it was falling down. Was it just shoddy building or the result of a serious earthquake here in 2004 that killed over 600 people? I didn't know. And it seemed rude to ask.

My sparkly Art Deco hotel was an establishment entirely out of place in its much shoddier neighbourhood. After my first Moroccan shower – hot water wouldn't be a given in future hotels – I went out for a stroll and immediately realised one challenge I was going to face in Morocco.

The market in Al-Hoceima was a dot compared to those in the country's bigger cities, but I still got lost. It contained all the elements I'd later learn to be part and parcel of larger *souks*: There was the stench of fish guts, tiny cages stuffed with live chickens and pigeons – notably there were no quails – stalls piled high with olives and dates, and mountains of multi-coloured fabrics. Here it all fit into a space not much bigger than a tennis court and still I lost my bearings.

But the ghosts of that previous visit to Morocco were already being exorcised. Although the only white face in these narrow corridors, I didn't feel unwelcome. If I caught someone's eye, it was followed by a smile, not a murderous stare. Morocco felt like it was going to be more Fred Flintstone than Fred West.

My hotel included a café. Once I'd taken a seat there, its menu seemed uninvitingly western for someone on the prowl for the weird, but maybe it was better to ease my way into this new continent's food gently. I ordered a plate of *viande hachée* – minced meat patties – with chips, a tomato and olive salad, and a couple of mint teas, the whole lot under five euros. It was all tasty enough, especially as it was the first non-bread food and non-water drink I'd had since I'd left Melilla thirty-odd hours earlier, but it lacked the anticipated excitement of that stuffed camel spleen.

Today being a Sunday in January, Liverpool and Everton were battling it out on a big screen. Moroccans love their football. Life here didn't feel much different to Spain's Costa del Sol except that none of the clientele had a beer in front of him, and, yes, every single person in the room *was* male.

As I ate, I watched the match. Despite there being just one goal, the Arabic commentator was close to orgasm the whole time, such was his breathless hysteria. He only exhaled three times per half.

After the game, seeking something sweet, I visited a patisserie and bought a trio of pastries. With its French influence, I'd assumed cakes here would be of a high standard. Sadly, if they'd been influenced by any region, it was the Sahara. They were a bit on the dry side.

But after today's effort, this still wasn't enough and the real highlight of the day would arrive in the form of my second dinner. I was determined to find an alternative to the soft option of the hotel's menu. A couple of places advertised themselves as restaurants, but they were full of men huddled over coffees, eating nothing. I was about to give up when somewhere caught my eye, a dark corner of the street garishly lit with flashing green and red strip lighting. It suggested a brothel rather than a fine diner, but I could see a man behind a counter surrounded by kitchen implements. There were no customers, mind.

I went inside. It was an oddly decorated place with a

grubby checkerboard floor. The lower halves of its walls were tiled while the upper part was painted lime green and covered in a brightly coloured collage of fruit photos. It was like someone had overdosed on Skittles and then violently puked on the walls.

To announce what I hoped would be a passionate affair with their food, I chose the Moroccan organ most associated with love. Here it's the liver rather than the old ticker. On any "I Love Marrakesh" t-shirts, do they exchange the customary red heart with a sloppy pile of brown stuff? That could send a different message entirely.

My choice was a Moroccan classic, the lamb's liver sandwich. The meat was chopped, lightly grilled and served with salad on a partly hollowed out baguette and a decent sprinkle of cumin. It came with crunchy chips and another sweet mint tea, a drink I was quickly becoming addicted to. It was all utterly delicious, the liver still soft and juicy. Why don't we eat more of it in the West? It's cheap, flavourful and as healthy as the animal it comes from, although this isn't saying much if your farmer gets his sheep smacked off their tits on antibiotics. It didn't matter. Gastronomically speaking, I'd finally arrived in Morocco.

*

Meanwhile, unknown to me, 6,000 miles away on the other side of the planet, a few dozen people had developed a nasty, persistent cough, and it was only going to get worse.

Chapter 2: Mountains of Drugs

The Rif Mountains and Chefchaouen

The next morning I wandered downstairs to the café, the hotel's passageways smelling deliciously of cumin. There was a choice of breakfasts and so I went for the most Moroccan, a pile of *msemen*, a spunky sort of thick, crispy but pleasantly chewy pancake, served with olive oil, apricot jam and some olives. It also came with a couple of triangles of La Vache Qui Rit, a French take on Dairylea. At the time, the fake cheese had seemed inauthentically out of place, but it's actually produced here and I'd soon discover it's included with *every single* breakfast in the country. It's as Moroccan as a carpet and even easier to spread.

Today I'd be heading towards the country's Danger Zone, the Rif Mountains, the home of its cannabis farms and the bruisers who protect them. The range's name inspired the word "reefer". I could have avoided them and stuck to the coast, but where'd be the fun in that? Besides, these hills possessed a jewel in the form of Chefchaouen, the Blue City, and apparently you can't claim to have "done" Morocco if you don't see it.

The climb out of Al-Hoceima inevitably included more pain and a great deal of pushing. Even lugging the bike up its steep pavements was hard work. And then suddenly it wasn't. I turned around to see a smiling policeman giving my machine a little physical assistance. Once he'd had enough, I continued on my way, wearily pushing alone. But this time it suddenly became even more difficult. I spun around again and saw an old woman leaning on my bike for a rest. That's how slowly I was going.

I eventually left civilisation behind. For a town that had seemed so high from the bottom of yesterday's daunting climbs, Al-Hoceima now lay far below me, orange fumes hanging over the city like the world's worst fart.

I was now entering a different land, but one that felt familiar. The mental image most people have of Morocco is of a dry, dusty desert. But here the landscape is almost identical to what lies on the other side of the Mediterranean at this time of year. Its green hills were studded with olives and cacti. For the most part, Spain has turned its back on cultivating its awkward slopes. There, the ancient terraces that converted steep gradients into manageable shelves of possibility have now mostly crumbled. In Morocco it's a different story. The farmers here are still busy. But give it a decade or three and the terraces will be gone and replaced by slimy Moroccan estate agents flogging expensive but cheaply built villas to wealthy northern Europeans.

I was getting through a lot of water and so I stopped to buy two more bottles. I also had two empties to throw away. The shopkeeper didn't want to take them, but he popped the bottles into a crate belonging to the shop next door. Problem solved, or at least reassigned.

Plastic and waste in general are big issues in Morocco. Today, on a hillside with some of the most glorious distant views I'd ever seen, the situation at my feet was depressing, a huge area littered with thousands of carrier bags, several entangled in each and every thorny shrub. In 2016, Moroccans consumed 25 billion plastic bags a year. Now they're banned entirely. But unless someone can be bothered to clean up the hills, these old, undead bags will continue to haunt them for decades.

Approaching a village, I saw a sight that triggered a mental warning: Kids! I'd read about their love of lobbing stones at passing cyclists. A small group of twelve-year-olds stood in the distance. One of them bent down to pick up a rock. His mate was already tossing one in the air. I may have been wearing a helmet, but I didn't want to be stoned to death. Don't you normally get to commit adultery before that happens?

I decided to tackle this situation psychologically. I needed to make myself human in their eyes, someone like themselves who'd prefer not to get hit in the head with a rock. But I wanted to add another element. I cycled directly towards them, stopped, stared the largest one in the face and yelled *"Bonjour!"* in a voice that hopefully conveyed both humanity and mental instability. He shrunk back. I smiled widely and I shouted the hello again. The group shared concerned stares. At least they weren't throwing things. One last time, I bawled a kindly greeting at them. One of the smaller kids bleated a meek reply. I think he just wanted shut of me.

"Merci bien," I said, with what I hoped was a manic grin, and pedalled off, unstoned.

The views of the distant High Atlas Mountains kept me captivated for what was a long and strenuous day. With no reason to believe I had any chance of success, I stopped in the 2,000-strong village of Bni Hadifa and asked a couple of guys if there was a hotel.

"No, there isn't," the first one replied.

"Oh yes, there is," responded the second.

This uncertainty suggested tonight's digs weren't going to be a shiny, obvious sort of establishment. I was given directions, but they didn't work.

"Turn right at the *lavage*," another guy told me. This is usually the word for a car wash, but here it was a scruffy bloke with a bucket and a sponge.

It took the unsuccessful help of four more people scattered around town before I concluded it was the first guy who'd been telling the truth all along.

I tried one last time and luckily the young fella I asked walked me directly to the hotel's front door. No wonder I hadn't found it. It was the size of a terraced house and, being as charitable as possible, looked what you might call "distressed".

I walked in slowly. The insides matched the grimness of the outside. There was no one about.

"*Bonsoir!*" I yelled. Nothing. I tried again, but still there was silence. I wandered down a corridor and, through an open door, saw a woman lying in bed. She, the owner's wife, jumped up, jabbering something and then showed me a room.

"*Combien?*" I asked.

"*Cinq,*" she replied.

Five? Surely not. I took out a five dirham coin and gave it to her.

"*Cinq?*" I said unsurely.

Of course not. Morocco was cheap, but it still wasn't 1970s India. Apparently, she'd meant seventy. Obviously.

The space I paid for was not so much a room as a cell, two metres by two metres filled entirely with a double bed. The ceiling was bare concrete, the rough walls painted salmon pink. The blue door, with its busted lock, matched the peeling paint of the single window frame. It was the sort of place you could imagine Terry Waite chained to a radiator. Except there was no radiator. That said, it was all I needed.

The owner appeared and his wife squealed excitedly that they had a guest, and a Frenchman no less, which says more about her French ability than mine. He demonstrated how to lock my door from the inside using the bolt. That was as good as the security got. If I left the room, I had to slam the door shut, but to get back in again I just gave it a little push.

I needed food. While hunting for my room I'd passed a

restaurant with an outdoor grill. Tasty wafts of barbecued meat had almost caused me to delay my search while I grabbed some calories instead.

It was now half five and the sun had disappeared behind a nearby hill. After a warm afternoon, the sudden drop in temperatures made the mountain village feel Arctic. Wrapped in two fleeces, I returned to the grill on foot, pointed to whatever was being cooked and told the chef I'd have one of those. I didn't care what it was. I took a seat inside.

Normally the concept of indoors is one that suggests warmth. Here, however, the double doors that made up the entire front end of the restaurant were wide open. My breath formed thick clouds.

Unlike last night's place, tonight's had customers. Three women were sitting in the corner, sharing a plate. Two other groups of men came in while I waited and ordered the same as me. This was little Bni Hadifa's most happ'nin' joint.

For a few minutes I sat there, taking in my surroundings but mostly blowing out great plumes of cloudy breath and pretending I was a dragon. The pea-green walls clashed uncomfortably with the old, brown vinyl tablecloths. But that didn't matter once the food arrived, a bowl of olives and a decent-sized plateful of minced meat fingers with salad, bread and sweet tea. Mince, formed into a shape and grilled, seemed to be Morocco's default option, at least in the parts I'd experienced so far. I hadn't seen a hint of tagine anywhere.

I walked home in twilight under a large, bright moon with the discordant tones of the muezzin's call to prayer rattling through a desperately substandard PA system.

"Steven!" someone shouted.

I kept walking. Obviously, it must be a different Steven. No one knew me in this town. Hell, no one knew me on this entire continent.

"Steven! Mister!"

I turned around and saw a portly but smartly dressed fella heading towards me. His excellent English was the first I'd heard since the border. He introduced himself as the local chief of police. Oh, bloody hell. What had I done now?

Apparently, he had to ask me a few questions. Back at the hotel, he checked my passport and my intended route.

"Do you check every visitor who comes here?" I said.

"Yes," he replied. "All the foreign ones."

I wish now I'd asked him how many people that is. I doubt it's more than a few.

"Are you married?" he said.

"No, but I have a girlfriend," I replied. Yes, he probably thought, the typical answer of the homosexual, a crime which is punishable in Morocco by three years in prison, and a real prison rather than my hotel room.

With my inquisitor satisfied, I disappeared into my cell for a lie down. My bed was odd. The mattress felt like it was stuffed with cardboard, one half of it at least two centimetres higher than the other, but, given the air temperature in this unheated room, I was loving the thick blankets. Terry Waite never had it this good.

During the night, I heard a rustling in a bag I'd left on the floor. I suspected a creature of some sort and had a look. I assumed it'd be a cockroach but hoped for something more entertainingly African, like a meerkat or a gazelle. My ensuing torch search under the bed found nothing alive, but I saw things I wish I hadn't, including months, maybe years, of dirt, discarded tissues and several ancient cigarette butts. Would they really wash these sheets, and these two thick blankets, after my seven euro stay?

*

I was being lucky with the weather. This time of year is when Morocco gets its precipitation. And cycling at an altitude not far off a thousand metres would mean freezing rain or even snow. The evenings may have been chilly, but the days stayed sunny and warm. In Britain, a daily temperature fluctuation of five or six degrees is normal. Here it was around four times that. I think this is what the menopause feels like.

The views continued to be breathtaking. Near black, lumpy, lava-like hills with shiny surfaces sparkled in the sunlight. And the mountain roads were still dotted with others, even in the most remote of places. A man lugged barrels on a hairy donkey while a young boy sold bread near a viewpoint. Three girls tore across the road, intending to block my way and sell me prickly pears, but screamed and changed direction when an overtaking car nearly ran them over. There was rarely a chance to feel alone up here.

Today was a short day of fifteen hilly miles. Around lunchtime I looked down on my target, Targuist. The town may only have housed 11,000 but from my viewpoint it was a little city. I descended steeply to its centre and met with Moroccan market madness, its streets thick with people.

I hadn't yet found the bed MAPS.ME had promised and so asked for help. Apparently, I was standing right outside the building, despite no obvious clue it was a hotel. Inside I secured myself a clean room for a meagre four euros, the cheapest ever in the whole history of my travels. It even had WiFi. Three weeks here or one night at Premier Inn Doncaster, you decide!

While bringing my bicycle inside, I was accosted by an old, grizzled beggar. He pointed to a bottle strapped to my bike frame. Who was I to deny him his human right to water? I mean, I wasn't Nestlé, was I?

Before exploring the town, I would get something to eat. I entered my hotel's attached and bustling café where dozens of men sat around smoking and watching, or at least facing, a wall-mounted television.

"Have you got anything to eat?" I asked at the counter.

The staff looked at each other as though telepathically checking if that was indeed an option here.

"An egg?" came the minimalist reply.

My lunch arrived, fried and in a little bowl accompanied by bread. Moroccans don't normally use cutlery and none was forthcoming today. Have you tried to eat a fried egg using only bread? Once half the yolk had dripped down my arm, and snatching at the egg white with loafy pincers had failed miserably, I took out a plastic knife and fork I'd been carrying for just this emergency, a typical European failure. Top tip though: Cumin on a fried egg is wonderful.

My beggar was outside and making a nuisance of himself. A young waiter had already thrown him out of the café, but he was back again now and, through the window, I could see him on the street having a furious argument with an empty plastic chair. He fumbled in his capacious trousers, searching for the necessary organ from which to spray his invisible opponent. The young waiter leapt out of the café and chased him down the road. The beggar was clearly as mad as a cactus juggler.

Over the general hubbub of the street market, the call to prayer kicked off. This muezzin's style was particularly unpleasant, like someone doing a bad impression of a failing car engine or that annoying Crazy Frog thing. Surely in a country of 36 million they could find one person able to sing.

It was time to hit the streets and see what Targuist was all about. I was met with a wall of people, a mix of women and men, the latter dressed in winter *djellabas*, the thick, warming, coarse fabric smocks worn over their normal clothes. Younger blokes carried huge half-cows through the crowds to deliver to a butcher and be hung outside, unrefrigerated except for the cool mountain air. A starving kitten was chased from the legs of a stall piled high with sardines and took shelter under a parked car. A bull of a man sat outside his blackened workshop, bent over his equipment, welding.

All available products were built into mini-mountains: dates, olives, oranges, strawberries, spices and brightly shining silver tea pots. Young workers pushed metal trolleys through the dense crowd, a human corridor naturally forming before them by the threat of painfully bruised shins. While Targuist definitely felt crazy, it didn't feel poor. Many of the buildings might have been on their last legs, but the people weren't.

I turned down an alley that brought me to another market, this time mostly fruit and veg, on waste ground the size of a football field. People here were even more densely crushed together. The stalls were constructed of tarpaulin and wooden poles set at sixty degrees to the earth and then pegged to the ground, usually in the middle of the footpath between the stalls. The local health and safety officer was nowhere to be seen. The produce – bananas, pineapples, tomatoes, peppers and huge clumps of herbs – looked like it had been picked this morning. Maybe it had.

I escaped the chaos and spied a bakery. Let's see if this one could do better than Al Hociema's. After all, one egg was no lunch for someone who'd cycled a mighty, er, fifteen miles today. I bought three large cakes for a grand total of seven dirham, but once again they were disappointing. My new goal, as well as my quest for the holy quail, was to find a decent Moroccan pastry.

In the evening, after another lovely grilled mince sandwich – I'd have chosen something else had there been an alternative – I found a café, the only one not already rammed, for what was becoming my evening fix of sweet mint tea. Twenty blokes, many smoking, once again faced a television. Their hooded djellabas gave them the look of a band of cloaked Jawas from Star Wars.

The room was dark and noisy, but more unsettling was the Arabic news channel, showing launching missiles, a downed airplane and explosions in cities populated by folk who looked remarkably similar to those at the tables around me. Who knew what was about to be unleashed on the world?

*

For someone in my physical condition, today was going to be a long one, made worse by lumpy terrain and a height gain of 1,600 metres. Basically, it'd be like riding from sea level to the top of Ben Nevis and then discovering you still had to cycle up the Gherkin and Big Ben's clock tower. Such geographical references won't mean much to anyone outside Britain. So for Americans and Europeans, it's like riding up the Empire State Building four times or to the very tip of the Eiffel Tower five times. For Germans, it's like cycling up 829 David Hasselhoffs.

But this wasn't the biggest problem. Today's route would take me through Issaguen, close to the country's drug centre. Morocco is the world's largest producer of hashish and most of it comes from here. According to one French minister, 80% of Europe's cannabis originates in these hills. Guide books warn you not to linger.

This home-grown drug is officially illegal everywhere in Morocco – it's also criminal to be *with* someone who's in possession, even if you're entirely unaware – but the police turn a blind eye in these parts. In fact, this region isn't policed at all. The authorities hang around its edges with roadblocks and arrest anyone foolish enough to buy any. Stories tell of dealers working in cahoots with the police, who return confiscated ganja to be sold again while receiving a cut for their trouble. Who knows if this is true? Whatever the facts, Moroccan police seized close to 180,000 kilos of cannabis in 2019, more than four times what the UK did. But maybe they only found so much because their coppers keep handing it back to the dealers.

It was a bright morning but cold enough to have me wrapped in a fleece. The scenery remained spectacular, every ridge picked out by the low, newborn sun. Impenetrable puddles of mist obscured the valley floors. Cars tooted and people waved, often shouting me a lusty *très bien*. I hadn't had this much encouragement since my dad taught me to cycle.

On the edge of one village I passed a primary school and noticed a common theme, decorated as they were in a strange mix of cartoon characters and socialist realism. Today's school had Tom and Jerry separated from Daffy Duck by happily dancing, hand-holding kids. Yesterday I'd seen Mickey Mouse and Donald Duck marching along with children carrying the Moroccan flag. It was like Disneyfied Soviet propaganda with a blind eye turned to trademark infringement.

I needed to reach Issaguen by half one if I'd any chance of making Bab Berred before dark. After climbing all morning, I was a few miles shy of my lunchtime target when everything changed. Rather than the occasional roadside dosser, loads of people appeared, traffic increased and the asphalt fell apart.

An old bearded fella, wearing a brown djellaba and skull cap, left the crowd to block my way, his arms ushering me to the side of the road. These new crowds made me feel slightly vulnerable. As there was nothing Old Beardie could be selling that I might want, I swerved around him. As I trundled past, he yelled something unpleasant-sounding. But maybe that was just my imagination. Perhaps there was a prophecy of a bike-riding westerner to whom he should leave all his worldly goods. This would've been a shame. I could see myself in that djellaba.

I passed more people, many shouting things at me, offers rather than abuse I think, but who knows? And then I hit

Drugsville. The crowds thickened further. Hundreds of people swarmed over the road. The low-level buildings gave the place the feel of a cowboy town.

"*Kif?*", the local word for marijuana, was shouted from the roadside and through rolled-down car windows. They were very open about their narcotics. I'd heard stories of the plants growing right by the road, protected by men with machine guns. I saw none of that, but I guess January isn't the time of year to see forests of weed.

The centre of Issaguen was full of potholes and it didn't get any better for several miles afterwards, which I guess was the limit of the drug lords' dubious jurisdiction. If this region didn't contribute to Morocco's tax bucket with the money from their drugs, that bucket wasn't going to pay for their public services. Let your drug barons stump up for your roads, which of course they didn't.

Not far through Issaguen, now at a height of around 1,400 metres, I noticed a pond, frozen solid. I entered a thick pine forest and, with the sun's warmth more effectively removed, it became even colder. At least the continual climbing provided some internal heat, until I topped out at 1,600 metres. Three hours of challenging cycling later, I spied tonight's home, Bab Berred, a town of 5,000, below me in the distance. Its name means "Gate of Coldness" and offers a fair warning to those approaching from the opposite direction, as my chattering teeth could attest.

Rolling down the hill, I saw a large hotel on the edge of town. Its front entrance was locked, but I found the receptionist in the restaurant next door and she let me in. I was the only guest. Wandering its empty corridors felt like *The Shining*.

For fifteen euros I got a large room the temperature of a meat freezer. Luckily, it came with an electric heater that pumped out a good deal of warmth, but only if I was within a metre of it.

I needed a wash, but without hot water there was no way I was having a cold shower in these temperatures. Better to be blackened by dirt than frostbite.

I crawled into bed under a thick blanket with the heater on the bedside cabinet a few inches from my face and slept for an hour. I was lucky not to set my hair on fire.

Dinner time arrived. I reluctantly crawled out of bed and put on both fleeces. With no light in my haunted hotel's corridors, I took my head torch, found my way to the front door and went outside. It was exactly the same temperature as my room.

The dark, unlit road provided a murky entrance to the town itself. An occasional set of headlights flashed by. I decided I'd stop at the first place that offered hot food. It wasn't far. An open-fronted, single-garage-sized eatery appeared through the darkness. The owner was sweeping out an unfeasibly large quantity of rubble, presumably from the boots of his lunchtime crowd. Either that or he had major problems with his ceiling. There was a vaguely intestinal smell about the place.

Neither the owner nor his assistant spoke any French, but this being a snack bar they worked out I wanted food, the little geniuses, and I was offered *bissara*, an unappetising grey soup made from mashed fava beans. Served with half a flat bread, it arrived at the temperature and consistency of molten lava. The soup was dressed with an extravagant swirl of olive oil and I was given chilli powder and cumin to jazz it up as I saw fit.

A metal spoon rested innocently in the soup bowl. Temporarily forgetting the principles of conductivity resulted in an embarrassing squeal. Instead, I attacked my meal carefully with torn up chunks of bread. As I huddled over my warming bowl, this felt exactly like the thing a weary traveller should eat on a cold winter's night, even if flavour-wise the soup tasted only of whatever was sprinkled upon it.

As my bissara cooled, its viscosity increased, becoming thicker and thicker until it was only one degree from hummus, but it was the central heating I needed.

I walked back through the darkness to the hotel and saw some lights were now on inside. Had the receptionist noticed my head torch – she seemed to live in the bar next door – or did we have another guest? I could certainly hear someone, although maybe it was those evil twins or that kid whizzing about on his tricycle.

*

After a week of sunny starts, I'd expected to see similar weather when I pulled back the curtains this morning. Weirdly, I couldn't see *any* weather. It took me a moment to realise today's blank canvas was actually dense fog.

Outside, I rolled my bike towards the main road. About to push my machine across, a rumbling truck's headlights instantly materialised not five metres to my left. Bloody hell, this fog was *really* thick, Joey Essex thick.

I fastened lights to my bike and hoped against hope it'd be enough. At least everyone would be driving slowly. There was another obstacle though. Near an unmanned police roadblock on the edge of town, portable, tyre-busting spikes had been spread out across part of the tarmac. They were easy to miss in these conditions. My tyres might claim to be puncture-proof but even so.

Once out of town, the fog thinned a little, enough to spot a roadside tip, basically a huge mound of rubbish. Wind picked up litter and carried it wherever it wanted. Maybe the country's scattered plastic wasn't the work of inconsiderate Moroccans after all, but rather bad town sanitation planning and the wind working in harmony. But I bet the locals had a hand in it too.

The road climbed while temperatures tumbled, assisted by a piercing headwind. At one stage, the clouds above me cleared and I could see snow on huge, jagged mountains. I pushed sometimes just to stamp warmth back into my feet. I was inconvenienced by my pre-ride sartorial choices. This wasn't the weather to be wearing sockless adventure sandals.

Having cycled through several small villages, all unknown to MAPS.ME's cartographers, the road dropped but the fog thickened, accompanied by a reinvigorated wind. As I passed through another collection of buildings, my core felt frozen and I stopped for some restorative tea.

The thick mist made it difficult to see which of the roadside businesses were cafés. I found one and entered, stamping my frozen feet. Inside, eight blokes, all in thick, winter djellabas, sat around, looking snug. It was a shabby little place but warm. No one drank but most smoked spliff.

I made a friend instantly. He came to sit at my table.

"*Kif?*" he asked.

"No, thanks. I don't smoke."

"Whisky?"

"I don't drink." My reply was only true of this trip. One of the reasons I'd chosen Morocco was to give my liver a break.

"Good man," he replied.

The conversation stalled.

"*Kif?*" he finally repeated.

My tea arrived and, with it, the beginnings of internal warmth.

"Ah," he smiled, looking at my drink. "Moroccan whisky!" He thought for a moment. "Do you know Morocco's drugs are the best in the world?"

"No," I replied. "I didn't know that."

"How much do you think one gram of hashish costs?"

How should I know? He might as well have asked me what it cost to land a moose on Mercury.

As I sipped my tea, a slyly smiling man came up to me and lent towards my ear. He whispered something so quietly I couldn't tell if he was speaking French or Spanish. All I caught were "Morocco" and "politics". I told him I didn't understand. Whatever it was, he hadn't wanted the others to hear and wasn't going to repeat it more loudly. Instead he wandered off.

The tea and the warm room had worked their magic. I left the bar and returned to my bike. As I stood there, Mr Sneaky sidled up to me again and whispered conspiratorially the same political message. It was still too quiet. What did he want? To recruit me as a spy? To reveal some horrifying truth about Morocco? To invite me into the toilets around the back?

As the road tumbled ever downward, the fog began to clear. By the time I reached the turn-off for Chefchaouen, total visibility was restored. From here it was just five miles to Morocco's Blue City, unfortunately all uphill.

A long hour later, I arrived at a glorious panorama that looked over the entire town. Having seen photos, I'd only expected a village but in reality 50,000 people live here, halfway up a mountain in an enlarged Costa del Sol "White Village" but one infected with a pale blue algae. For a long time, visitors weren't welcome here. The first Christians were allowed in only a hundred years ago, after the Spanish invaded. Until 1920, just three Christians had made it inside. Unfortunately, American missionary William Summers didn't make it out again. The townsfolk poisoned him.

There are various theories to explain why the place is blue. One is that the colour keeps away mosquitoes and, if true, this would've been important since it's the only region in Morocco with a recent history of malaria. Another proposal is that, back in the 1930s, the Jewish community living here painted it their favourite "spiritual" colour, matching the shade of their prayer mats. A more cynical theory, and the one

I'm leaning towards, is that someone in the 1970s thought it a cunning ploy to snare tourists. It definitely worked.

I found a hotel, as unheated as the last but fortunately with plentiful blankets.

"Where have you come from?" asked the owner.

"Al-Hoceima, through the Rif Mountains."

He looked aghast.

"Wasn't it dangerous? Did anyone try to attack you?"

Not that I'd noticed, although maybe that old fella near Drugsville had plans for my demise.

The blue medina could wait until morning. Finding an outdoor restaurant in a square in the newer part of town, I figured it probably better to eat early, while it was light and there was still a hint of warmth in the air. The place mostly sold snacks like pizza and paninis, but there were at least two genuine Moroccan originals.

The first was *harira*, a tomato and chick pea soup usually with some meat thrown in. It's traditionally the dish that breaks the daily fast during Ramadan. As it only cost five dirham, I wasn't expecting much, and that's exactly what I got. It tasted like watered down Heinz tomato soup with a dessertspoon of chick peas thrown in, along with a gnarled lump of unspecified meat. Still, it provided warmth.

Much better was the main course. Morocco offers a huge range of *tagines* – tagine is the name of a dish as well as the pot in which it's prepared – and so, as this was my first, I figured I'd start with the most basic and work my way up the pecking order over the coming weeks. The *kefta*, or meat ball, tagine came with an egg in the middle of its tomato sauce and, in this land of no cutlery, was to be eaten entirely with bread. It arrived at a temperature similar to yesterday's bubbling soup, and, when the tagine's lid was removed, it unveiled steam almost as thick as this morning's fog. They may have been humble ingredients, but egg, mince and tomato had never been better combined.

*

The meat of the Chefchaouen experience is not found in a tagine but in its ancient blue medina, and it was here I headed this morning. Outside one of its entrance gateways an older bloke in a heavy djellaba accosted me in English and walked alongside as I sauntered up the hill past the first blue houses. He dished out a throwaway fact or two and I soon realised, whether I liked it or not, he was angling to be my guide.

I told him I wasn't interested in looking around and that I was off to get breakfast. He pointed out a place I was already heading towards and sat down with me. I was too British to tell him to sod off. I asked him what he did for a living, as if I didn't already know.

"I have a shop," he replied, "but I also do tours." Ka-ching! "I take tourists into the mountains to photograph the marijuana plantations."

His lumpen physique didn't suggest a hillwalker.

"Where are you staying?" he asked. I told him. "Ah," he replied. "I used to work there."

I nodded, but I didn't believe him. There are literally hundreds of hotels here. He smiled with a kindly face and three teeth that couldn't agree on a common direction of travel. And there was plenty of eye contact. I felt like he was attempting to befriend me into submission.

"What's your name?" I told him and asked him his. "Omar. Like Omar Sharif."

As I was hungry, I ordered the restaurant's biggest breakfast, although still only two euros. As it arrived, Omar got up and wandered outside. Before me were a fried egg, a few pieces of non-pork halal sausage, some more pretend Dairylea, black olives, goat's cheese – this is a deliciously creamy speciality of Chefchaouen – all drowned in three millimetres of good olive oil. Tea, fresh orange juice and bread lay on the side. Once again there was no cutlery but a single toothpick. I used it to drag the fried egg clumsily towards a bit of bread and make an egg butty. I was getting the hang of this Moroccan way of eating. The yolk didn't even drip down my arm this time.

I thought Omar might have disappeared, but he was still waiting outside. Seeing I was nearly finished, he came back in. I had two choices now: either I could walk away with him in hot pursuit, shouting snippets of local wisdom and then have him fight me for an obscene amount of money later or I could negotiate now.

"How much do you charge for a tour?" I asked casually.

"For two hours, it's forty euros."

I laughed.

"That is *far* more than I can afford to pay."

"How much then?"

"Seriously, I can't do more than five euros. Just give me a short one."

He smiled.

"Since you're a good friend and you're a nice man – I had a Filipino here yesterday from London, not a nice man – I can do it for ten euros."

Wow, I was a good friend already. Maybe I should've asked him if I could borrow a tenner.

"No," I said, "five is the most I can pay." I wasn't going to play this stupid, let's-meet-in-the-middle haggling game. "Otherwise, it's no tour."

He thought for a second and then nodded.

"Five euros then," he said. "Seventy dirham."

Sneaky bugger.

"Five euros is *fifty* dirham," I replied. He started to grumble. "Fifty dirham or no tour?"

We left the café and re-entered the blue medina. There was a noticeable difference between the people outside and in. In the streets surrounding the medina, it was mostly old men in sombre-hued djellabas. Inside were both sexes, younger and usually in bright colours and shorts.

"Is this the most touristy place in Morocco?" I asked.

"Yes," he replied. "And lots of Moroccans come here. Since the King came to visit a few years ago. Now everyone comes."

The monarch only visited in 2010, but tourists have been coming here for decades. He imparted other information that seemed dubious.

"You see this arched door?" he said, pointing to a house. "It means lots of families live inside. A square door means it's reformed. Rich people, living alone."

"Rich people don't have families?" I asked.

He ignored that question. Instead, he explained the meaning of the name Chefchaouen, one that contradicted the story I'd already read in several places, that it meant "Look at the mountains!" Maybe it's better not to requote any information imparted by Omar.

"And here's a nice street," he said, indicating left, as we walked up the alleyway. "Take a photo."

I looked around the corner. A selfie-taking twenty-something had splayed herself out along its blue walls in full Instagram mode. The place was undoubtedly lovely, but it felt as fake as Christmas.

We passed a Chinese restaurant, hardly an original feature of the medina. But perhaps it merged the best of oriental and Moroccan culinary arts, a camel foo yung perhaps.

"Do you like Chinese food?" I asked Omar.

He shook his head dismissively.

"Moroccans never go in," he replied. "Just for tourists."

I scanned its outdoor photo menu. Not only was there no attempt at fusion, but prices were three times what you'd pay in Spain. No wonder Moroccans avoided them.

"I don't want to waste your time, Omar," I said. "When we've done fifty dirham, you tell me, yeah?"

I didn't want him adding on bonus tours for extra money.

"And this is where the Queen stayed when the Royal Family came to visit."

"Is the King popular?" I asked.

"Yes, very. He's a good man. A normal man."

Again, it was hard to know if this was the truth. King Mohammed VI's portrait was a feature of many restaurants and shops, but anyone who dissed him got locked up. A well-known Moroccan YouTuber, Mohamed Sakkaki, had been sentenced to four years just a week before I'd set off, and all he'd done was criticize the King's speeches. Imagine if there was a similar law in Britain for those speaking ill of the Prime Minister or Royal Family. To squeeze in all the offenders, they'd have to fence off an area the size of Lincolnshire.

Omar started his own interrogation.

"What do you do?" he asked.

"I cycle around. I write books."

"But where do you live?"

"Sometimes in Spain, sometimes in Britain, other places."

He smiled.

"You are a nomad."

I'd read that nomads – real nomads, I mean – were well-respected in Morocco. It seemed wise to agree with him. Besides, if he knew how poor I was, the less chance there was of a rumble later.

"Yes, I suppose I am."

We kept walking. A little up the road we passed a building. Through a window, I could see people indulging in an act of worship.

"Ah, a mosque," I said.

"No, that's not a mosque. Mosques are for praying *and* reading the Koran. This place is just for praying."

"Five times a day?" I asked.

"Yes."

"Do *you* pray five times a day?"

"Every day," he replied.

"And how often do you go to the mosque?"

"Every day." He looked slightly uncomfortable. "But I cannot go now because I like a drink."

"And that means you can't go?" He nodded glumly. "And what about kif? Can you go after smoking kif?"

"Yes, you can go."

But he'd lost his mojo. By accidentally winkling out that confession, I'd depressed him.

"Don't forget to tell me when my fifty dirham is up."

It was. He led me to the medina's main square where the grand tour was concluded. I offered him a fifty dirham note.

"Euros would be better," he said.

He pocketed the money while glancing around suspiciously. There were no more smiles, an end to eye contact. Our special friendship was over.

"It's not much to get a drink," he grumbled, assessing his payment for the last twenty minutes. "But I'll get one anyway."

He shuffled off barwards. If you consider the average salary in Morocco is only 500 euros per month, he hadn't done too badly. He'd made about ten cents per fib.

I wandered through the square. It was full of people obsessively videoing stuff rather than enjoying the moment. Behind a portable amp, a bloke thrashed at an electric guitar and crooned awfully. He should get a job as a muezzin. He finished murdering a pop classic to complete silence from the nearby café crowds.

"Thank you very much," he said to no one in particular.

Every shop in the square, just like most throughout the medina, sold souvenirs that had probably travelled farther to get here than the tourists, all the way from a factory in China.

For lunch I did what I usually avoid and sought out a chain restaurant, but since the company only had three outlets – its other two locations were Marrakesh and Fes – could it even be considered a chain yet?

Café Clock billed itself as "cross-cultural" and offered an interesting if expensive menu in an old building hidden away in the medina. There were great views of the whole town from its roof terrace. Its options were mostly vegetarian and vegan with an odd, and very original, nod to carnivores. After all, it was the only place in town – and, according to the waiter, the only place in the country – where you could sample a camel burger.

While waiting for my food to arrive, the call to prayer began and it became quite a battle. Being so high over the town, I could hear four separate muezzins competing for the faithful. It's rarely tuneful when only one of them is at it. With a quartet blaring away, we'd strayed into the realms of experimental jazz. Are muezzins really necessary nowadays? Surely there's an app for that. Actually, this problem was solved with the invention of the alarm clock.

The café may have been aiming for the cross-cultural but its customers were limited to Europeans and Americans. I suspect the prices dampened any Moroccan desire to eat there. Ten euros for a burger was a lot when a similar-sized snack on the street would cost barely a fifth of that.

But the food was good. Unlike more famous chains, the chips tasted like they'd been cut from a real potato. And my dromedary burger came with tomato, onion, cheese and chilli relish. It looked a little on the small side, but the meat was strong and tasty, a megabeef, the lowing offspring of an illicit union between a cow and Superman. Let's not linger on that image.

I left the medina through the gate I'd entered and the

tourist realm fell away. Morocco suddenly became more real, perhaps not as pretty, but not solely interested in the contents of my wallet.

Some aspects of Morocco were best kept outside the medina, away from those seeking a glossed over version of the country. On a backstreet I saw the freshest roast chicken shop in the world, about 200 live birds held on the floor, beak to cloaca, ready to be dispatched and cooked upon demand. There were no sell-by dates here.

I saw two people in wheelchairs today. It's easy to forget how far Europe has progressed with disabled access. As a bike pusher with heavy luggage, I share many a street obstacle with wheelchair users, and Morocco must be an absolute nightmare. Kerbs are often huge, rarely with a ramp at junctions and crossings. Pavements are uneven, and you could forget about navigating the cobbled medina, built on a steep hillside, unless you had tyres like a monster truck and arms the size of Popeye's.

I wanted to see how the other half lived, those Chaounis, for that is their name, who shunned the blue medina. The newer town had some admirably well-kept apartment blocks compared to what I'd seen so far in Morocco. It was no surprise the locals would rather offload their poky medina houses to a foreigner or business and move somewhere relatively flat and presumably free of damp. And local shops would sell useful stuff, y'know, like food rather than blue plastic houses.

Speaking of shops, something I couldn't help but notice were the hoardings of typical Moroccan shopfronts. Rather than shouting any textual clue to the nature of the business, this information was imparted by dozens of tiny photos of things they sold. Hardware stores showed miniature images of hammers and drills and welding masks and a hundred other items. There was good reason for this. Only three-quarters of Moroccans can read and write, up from just 50% twenty years ago. The pictures explained a shop's purpose even if written language was beyond you. But some stores didn't need to bother. Butchers displayed their wares on shopfront hooks, although in the poorer Rif villages fresh meat was replaced by large plastic carcasses. Or maybe Moroccans there had developed a taste for polyethylene steaks.

In the evening I returned to the medina. Once inside the alleyways, I was offered kif a few more times. Is every male in Morocco a dealer?

In the main square a new troupe had replaced the wailing guitarist. Three African guys in gold and black robes jumped up and down enthusiastically, shaking the tassels on the tops of their hats. It was a slim skill-set on which to build an entire act, but *Britain's Got Talent* has seen worse.

For dinner I found a place with a table of eight Spaniards sitting in an otherwise empty but clean-looking restaurant. I opted for a chicken tagine, the next one up the complexity scale after yesterday's meat balls.

The tea came first.

"Moroccan whisky," the waiter said, like he'd just made it up on the spot.

As before, the food arrived bubbling hot, but it was all a bit school dinners. A single chicken leg was surrounded by a pile of potatoes, green beans, carrot and fennel. It was cooked well enough but tasted bland. I'd expected Moroccan food to be rich with spices, but this dish hadn't even been visited by a salt cellar.

I'd exhausted what Chefchaouen had to offer. It was a pretty place, but in reality it didn't have anything that couldn't be provided by a typical white Spanish village, except some blue paint and that hump-filled burger.

After a day off the bike, I was looking forward to moving

on to two cities in Morocco's far north, including Tangier, the place that had put me off this country for so long. Was it going to be as awful as I remembered?

Chapter 3: A Tale of Two Cities

Tetouan and Tangier

I woke up to another day of bright sunshine albeit with refrigerated air. The sun picked out the mountain above Chefchaouen. It looked a challenging climb. I couldn't imagine old Omar getting up there to show kif to tourists, not unless someone on top had promised him a pint.

It was forty miles to Tetouan and I needed fuel. I stocked up with some gastronomic excitement, two surprise pastries to eat later on the way. Rather than Russian, I was playing *Moroccan* roulette, with buns rather than guns.

Starting high in the mountains, Chefchaouen gave me some painless rolling to begin the day, wrapped in fleeces to counter the air temperature that had already dusted the ground plants liberally with frost. The landscape looked sugar-coated and sparkled in the morning sunlight.

I got the largest climb done early and stopped for my breakfast at the day's halfway point. I pulled a mystery samosa-like pastry from my bag and gave it a sniff, unable to tell if it was savoury or sweet. Taking a bite, I was disappointed to discover it was filled with cream cheese, inoffensive but dull, like *The Mash Report* wrapped in filo.

This couldn't be said for my second pastry. Looking like a spring roll, it was stuffed with hundreds of thin noodles, all lying suspiciously parallel, like a thick tube of tiny worms. Its innards had a pinkish hue, but the flavour was bizarre, a bit sweet with a little background heat and an out-of-place fishiness. It felt like an experiment gone wrong or eating someone's wrist with the bone removed. It was bloody awful.

Moroccan pastries still weren't redeeming themselves. At least there was an open sewer at the side of the road to take my mind off the taste.

I shadowed a ridge of low, grey, jagged mountains northwards towards my destination. From its edge, Tetouan looked huge, its population nudging 400,000. The city promised a lot, if only because of one of its most celebrated residents. Sayyida al Hurra, the Pirate Queen, ruled here for 27 years in the sixteenth century. Her real name was Lalla Aicha bint Ali ibn Rashid al-Alami Hakimat Titwan – filling in forms must have been an absolute nightmare – but no Pirate Queen worth her salt was going to settle for a moniker full of bints and tits. Instead, the name she chose meant "one who is free and independent". "Free" was not a word you could ever use to describe the western Mediterranean while she was around. As well as controlling Tetouan, she plundered what she could, even carrying out daring raids on the Spanish mainland. But then, as always, a bloke came along and messed it up. To make matters worse, it was her son-in-law who nicked her crown. That must have made Christmases awkward.

I rode into the centre of town beside a pleasant river and arrived at a hotel. I was checked in by a young lad. An assistant hovered around too.

"And do you have anywhere safe for my bike?" I asked.

"In your room if you like."

"And what floor am I on?"

"The fourth."

"Do you have a lift?"

"No."

Excellent.

With my bicycle safely installed on my balcony, I hit the town and, without trying, found the medina, busier but with a little more room to breathe than the one in Al-Hoceima or

Chefchaouen. Almost immediately someone hollered in my direction. I looked over to a food stall.

"Something to eat?"

That fella could read my mind.

"You want a tagine?"

No, not if yesterday's was the norm. Instead, he had piles of freshly fried fish, and I pointed at those. He dragged out a tiny stool and invited me into his domain. From his mound of grub he grabbed a couple of sardines, a mackerel, a little flat fish and the large head of some other swimmy thing I didn't recognise. He threw them on to a paper-lined tray and placed it before me. Then came a wheel of bread, a salad of chopped tomatoes and cucumber, and a thick gazpacho-like sauce to dip my crispy fish into. It was finger food at its finest and utterly divine. This was what I'd come to Morocco for.

The fish stall was a slick operation. One man fried while another, who as far as I could tell was merely a floating head with a passing resemblance to Davros, stood behind a tall counter, chopping things and keeping a watchful eye.

At the far end of this counter was a small sink available to punters for a postprandial scrub-up. Everyone who used it had something with which to dry their hands, probably a necessity for good Muslims who pray five times a day and wash before each event. Of course, I had neither faith nor a towel. However, I *did* have very greasy fingers. I completed my lovely lunch and went for a wash. I'd just finished drying my hands on my trouser leg when Davros's hitherto unseen arm thrust a paper towel from behind his counter. Ah, so that's where they were all getting them from, the napkin-rationing King of the Daleks.

I continued through the market, a UNESCO World Heritage Site and well worth a look. Its roof was latticed, letting in beams of bright sunlight that made airborne dust twinkle like gems.

Most of the stalls here had a little green door fronting a tiny room, individually numbered up to at least 1,400. Between them, they sold everything from clothes to food to piles of phone batteries, but some stalls looked like nothing more than a car boot sale offloading a random collection of undesirables. One was selling a 2011 Playstation Pro Evolution Soccer game, an old mixing desk with missing knobs, a dirty pair of baby's trainers and an ancient hair dryer. So if you're on the lookout for any of those things, you know where to come.

In the alleyways between the official stalls, the more desperate spread out a rug on the ground and sold from there. One had nothing to trade but six pairs of tatty old shoes and a bottle of olive oil. What happens to his family if nobody buys today?

I continued through the medina, into a section that specialised in djellabas.

"Remember me?" said a young male face, suddenly appearing from one of the larger stalls.

"No."

"From your hotel. I work here during the day." I really didn't recognise him, but maybe he was the receptionist's assistant. "Come, I have something amazing to show you."

Cool. I was hoping for a magic pony or an eight-armed woman, but reality, as always, was more prosaic.

"Very good," I said drily, as he showed me a back-room loom that no one was using.

"And here's my uncle!" the lad yelled excitedly, handing me over to the real salesman.

"Hello, uncle!" I said, giving him a little wave.

"Ah, my friend," the older man started, presumptuously I felt, "you've come on a *very* special day."

"Really? Why is it so special?" I asked, summoning all the wide-eyed gullibility I could muster.

"Because *all* the market is open!"

Mmm, just as it is *every single day* except Friday. Carry on and lie to me some more, I didn't say.

"So," I asked, "how long does it take to make a djellaba?"

Uncle Bullshit made a serious face.

"Two days. And then the embroidery starts."

"And you make everything here?"

"Oh yes."

Belm! If they take so long to manufacture, he'd produced a hell of a lot of stock for a single loom. They're probably knocked out *en masse* on an industrial estate in Casablanca.

"Come," he said. He hurried me to another storeroom, one stuffed with carpets. "Look at this one." He picked up a rug and jabbered a series of forgettable technical details. "And," he continued, his voice full of mystery, "no two are ever alike!"

"Is that some sort of conformity issue?"

He smiled but didn't answer.

"The Inkyschminky tribe from the High Atlas make very special carpets," he said, as I loosely recall. "Always in the colours of their animals," he continued, while unrolling a black and white rug.

"Lots of zebras and pandas up there, are there?"

"Nice, yes?"

"Yeah, very nice. Oh, I wish I had a house," I said, assuming it was my turn to start lying.

"You *have* a house."

"No, I don't. I'm on my bicycle."

"You have family with a house," he said, attempting a Jedi mind trick on me. "We can parcel up and send it."

"No, I don't. I live on my bike."

"You are like nomad?"

"Yes, I'm like nomad."

I'd embraced Omar's description of me. I felt it provided

some protection from annoying salesmen.

"Nomads have carpets," he continued.

"Do they really?"

"Yes, smaller ones, like these." He rolled out something the size of a bathroom mat. "They take them everywhere they go." Yes, on their bloody *camels*. "You can take a small one."

"I've no room in my bags."

"A djellaba then. For the cold."

"I've no room."

The young fella who claimed to have recognised me from the hotel said something to his uncle that sounded despondent.

"OK then," his uncle said sadly. He'd given up, but now he wasn't my best friend any more. In fact, he wouldn't even show me out of his shop. He may as well have kicked me up the arse as I left.

Call me Captain Sceptical, but I was even thinking perhaps his nephew didn't work in my hotel at all. I needed to come up with a suitable response for the next time someone tried this approach.

"Remember me?"

"Of course!" I could reply loudly, slapping him matily on his back. "Still shagging your sister?"

Once I'd found my way out of Fantastic Fabrications Ltd, I escaped the people-stuffed corridors of the market and realised I needed a drink, but not an alcoholic one. In a town centre café, I sat watching the main shopping street for an hour with two teapots of mint tea. My name is Steven and I'm a tea-aholic!

Tetouan felt much more cosmopolitan than the Morocco I'd seen so far. Remove the Arabic script from the shopfronts and this pedestrianised cobbled street could have been anywhere in Europe, perhaps not Paris or Barcelona, but certainly somewhere farther east.

Hawkers danced from table to table, selling anything portable from cigarettes to tissues to buns. A toothless Bill Murray-lookalike approached me with his old violin. He held it upright in front of his chest and played it, maintaining eye contact and a large, goofy smile. He was really going for it, pulling a face like a guitar hero. And he was well in tune too, but the overall effect was more for comedy. He suddenly stopped, but I kept on smiling and gave him a coin while he waltzed away happily.

*

I'd given myself another day to see more of this crazy city. First, I'd get me some culture. Tetouan had a modern art gallery and, if it was anything like those in Europe, it'd be a lot of stupidly pretentious fun.

Unfortunately it wasn't, and I think that was the fault of Morocco's establishment rather than the gallery itself. Modern art is supposed to be subversive, but subversive isn't allowed in Morocco. In late 2019, the rapper Gnawi wrote a track about police corruption and found himself sentenced to twelve months in jail. The year before, a Berber Banksy, Axil Tinsti, was arrested for graffiti depicting anti-state political leader Nasser Zafzafi. There are plenty of other examples.

As a result, today's art was mostly insipid, the sort you'd see at a market. Perhaps that explained why I was the only person there. The security guard even switched the lights on especially for me. I was done within fifteen minutes.

I walked back to town via the fish market, noisy and still freshly smelling, the ground outside wet with the melted ice used to pack the creatures in plastic crates. Men yelled their prices and hauled large tubs of sardines from one transit van to another, to be sold at a destination further south. Inside, there was more variety. A fishmonger stood at his counter, huge knife in hand, about to dismember a tuna the size of a large child.

I was hoping the medina, much quieter this mid-morning, was going to provide a lunch of yesterday's quality, but I'd taken a wrong turning. As I stood on a corner deciding which way to go, an old bloke in a mustard yellow jacket approached me.

"You have the beard of a Berber," he said.

I'd no idea if this was a compliment or not. I mean, was it akin to "you have the appearance of a sage, my wise old friend" or more of a "you're a bit of a Peter Sutcliffe, ain'tcha?" I don't know. Maybe Berbers are right buggers.

"Thanks," I replied, deciding to be gracious about it.

"You should stay in Morocco," he continued. I planned to, at least for the next ten weeks. "What are you looking for?"

"Just the market. But I realise it's here."

I set off walking with Colonel Mustard at my side.

"I like your jacket," I lied.

He chuckled.

"I got it from a flea market," he said. "By the way, I am Mohammed."

We shook hands and continued walking. He asked where I was from. I told him.

"I'm famous in England," he said. Bullshit alert!

"Really?"

"Yes, you know the Hairy Bikers? I worked with them when they came here."

"How did you help?"

"I got their ingredients."

Mmm, I'm not sure that counts as fame. Even a show as low-rent as Celebrity Driving School didn't include some high-up's personal shopper.

"There's a very special viewing point here in Tetouan," he told me. And then for the next couple of minutes I followed him up a series of stone staircases, through narrow alleyways, until we emerged on a platform looking down on the city's rooftops. A mist rose from yesterday's river and hung in the air, shielding the base of the mountains beyond.

"Very nice," I said, taking a snap. "Do you mind if I take one of you, Mohammed?"

"Not at all."

Click!

"If I meet the Hairy Bikers, I'll show them this and ask 'em if they remember you."

He coughed suspiciously, like he hoped I'd rather not. Surely this wasn't another Moroccan telling a porky?

We continued walking together and chatted about Morocco.

"My favourite place is Asilah," he said. "I don't like Marrakesh. They are just after tourist money."

Mmm, and you aren't? By now, I'd realised this constituted a tour and so I asked him what he did for a living.

"I used to design carpets – I wasn't a weaver! – and worked with leather. Now I'm retired, I show people around."

Unofficially, obviously. But money would definitely be involved.

He threw out details. Apparently, in the medina there were 25 mosques and twenty *hammams,* steam baths where you get massaged or, more accurately, physically attacked in the name of good hygiene.

"How often do you go to the hammam?" I asked.

"Twice a week."

"Don't you have a shower at home?"

"Yes. I shower every day."

Clearly his hammam visits weren't a cleanliness issue. Maybe he just liked being touched by other men.

He showed me the tanneries – a series of liquid-filled pits where leather was worked by a handful of fellas – to a place that sold natural remedies and finally a carpet shop. I nipped that one in the bud early on.

"I don't want to waste your time," I said to the owner, "but I have *absolutely no desire* to buy a carpet."

The man nodded and said no more. Had it always been that easy?

The route took us through the medina. I even saw "the guy from my hotel" but he didn't recognise me today. He did however laugh as Mohammed and I walked by.

"Hey!" he called to me. "When you're done, just give him five dirham or something."

Mohammed cringed.

"Ah, boys," he said. "Having a little joke."

This was a good time to discuss finances.

"So, are you going to charge me a lot of money?" I asked.

"An official guide is 400 dirham," he replied.

Forty euros?

"But you're not official."

"I charge half."

And it was now I realised something, a stupidly obvious thing really. And that was that all the power lay with me. If you negotiate a price and later renege on it, that's hardly fair. But until an amount has been agreed, anything's on the table.

"Well, it won't be that much," I said. "It'll be five." He choked. I'd made a mistake by switching to euros in my head. "Sorry, I mean it'll be *fifty* dirham."

"But Steven, I took you to the top of the town. Even official guides don't do that."

I'm sure they do. This wasn't London. There weren't *that* many sights.

"Well, it's fifty, just so you're clear. If you'd wanted more, you should have negotiated beforehand."

"You are a hard bargainer," he said. I'm really not. "For you, one hundred."

I smiled.

"No, it's fifty."

"Eighty."

"Fifty. No, I tell you what, I've got a fifty dirham note in my wallet. But if I have a ten dirham coin as well, I'll give you sixty."

For the sake of future visitors and Morocco's image abroad, this shouldn't be encouraged, but he was an amiable old duffer.

"Got that? It's going to be sixty, so feel free to stop the tour whenever you like."

"I always finish my tours," he said proudly. But two minutes later, we came to a halt. "Your hotel is around the next corner."

I still hadn't eaten. I popped back to my room to get my sunglasses in the belief that lack of eye contact would deter the grifters, but of course it didn't make a sod of difference. I walked back through the now bustling medina, salesmen howling out their fish prices, one feeding a sardine to a cheeky stray cat. I was on the hunt for grilled food.

"You want to see the tanneries?" a bloke shouted towards me.

"No, I saw them earlier," I said, continuing to march along.

"Hey, we're not all guides, you know."

"Yes, you are."

Outside the medina, I could smell smoke and food. I followed my nose to a tiny counter full of meat, behind which was a grill. Whole chickens hung from a metal bar at eye level, their tongues grimly lolling. I didn't even know chickens *had* tongues.

I pointed to some skewers of meat in his cabinet and asked the owner for a sandwich. Ten dirham got me a very tasty half a bread full of grilled turkey, tomatoes, onions and olives. You can eat well for next to nothing in Morocco if you follow the locals. I mean, don't stalk them or anything.

While waiting for my lunch to arrive, the kitchen's extractor fan, cobbled together with tin foil and tape, made worrying noises, juddering clunkily like it was about to explode. The owner repeatedly unplugged the fan, waited a moment and then retried it. Thirty seconds later, it was quaking again. It was only a matter of time before something went bang and his customers were pulling fragments of chicken beak out of their faces.

I came back to the hotel via a bakery. I chose two filo pastry rolls because I was fairly certain they'd be sweet. They were, after all, covered in dozens of bees. They were crispily nutty and tasted deliciously of orange blossom. Possibly with a hint of wasp dribble. This was a valuable lesson. Ignore the French-style pastries and stick to the more traditional ones.

I was enjoying my time in Morocco, the mountain villages, the busy cities and everywhere in between. But how would I feel tomorrow, when I finally returned to Tangier?

*

The ride to Tangier was a five and half hour slog on an unlovely, traffic-heavy dual carriageway. A few of the dumber truck drivers hadn't worked out there was a second lane they could use when overtaking me at speed. A couple of them got closer enough for the ol' sphincter twitch. It was comfortably the most unpleasant cycling experience in Morocco so far.

Much more fun was bombing through the busy city streets of Tangier itself. And what a transformation! My 2002 memories of the town were of a scabby, shady-looking cesspit of half-crumbled dives. In today's bright sunshine, its seafront looked more like Nice. It was now the eighteenth richest city in Africa. It had clearly had some work done.

On my way through town, while swigging some water on a busy street, a small but well-built African lad started talking to me. He wore a black leather jacket and, oddly for such a warm day, a red woollen cap that was pulled over one eye.

He told me his name was Emmanuel and that he was Nigerian. He'd had one hell of an adventure to get here, crossing the Sahara, illegally negotiating the borders of Niger, Mali and finally Morocco without a passport.

"And you live here now?"

"I'm sleeping rough. But I went to a charity today to see if they can give me something."

"Can they?"

"Yeah. But in a day or two. I'll survive. Where you from?"

When I told him, he looked around me, checked out my arse, then bent down and squeezed my calves, like he was a slave trader weighing up a possible purchase. If he bought me and sold me on, he wouldn't make enough to buy a sandwich.

I wished Emmanuel well, continued to the medina and tried to find the hotel I'd stayed in last time. It wasn't there, but a smaller one stood in its place.

"And how much?" I asked.

"Normally 150. For you 120."

"And do you have a safe place for my bike?"

"Outside?"

"No, thanks," I said, turning to leave. "I'll find somewhere else."

"One hundred!" he yelled.

"It's not about the money. I need somewhere safe for my bike."

By now I was on the street.

"You can store it in the café next door!" he screamed, panicked.

I hadn't realised getting a discount could be so easy.

I went into the medina, expecting to be pounced upon by chancers, but it never happened. Everything looked completely different. The atmosphere was friendly and unthreatening. I knew that Morocco had made efforts to clamp down on illegal guides, but I hadn't expected it to be so successful here.

I eventually came to the Grand Socco, the medina's largest market square, although in reality now a roundabout complete with another non-functioning fountain, a feature of every city I'd seen so far. It was ringed by dozens of restaurants. I hadn't planned to eat just yet, but after today's effort on an empty stomach, the edges of my vision clouded, a sign of hunger-induced low blood pressure and imminent unconsciousness. I threw myself on to a seat and a waiter thrust a menu into my hand. It was probably for the best.

I ordered another disappointing harira, that tomato and chick pea Ramadan soup, prepared as cheaply as last time. Who knows, maybe it's always that bad. The main course though was an improvement, just, a fish tagine, despite the fact it was clearly made from tinned sardines in a country where fresh sardines are cheaper than air.

I continued my exploration of the medina. As usual for Morocco, loads of people milled about but, unusually, a lot of them were young women or mums with kids. Tangier didn't contain an ounce of its former dodginess. Had it changed? Had I? Was I now so acclimatised to the more Moroccan bits of this fascinating country that the tourist areas now felt boringly safe?

*

I got up and hunted for my standard breakfast, but maybe Tangier wakes up later than other cities in Morocco. I could only find one open café, a dark morgue of a place that struggled to rustle up a croissant. Inside with me were five Moroccans, staring vacantly at a 24-hour news channel. The telly went into automatic shutdown mode, counted down and switched itself off. Everyone continued to stare at the blank screen. Maybe no news is good news.

Unsated, I wandered through the medina's indoor fruit sellers, their wares eventually giving way to meat. A more deathly smell hung in the air than at your usual British butcher's, possibly because nothing was refrigerated. Tripe and other innards dangled from bars across the front of the stalls like props in a horror film. Dead rabbits drooped, yet to be skinned. And then came the fish market, the busiest section so far. Piles of sea bream and bass sat beside squid and octopus and a thousand other species in a display that would make any cook's heart sing. It would've been great to have a kitchen to take advantage of all this fresh loveliness. Still, I'd find another solution at lunchtime.

I wandered blindly around the medina's tiny streets, getting myself thoroughly lost and not really caring. I just took any turn that felt instinctively right. Only occasionally was their any nod to modernity here. I could have been strolling these crumbling alleyways at any time in the last 1,000 years. Maybe the Pirate Queen had popped over from Tetouan and walked these very streets, probably slapping a few blokes and nicking some shopping.

A little kid asked me if I wanted to see the Petit Socco, honing his skills for when he was a fully grown tout. From what I'd read, it was a noteworthy smaller version of the larger square I'd seen yesterday, and it was just about the only place left for me to see in Old Tangier. I accepted and he took me there – it was only two turns away – for a single dirham. Disappointingly, it was the street where I'd had this morning's croissant and had already walked through three times in the last few hours. It was only a square if you used your imagination. Apparently, this was once a thriving spot for drugs and prostitutes. You could almost certainly still buy drugs here, but its other former illegalities had now been replaced by knock-off Barcelona shirts.

It was only eleven and I sat down for a tea. Perusing the

menu, I realised I was still peckish and noticed something on my Moroccan Food hitlist, *khlea*. This is meat, usually beef or lamb, cut into strips, marinaded in garlic, coriander and cumin and left to dry. It's then cooked in a mixture of water and fat, left to dry again and then stored in more fat for up to two years. By all accounts, it wasn't very nice, but that was no reason not to try it. Mine came chopped up in small pieces and added to something approaching an omelette. Because it's stored in fat, it's juicier than your typical jerky, but it was very stringy and had an unappealing stale background flavour, like something you've eaten from the back of your kitchen cupboards and then realised was four years out of date.

I wasn't spending *all* my time eating, despite what you're probably thinking, but lunchtime rolled around soon enough and what a lunch it was. I wandered in the direction of the seafront and discovered a terrace overlooking the fishing port with half a dozen fish restaurants. I'd obviously found the right place since, among the crowds, I couldn't see a single white face.

At the end of the terrace was a fence of tall metal bars. Like a prisoner, I looked through them and over at the bustling harbour below.

"How do I get down there?" I asked a passer-by.

"*Interdit*," came the reply.

Oh well.

One restaurant was larger than the others and full of people. As I looked for a table, I uttered the single word "Fish?" at a passing waiter, who seated me and laid me some cutlery.

"Fish. Sixty dirham," he said.

"Good."

"Salad fifteen."

"Fine."

Bread arrived, as did a bowl of dipping sauce. And then came a huge plate of juicy prawns and crayfish. I'd been hoping for some actual flippy-floppy fish rather than shellfish, but they were extremely tasty. This'd do.

I'd nearly finished my plate when I realised my pink crustaceans were merely an *amuse-bouche*. A mountain of fried fish arrived, along with a salad that alone could have fed a family of four. I picked my way through lip-smacking sardines and flavourful flatfish and piles of squid rings before uncovering the star at its centre, the largest red mullet I'd ever seen. The salad was also excellent, with tomatoes and potatoes and carrot and beetroot and lettuce and tuna and egg. I left half of it and that never happens. I am, after all, an exceptionally greedy pig. This had been a feast, and all for the cost of two Starbucks Caramel Frappuccinos.

With difficulty I walked back to the entrance of the fishing port. I wanted a proper look at the boats that delivered such an excellent meal. A sign said photos of the port couldn't be taken without permission. I approached a policeman and asked if I could go inside and take some snaps. He scowled at me and barked such an emphatic negative you'd think I'd asked permission to fondle his wife.

Tangier had been almost disappointing in its lack of horror and, strolling the medina, it was now how I'd imagined it would be back in 2002, an easy introduction to Morocco. But it's not like this for everyone. Recently an English woman was filmed here attacking a stallholder because she didn't approve of his cage-confined chickens. She even bit the fella. Maybe that's why it all changed. Perhaps they're now terrified of us.

It was time to turn south and explore Morocco's other coastline, its Atlantic one, all the way to Agadir, well over 500 miles away. And if anyone started any trouble, all I had to do was bite 'em.

*

That mystery coughing disease on the opposite side of the planet had begun to spread. Cases had already appeared in Thailand and Japan. And last week, it claimed its first life, a 61-year-old Chinese man. Tomorrow, January 17th, it would take its second.

Chapter 4: The Worst of Morocco

Asilah, Larache and Kenitra

I was woken at eight by a proper ruckus. It was coming from reception, several blokes screaming and smashing the hell out of each other. Ever the superhero, I figured I'd give it a few minutes before I headed down there. Maybe a tout had taken the piss with the wrong crowd of tourists, or that English woman was back to finish eating the rest of Tangier's chicken salesmen.

It took me an hour to escape the western capitalism of modern Tangier and its boring predictability, the same old omnipresent chains. Tangier may have been sanitised since I'd last seen it, but morphing it into a carbon copy of everywhere else surely can't be the best solution.

From a busy dual carriageway I turned on to the N1, the country's old national highway that hugs the Atlantic coast. Now, at least in certain sections, it was forgotten and almost unused. A motorway had rendered it redundant, thankfully. The peaceful riding I'd experienced in the Rif Mountains returned, except now there were no hills to toil up either.

As the N1 was on the beach here, property development had taken off. The shells of new apartments were being erected right beside ghost estates, those that were partially built and clearly abandoned. Huge roadside hoardings advertised properties for just 40,000 euros. Cheap, yes, but the signs in Arabic showed a price of only 20,000. Maybe it was cheaper for locals. After all, a rubbish kasbah I'd visited in Chefchaouen was ten dirham for Moroccans but sixty for the rest of us. At any price, it didn't look like anyone was buying, but maybe that'd change if a construction company ever finished a property.

As I headed southwards, the beach became wilder and vaster. Huge waves hurled themselves violently on to the sand. Eventually, I reached Asilah, a popular destination at warmer times of the year for Tangerines, given its proximity to their city. This was my first chance to see a mid-sized beachside town. What would it be like? Would the fact it was once home to El Raissouli, an early twentieth century bandit and kidnapper, who famously targeted foreigners, have rubbed off on the locals? Yes, it would. Very much so.

I'd decided to stay at the Belle Vue hotel and headed to its supposed MAPS.ME location, but it wasn't there. No problem, I thought, I'd find a different one. After all, there wasn't a shortage.

"You looking for the Belle Vue?" asked a tall lad of about fifteen. "It's here."

I thought he was just going to show me around the corner, but instead he set off at a sprint and I followed him for a couple of minutes before we reached the hotel. I checked in while he hung around awkwardly.

"What about something for me?" he said, interrupting the registration process.

I delved into my pocket and extracted the only coin I had, a five dirham piece. He went bananas.

"It's not enough!" he yelled.

"I'm sorry," I replied, turning back to the receptionist.

"I can't buy *anything* with five dirham!" he said aggressively.

What was I supposed to do? Give him enough for a car?

"It's all I have," I said, bored. "You should have told me you wanted paying beforehand. I've done 400 miles without your help."

The interesting thing is how he knew I was specifically

looking for the Belle Vue when I wasn't really anywhere near it? Maybe he'd added its fake location to MAPS.ME in order to effect this scam. And his crime had paid, just not very well.

I explored the town. There was one near unavoidable street that on each side contained an endless row of nasty-looking restaurants aimed squarely at tourists. And because there were hardly any visitors around in January, the eateries' touts had me almost to themselves. I should carry an air horn for times like these.

It wasn't only the restaurateurs who were annoying. An artist sidled up to me. If you want an image and are of a certain age, he looked like a diminutive Moroccan version of Grange Hill's Scruffy McDuffy.

"I'm not interested," I said.

"I'm not a guide," he replied.

"I don't care. I'm not interested."

I accelerated and he kept up with me, banging on about his work.

"I don't use canvas," he said, not tiring. I went faster. "I use cement bags." He flicked out a painting before me, a useless streak or two on a torn off bit of paper bag.

"It's very brown, isn't it?" I said.

"This key..." he started. I strained my eyes to locate a key. I couldn't. "This key symbolises her liberty." I didn't know who the "her" was and it didn't matter. It was pretentious, which is forgiveable if it provides a laugh, but it was also rubbish.

"I'm not interested."

By now we'd covered about 500 metres. He hadn't fallen behind. He probably clocks up a few hundred miles every day shadowing tourists until they eventually give in and buy his crap. But I wasn't going to, and he finally got the message.

An hour later, I needed calories and found a Moroccan fast food joint. While eating at my roadside table, unable to escape, my artist came past again. I nodded to him ironically, which was a mistake.

"You want me to tell you how much my paintings are?" he asked.

"Not really. But feel free," I replied uninterestedly.

He dragged himself closer to my table and unsheathed a roll of drab, brown splatters.

"Usually they're 150 each, but for today 100."

"Right then. Thanks."

I fell silent.

"How many do you want?"

"None. I'm on a bike." Why do I always have to provide an explanation for not buying? "No" is answer enough.

"Look, you can roll them up like this," he said, demonstrating. "Fifty to help a struggling artist."

There was a good reason he was struggling as an artist.

"No, thanks."

Then he got annoyed and sarcastic.

"What? You want one for free?"

"Not really."

That's gotta hurt. He stood up and threw out a dismissive arm.

"I don't know what you want," he spat. What I wanted was for him to disappear. "You ask for the price..." No, I didn't. "...I give you my best price and you still don't want it."

"What can I say?"

He stamped away, fuming, or at least pretending to fume. But we weren't done with all the people I'd slighted today. My erstwhile hotel locator then walked past.

"Five is not enough," he said, repeating his earlier whinge. "Are you happy now? Was it worth it?"

Actually, no, five wasn't worth it. I'd been robbed. But the slimy smile he'd added during this flyby made me suspect he'd returned to the hotel in my absence and done something to my bike, snipped a cable or two, ripped out a handful of spokes. After all, it was stored at the bottom of the stairs and he may have seen me put it there.

Now I couldn't enjoy the rest of my dinner. I wolfed down what remained and hoofed it to my hotel. Fortunately, I found my bike unscathed, unless, that is, he'd done something more subtle, polonium in my seatpost perhaps. Unlikely, I admit. The only thing he radiated was the spirit of that old bandit, El Raissouli.

I returned to the streets, needing something sweet to eat. I found a café to sit outside and had a *pain au chocolate* and tea. Being the only white face in town, I caught the eye of a man who walked past. Oh joy. He introduced himself as Rachid and sat down beside me. He didn't order a drink but asked me about my trip. He seemed a little sad.

"Do you work?" I said. If he told me he was a vet or an accountant, I could relax and this then wouldn't be yet another attempt to extract money. But of course a vet or an accountant would probably be at work at this time of day.

"No," he replied, "well, when I can."

"And what do you do?"

"I'm a guide."

Jesus Christ! Is that how everyone in Morocco makes a living? But he didn't seem in the mood for selling his services. We talked about prospects in Morocco, about wages and retirement. This topic didn't raise his spirits.

"Is there a pension in Morocco?"

"If you work for the government, yes."

"But no one else?"

"No."

I guess that's why everyone here has kids. You'd need them to feed you when you can't feed yourself, just as it used to be everywhere. And how it'll be again when we all live too long for Ponzi pension schemes to function.

"Have you seen the medina?" he asked.

Here we go.

"Oh yes," I lied.

I finished my tea, thanked him for the chat and then went to find it, but it wasn't all that. It didn't feel like any of the other medinas I'd seen, lacking the bustle of Tetouan and the colour of Chefchaouen. It was entirely flat and cleanly painted white, with forgettable street art, unmemorable for the same reason as Tetouan's art gallery. Anything subversive would've been removed. The whole place felt sterile, and this would be the one and only time I'd say that about anything in Morocco.

I *did* find a gorgeous, green Islamic doorway. It was surrounded by small, attractive paintings of shells and hand prints in a pretty cobalt blue. Unfortunately, it took me a good five minutes to get a photo because another nineteen-year-old Instatramp was modelling in front of it, pulling poses like Vogue-era Madonna while her thirty-year-old boyfriend snapped away. The shapes she threw were unintentionally amusing. Imagine if Victoria Wood had been told to act "all sexy, like" and you're halfway there.

And that photo, that *one* photo, was the highlight of my entire visit to Asilah. From the minute I'd arrived, the whole place had left a bad taste in my mouth. If I'd thought the rest of the country was going to be like this, I'd have turned around and gone home. Only go there if you love hassle or really shit brown paintings.

*

The National Highway moved away from the coast and climbed. The property developments gave way to green fields. It could've been England in springtime except, obviously, for the plentiful sunshine.

Halfway to today's destination, Larache, I met Gustav, a German who'd started back in November in Agadir. He'd done the hinterland and was on his way home.

"I don't like the coast," he said. "But inland is wonderful."
"Any recommendations?"
"Everywhere."
"Except the coast?"
"Yes, except the coast."

Cycling into Larache, the town looked impressive, with a rocky coastline battered by an angry sea. A crumbly old fort, keeping lookout over the waves, sat among colourful houses that tumbled down the surrounding hillside.

I stopped to take a photo from a large piece of waste ground, thereby indicating to the locals I was a tourist and justifiable target. In the far distance I noticed old men shuffling towards me, arms outstretched like zombies, presumably about to offer their services as guides. I cycled off before they could sink my opinion of the town as low as Asilah's.

Larache is home to around 125,000, but it never felt that big. I arrived in a pretty main square, built by the Spanish, architecturally different to what I'd seen elsewhere in Morocco, and found a hotel for just seven euros. Such a price only got me a shared bathroom and, technologically speaking, an eighties themed room, i.e., electricity but no WiFi.

Seeking a link to the outside world, I returned to the plaza and found a connected café. While sipping my mint tea on its terrace, a grey-bearded fella in a red woollen cap came down the road. He was eating a small bowl of spaghetti and plonked himself at the next table. He had the face of an affable madman, which made me warm to him immediately.

"Ah, you're English!" he said, before telling me his name, which involved the accidental ejection of a sizeable quantity of pasta. "But just call me Ash."

He gave me a shortened version of his life story. He'd lived in London for thirty years with his police officer wife, also

Moroccan, but they were now separated.

"An 'uncle' moved in with her," he said. "She cheated."

"And then what?" I asked.

"I got deported."

I assume there was a missing link between those two events, but I didn't pursue it. This had all happened ten years ago.

"What was your job in London?"

"I was a bodyguard."

"For anyone famous?"

"Yeah, Michael Jackson, Whitney Houston, Bob Dylan."

I'd no idea if Ash was another Moroccan fantasist, but I rolled with it.

"An armed bodyguard?"

"Yeah, I was licensed. Had two guns."

"Did you see any trouble?"

"Only when getting drugs for the stars."

He had a good amount of spaghetti in his beard and seemed to annoy the people around him for some reason, possibly because he'd brought food from elsewhere. One staff member marched on to the terrace and made as if to hit him. Ash stood up and so the fella grabbed his chair and threw him out. My madman walked away, shouting and scratching his arse through his baggy trousers.

"People here are stupid," he yelled to me. "Only interested in money."

He came back a little later, shouting theatrically at the staff and customers, who started to laugh at him. It felt like he was putting on a show. Ash chuckled too before wandering off.

I paid up and left but saw Ash again up the street.

"What happened?" I asked.

"They're jealous," he replied. "Because I was speaking to you in your language."

Ah, so it was *my* fault.

After a kidney sandwich, I headed to the town market, an attractive place in blue and white with huge murals high on its second storey walls. The stalls themselves seemed down on their luck. Larache doesn't pull in tourists like the other towns along this coastline, which was probably the reason the touts stayed away and made it a more enjoyable place to be.

I headed further into the medina, down a narrow passage. Up ahead I could hear a kerfuffle, high-pitched screaming, like a bunch of girls having a fight. I walked towards it and that was exactly what I found. Eight women, ranging from fashionable teens to black-smocked grannies, were tugging and yelling at each other in a huddle that rumbled up and down the lane depending upon who had the upper hand. A crowd of locals stood by, stepping backwards and forwards as necessary and sharing flabbergasted glances. From their expressions, this wasn't normal behaviour. I retreated, lest I got caught up in its female unpredictability and had my genitals torn off.

Seeking nature rather than humans I strolled to the seafront. The fort stood solidly at one edge of a splendid bay, cliffs all around its large waves. Unfortunately, just over the promenade wall was a mass of trash. The authorities clearly didn't care, otherwise they'd install the odd rubbish bin.

Darkness was descending. I returned to the streets near my hotel. My conversation with Ash wasn't going to be the only one I'd have with a former London-based Moroccan today.

"'Ey! 'Ello! Wotcher. You English?"

I turned around, expecting to see Danny Dyer but instead saw a man in his fifties as Moroccan-looking as everyone else in town. In Britain, I'd have thought nothing of it, but here his accent was fascinatingly out of place. I stood by his streetside table and we chatted.

"Are you a Cockney?" I said in the same starry-eyed tone

I'd use to ask someone if he were a wizard.

"I'm an East End boy," he replied, smiling and guffawing like Sid James. "I was a right villain."

"What did you do?"

He chuckled to himself.

"What didn't I do? I was a bad 'un. Thieving, burglary, you name it."

Go for it, Steven.

"Did you kill anyone?" I asked, hopefully with a cheeky, please-don't-stab-me smile.

"Nah, nuffin' like that. Come 'n' sit daahn. Talk to me."

So I joined him.

Mustafa had been taken to London as a youngster before eventually being deported for his crimes. It was odd that, until this morning, I'd never met anyone in my entire life who'd been deported and yet he was my second today. Maybe everyone in Larache is an exiled ex-Londoner.

"Would you like to live there again?" I asked.

"Yeah." He looked around. The streets were crowded and people streamed past us thickly. "But in London, you don't go out at night. Full o' villains."

"Like you?" I said.

He laughed.

"Yeah. But not any more."

"You must have gone out to pubs though?"

"Oh yeah. Lived in Whitechapel. Used to drink in the Blind Beggar, y'know, same place as the Krays." And then his language demonstrated how long it'd been since he'd left London. "Y'know, one of 'em was a puff?"

Mustafa had come back to Larache to look after his dad, who'd died two years ago. Like a typical Eastender – that is, someone from the TV soap – his life seemed full of turmoil.

"Now I live in my dad's 'ouse. But my stepmum's a bitch. I 'ave to do what she says. If I want to throw you out, she tells me, I will do."

"Don't you have other family you could stay with?"

"I've got four brothers and two sisters. But I don't get along wiv most of 'em. Two of 'em are proper alkies."

"Ah."

Then everything veered sharply off-topic.

"You a religious man?" Mustafa asked.

"No."

"I wasn't either," he said. "But then I 'ad kif."

"Marijuana?"

"Yeah. I was buzzin'. I climbed up on my roof an' looked up. Allah, I says, please forgive me for ev'ryfink I've done. An' I 'eard 'im speak to me:" He lost his cockney tones and instead channelled Charlton Heston. "I forgive you!"

I struggle to stay serious with conversations like this, always wanting to jump in with a stupid quip, but this wasn't the time.

"You mustn't do anyfink bad no more," he continued, quoting Allah.

"And did you?"

"Naah. I'm an 'oly man."

"That's good."

"I mean, I don't pray or naffink. But I'm an 'oly man. I used to drink. A lot. But you need to be clean for the angels."

We'd been talking for twenty minutes when I realised I was taking on the role of not just his confessor but also his therapist.

"Been with the wife since the seventies. But course, we don't sleep togevver no more."

"No?" I replied uneasily.

Before I could put together a proper response, Mustafa presented the reason for this lack of carnality all too graphically.

"When she eats, she doesn't vom or naffink, but it comes

out, know whaddamean?" he said, lifting himself slightly from his seat and miming a small explosion from his rear end. It seemed too big a job for Imodium. I steered things in a different direction.

"Do you have a lot of friends here?" I asked.

"Nah. In Morocco, people fink you're naffink if you 'ave naffink. If I 'ad a big factory or sammink, I'd 'ave loads o' friends." He shook his head sadly. "Lots of Moroccans ain't good people."

"There must be some good..."

"The world is goin' to shit," Mustafa interrupted. He sounded like my dad. I suspect that, had he stayed in Britain, he'd have been a Daily Mail reader too. But not everyone was a monster.

"I met some Italians the other day. Lovely people. They wanted to take me wiv 'em."

So I wasn't the only one to hear his tales of hardship.

"Why didn't you go?"

"Ill," he replied. He showed me a badly scarred leg. "Second floor."

"A fall?"

"Yeah." Maybe he should stop climbing on his roof while high on kif. "And then there's the wife."

He was about to repeat his earlier mime. I nodded pre-emptively. He sat back in his chair and looked directly at me.

"You're a good man," he said finally. "Talking to you 'as made me feel calm, good. You took the time to talk to me. No one does that any more."

I think he'd taken the ear I'd lent him as that of a caring psychiatrist. In reality, I'd been slightly overwhelmed at the presentation of so many woes.

"If you come back to Larache, you come an' find me, right?"

I would, honestly, but I'd hope Mustafa's circumstances

were improved. They could barely be any worse. At least he had his god and his wife. Maybe he could ask the former to sort out the latter's bottom problems, especially as her bowels seemed to be moving in mysterious ways.

*

I got up and walked to yesterday's WiFi café. Since I'd gone to bed, someone had smashed a shop window, its remnants all over the pavement. Maybe Mustafa had turned bad ways again. I didn't suppose anyone would come to clean it up. Eventually the shards would be kicked into the road and carried away, lodged in the tyres of passing cars. Who needs street sweepers?

I rolled out of town. On its edge I stopped to buy water. A young fella in front of me was buying a small cake and a single cigarette. The shopkeeper accidentally dropped the fake cream slice on his counter, partially destroying it. Instead of getting him a new one, he just handed it to the lad in its smashed up form.

Today's ride was flat and rather dull. I took a shortcut through farmland and polytunnels. Distant women were bent double in fields all day long while men got the clearly much more physically demanding job of driving around little tractors with their friends and making choo-choo noises.

Based on my guidebook's description, I'd been looking forward to today's destination, Moulay Bousselham. The book painted it as a quaint fishing village. In reality, it was an out-of-season hole. It had a large, lonely beach and a small bay full of old boats, but these were away from the town itself, which consisted of nothing but overpriced restaurants, at least by Moroccan standards, all offering the same unimaginative options. This was the last place I'd find my holy quail pie.

I'd originally planned to camp here, but since the site wanted seventy dirham, the price of last night's bed, I figured

I'd find a cheap hotel instead. Through the back of what seemed a clean and modern café, the manager led me down corridors of jumbled tiles to a scuzzy room containing windows that rattled in the breeze with three camp beds covered in paint that had flaked off the walls. It was supposed to rain tonight. This room might have only had the comfort of a campsite but, for more or less the same price, at least I'd be dry.

After a sub-standard pizza dinner, I revisited the beach, the only sight that Moulay Bousselham had to offer, and strolled the town some more. Every pavement was broken. Young fellas hung around, bored, on streets corners, giving the place a slightly menacing air. The locals couldn't even be arsed to offer illegal tours, presumably because they had nothing to show.

So far, Larache aside, Gustav the German had been right about this coast. I was hoping it'd improve soon, but I'd have to wait a while before that happened.

*

So far, the roads I'd cycled on the west coast of Morocco had been filled with places that felt either like failed mid-eighties Spanish property projects, poverty-stricken Moldovan farmlands or, in yesterday's Moulay Bousselham, like a Ukrainian attempt at a small-town tourism, minus the tasty food and beer. Today felt very different, like sub-Saharan Africa.

The flat, monotonous strip of tarmac ran mostly through wilderness. I'd sense a change by the sudden appearance of mud on the road. Around the next bend would be a painfully poor village that stretched for a mile or so. The main occupation in town, and one only available to men, was staring.

Another visible vocation was death. In one village, a man sat beside the road, despatching chickens. Six or so bundles of motionless feathers lay around him. A final bird squawked its swansong as I cycled past.

In the most desperate of these places, every building was constructed of unfinished breeze blocks. Unusually for Morocco, this even included its ubiquitous mosque, which elsewhere was generally the least worst building in town.

Chickens, bony cows and sheep picked through the piles of plastic at the roadside. These unplanned rubbish tips also adversely affected the wildlife. A gull flew overhead, a metre-long plastic tape wound around its leg. With so many men sitting idle, it'd still never occurred to anyone to say, "Y'know what? Why don't we tidy up this shithole?"

Despite being a school day, the roadside saw plenty of children, but this wasn't because there were no schools. They just weren't being used, thereby creating another generation trapped in such poverty. At the end of one village, an eight-year-old boy stuck out a hand for a high-five, which I missed, distracted by his younger sister rubbing her fingers together in the international symbol of "Gimme money, rich boy".

Many of the villages had speed bumps, as if the only response to seeing these awful places was to rush through as rapidly as possible. Similar-sized settlements in the Rif Mountains had hardly been dripping in gold, but at least they didn't look like everyone had given up. Passing through as quickly as I could was a depressing experience.

I'd read a blog of a bloke cycling around Morocco. Somewhere near here, a gang of locals had spread themselves across the road in order, he thought, to intercept him. At times today it felt like this was happening to me too, but they were just walking on the asphalt because it was easier than negotiating the rough ground at its sides. Still, these villages gave me the creeps. The poor sods here had nothing and I at least had a bike and some bags and almost certainly a little money. I'd have been an easy target.

Things took a more surreal turn later in the afternoon. In one village a teenager yelled something repeatedly as I passed him. I was too slow to realise he was wiggling a phone and saying "photo". It happened again a couple of hundred metres farther up the road. This second guy was taller, better built than the first, and in his hand was a sickle, the sort that could easily take off a head if it were attached to someone declining the opportunity to provide a donation. It was wisest not to stop.

Later, a young teenager tried to keep up with me on his bicycle. Racing him at least passed some time on this monotonous track. Once he'd fallen behind, I stopped for a slurp of water, but he reappeared again in seconds. The race continued. He cycled at my side and asked for money, rubbing his fingers together.

"A million!" he yelled, more than a little presumptuously.

Just as he faded away, another race started, this time between me and a donkey and cart controlled, in a manner of speaking, by a group of girls. Initially, I raced them too, but in order to gain an advantage they thrashed the hell out of their beast. I didn't want to be the reason for animal cruelty, and so slowed down and let them win. But while distracted by the girls racing ahead, from nowhere came Pugsley, that weird little black-haired freak off *The Addams Family*, screaming at me and waving an axe in the air. That was an image too far and I put on another spurt that carried me all the way to the outskirts of my destination. Phew!

Kenitra was a proper city, home to 430,000 people, and its busy streets were quite a shift in mood. To arrive though, I first crossed a huge, shit-brown river. Given the appalling stench, it wasn't difficult to ascertain the reason for its colour. I didn't feel I was seeing the best of Morocco these last few days.

I hit the centre and, after a day of empty roads, traffic

reappeared. Lots of it. As I waited at some lights, a bloke on a scooter tapped me on my shoulder.

"*Bonne route!*" he said, handing me a couple of fresh pears.

This is a good time to mention Moroccan traffic lights. Cycling through Europe, there are two different systems in operation. Some countries, like Britain, have two full-sized lights, one where you stop and another several metres in front that the lead driver can more easily see. In other places, such as France, the second traffic light is replaced with a miniature one on the main traffic light's pole for the benefit of the driver in front. Morocco has found a cheaper solution. There's just a single set of lights at the place where you stop, no second set, miniature or otherwise. If you're at the head of the queue, you only know it's time to get moving when everyone behind is blasting their horn and wishing death upon you.

Despite its size, research had shown that Kenitra was not only light on cheap accommodation, but on any accommodation at all. So when I passed a grand-looking hotel in its centre, I leapt at the opportunity and was prepared to take a hit cost-wise. At least, I thought, it'd be a chance to discover what "nice" Moroccan hotels were like, rather than my usual cheap but often squalid affairs. Yes, I got a functioning television and crisp bed linen, but for my 45 euros – remember, that's eleven times the price of my cheapest Moroccan place – it was still fairly shabby. Each old school bathroom tap turned smoothly enough, but you obviously have to pay more if you don't want the entire spout to twist along with it.

Today hadn't been my best and I wanted it to contain at least one highlight. I found this in a chicken shack. Half a roast bird, with tasty and crispily blackened skin, was served alongside a decent portion of chips, a dhal-like lentil dish, a spicy spinach one and a gorgeous tomato dipping sauce.

Throw in bread and a drink and it cost just over three euros. On a day when I could've fallen foul of a cock with an axe, my day had been saved by a chicken.

In the evening I headed to a café to get my daily fix of mint tea. Being in an actual city, this one felt more like a trendy bar, a place you'd sip cocktails in London. I sat on a large, comfortable sofa watching Moroccan pop videos on a huge screen. I'm aware that music videos are often aspirational and don't necessarily represent any sort of truth, but these were filmed in a Morocco from a different dimension. They contained women for a start and, in reality, you could travel for quite a long time around certain parts of Morocco without realising women live here too. And these women also possessed skin!

But the biggest fantasy created by the video's director wasn't human. When one of the singers hoofed it through a forest, I watched the screen, thinking there was something remiss. But what was it? Ah, yes, where was all the plastic crap? A drone-mounted camera screamed into the sky to provide a wider shot. You could see for at least a square mile, and not a single wrapper. You have to feel sorry for the poor intern who picked that lot up.

C'mon, Morocco, raise your game.

Chapter 5: A Camel in the Capital

Rabat and Casablanca

I was now in the six-million-strong conurbation that stretches from here in Kenitra through Rabat to the south of Casablanca. To avoid the busiest main roads I took a more interesting route through the city's backstreets and suburbs. I even found a bicycle path. Painted blue, it started nowhere of importance and finished in a similar location 300 metres farther up the road. It looked like Kenitra city council had taken cycle infrastructure advice from Britain.

The mood turned grimmer as I travelled through the poorest corners of Kenitra. A city whose centre was so modern came apart at its edges. I passed row after row of shed-sized shacks with breeze block walls and corrugated iron roofs. Judging by the amount of washing that hung outside, there were crowds of people living within these tiny places. It was reminiscent of Delhi's roadside slums and all a few miles from an opulent city centre. The Organisation for Economic Co-operation and Development (OECD) says Morocco is the most income-unequal country in Africa. And this in a nation whose leader was once hailed as the King of the Poor. Maybe there are so many poor people to be king of because he has all the money. Even back in 2013, his personal wealth was two billion pounds and rising.

The road became a packed mud path, more like sub-Saharan Africa again. From out of a house, a muscular mongrel leapt towards me, teeth flashing, snarling and slavering. It took a lunge but just missed my foot. I yelled and it backed off but immediately jumped at me again. I shouted a second time. A small boy came out of the house after hearing the commotion, presumably to see if they needed to bother feeding the dog this morning.

Eventually, I ran out of lanes and was thrown on to the main road to Rabat, the capital of Morocco. The day was warm and dry and everything was going well until I hit the bridge to cross into the city and realised, as a cyclist, I wasn't allowed on it. A five mile detour later, I reached the centre. Heavily armed uniformed men walked around in threes. Either security was tight here in the capital or someone was having one hell of a fancy dress party.

After dumping my belongings in a hotel in the busy medina, I went out to explore. I passed a stall selling msemen, those thick, flaky pancakes I'd already had for breakfast a few times, but here they were a rich orange-red. I bought one, warm and wrapped, for three dirham from the smiling saleswoman. Their colour comes from minced and fried onion and pepper woven into the pastry and they're extremely tasty, so tasty that I immediately returned to her stall and bought a second.

In the evening I met up with Juan. If you followed my previous journey to war-torn Nagorno-Karabakh, you might remember Juan as the friendly bike repairman in Spain's Murcia. Our paths had crossed on this trip too. He was on his way to Senegal, a total of 2,500 miles through the Sahara and Mauritania, raising money to build schools there.

We went to a poky café, sitting inside on this chillier evening. Weak fluorescent bulbs dimly lit the place. The interior designer had gone for the usual sickly pea-green colour scheme. Food and drink options were penned up on a large white board. Tea was three dirham, soup five. It felt like the café and its prices hadn't changed for decades. If they'd had a telly here, John Pertwee would still be Doctor Who.

I walked back to my hotel through the lanes of the

medina. Things were bustling tonight. I caught a glimpse inside a mosque. It was quiet, just a handful praying, but I was surprised how plush, how neat and tidy, it seemed. It was almost like the outside world was deliberately kept tatty to differentiate it from God's house. Maybe that's why no one bothered to pick up all those plastic bottles.

I continued through the godless streets. The occasional bright light threw everyone into relief. A woman carried a freshly killed, still unplucked chicken. Cats padded around corners, looking for titbits. Merchants sat in front of huge rolls of material or in mini hardware stores piled high with teapots and tools. Tiny bakeries sold mountains of dry-looking biscuits that teetered precariously. And then there were all the pharmacies. There are twice as many per head of population in Morocco than the UK. Is everyone sick here?

A motorbike burst down the medina street and braked quickly when met by a wall of shoppers. An old woman pushed her mother in a heavy wheelchair, neither looking happy. On a rug a beggar sprawled himself, the first Moroccan I'd seen in shorts, worn here to accentuate his revenue-generating stump. All of life was in the medina and a lot of it looked painfully difficult.

*

I spent the next day wandering the city. It didn't feel like a capital, lacking the size or chaos I'd expected. With 577,000 inhabitants, it wasn't even as large as Tangier. I'd have to wait until Casablanca for the real madness. It's nearly six times the size.

The city was pleasant enough. I walked to the new town and saw its Art Deco cathedral and the Kasbah of the Udayas, a little like Asilah's medina but without the sterility. And not once was I approached by a tout. A lot of visitors avoid Rabat, which probably explains why the faux-guides are elsewhere, but this is reason enough to come here.

I returned to my hotel from a different direction, one that just happened to take me down a medina alleyway specialising in traditional grub. Oh lordy! What I saw there wasn't even on my Weird Moroccan Food List. Here was my chance to try a roasted camel's head.

It was quite a disturbing sight to behold. With half its barbecued flesh peeled away, much of its skull was visible, which seemed to consist of two mammoth tusks. A camel's head is massive. Obviously, you don't eat the whole thing.

I pointed at the smouldering mass of meat and the stallholder gave me a look that said, "Oh, this is going to be fun!" He invited me into the little eatery behind him. A few minutes later a sandwich arrived, a whole flatbread split in two and opened up to form pockets into which was stuffed a huge pile of roasted camel face. Liberally sprinkled with salt and cumin, it tasted like pungent, fatty lamb. As far as new experiences go, it was up there with my first ever pint of gin 'n' tonic, in that it was delicious but probably best for my health not to indulge too often. The meat was soft and a bit chewy, the sort you find still stuck in your teeth an hour later for an additional treat.

Feeling I was on a roll of interesting food after yesterday's flavoured msemen and today's dromedary delight, I went on the prowl for further goodies in the evening.

"Is that a pastilla?" I asked a bakery assistant, pointing to a filo disc about an inch thick, the first time I'd seen one in real life.

Yes, it was, and they had two different varieties. Neither of them contained my holy quail, which wasn't particularly surprising, but this was a good place to start, right at the bottom of the pastilla pecking order, with chicken. The second one contained seafood, a variety I'd never heard of and, once I'd tasted it, I realised why no one was talking it up.

What differentiates a pastilla from any other chicken pie is its unusual topping. It is liberally coated with icing sugar and cinnamon, a combination of sweet and savoury that won't appeal to everyone. My chicken pastilla was interesting, tasting both wrong and oh so right at the same time, like a main course and pudding all rolled into one. Don't imagine roast beef flavoured ice cream. That'd only work in Heston Blumenthal's head. Think turkey and cranberry sauce.

*

I had a cold, which was unusual for me. The sniffles usually pay a visit every third year or so. It wasn't much of a surprise in Morocco though. Everything you eat has been touched by dozens of people. It wasn't uncommon to see customers leafing through the piles of flat breads on a shop's counter, picking each of them up in turn and then buying one at the bottom that looked identical to all the rest. Every sandwich I ate contained the sum total of a village's bacteria. By rights, I should also have had cholera, diphtheria and smallpox. Thank Christ for all those pharmacies.

I cycled out of town along the coastal promenade, dismounting every few hundred metres to clear the massive kerbs of each and every side road. I said hello as I passed a policeman and then saw a sign suggesting I shouldn't be cycling there at all. The law, apparently, would rather I be on the busy dual carriageway alongside it instead. I figured I'd chance it on the quiet and beautifully wide, almost pedestrian-free prom. Besides, that copper hadn't said anything. Up ahead I passed two more policemen. I nodded at them and waited to be rugby tackled to the ground, but they too said nothing. Who knew what the rules were?

I reached the edge of town and continued onward, now into a strong, wearying wind. The rest of today was an untidy mess, a holiday home wasteland. There were loads of abandoned apartments, but new ones were also springing up beside them. All the billboards for the properties, as well as for other aspirational businesses, like gyms and high-end restaurants, featured humans with my skin colour. Buy this expensive stuff, they seemed to say, and you too can become white.

One particular housing project was painful to view. Old faded billboards, each attached to a different house, contained a single marketing power-word like Excellence, Luxe and Prestige. The houses weren't finished and never would be. They certainly didn't look like the elegant artist's impression that shared the space on those single-worded billboards. The buildings were already crumbling, their roofs caving in. It looked like money was wasted for fun, which wouldn't be so criminal if Morocco wasn't a country with millions of people desperately short of it.

Today's target had been Casablanca, and to reach it was only a sixty mile journey, but with an increasing headwind, my cold-weakened body and an impending rainstorm, I made like a parachutist and bailed.

Fifteen miles from Casablanca is Mohammedia, a town that sounds like an Islamic internet company. It was a soulless place, a long, thin, dual carriageway hugger. Online sources told me 200,000 lived here, just another part of this enormous conurbation. In reality, it looked like they'd planned for 200,000, but only a couple of hundred had turned up. There were scores of empty apartment blocks on the edge of town. The centre was marginally busier, but there I didn't see a single pavement that wasn't broken. It looked like The Hulk had paid a visit.

It wasn't just the infrastructure that was shafted. Thanks to a nearby oil refinery, the air was bad too. Local pulmonologist Dr Hamid Kerrat was interviewed by Arab news media organisation Al-Araby Al-Jadeed in 2018.

"At times, black dust envelops the city and can be seen on car windows and house rooftops," he said. He claimed this was why so many locals, especially kids, developed asthma. There's a good reason why Mohammedia isn't listed in Morocco's holiday brochures.

On my way in, none of the hotels I'd found online existed in reality, or they existed but were no longer hotels. In the centre I finally located the plush Hotel Fedala, a charming, riad-style place, heavy with gorgeous Moroccan tiling. However, I didn't know any of this yet, because upon arrival the reception staff were sitting in darkness due to a power cut. I was led to my room by a woman with a torch. It added an air of excitement, like I was off searching for treasure with Lara Croft.

Despite the rain coming down, I decided to see what the town had to offer. On my way out of the hotel, I asked the now illuminated but seemingly lower-ranked of the two receptionists what time breakfast was. She looked at me oddly.

"It's tomorrow," she replied.

Yes, I know that, I'm not a moron. I wasn't expecting it at eight o'clock tonight.

"Good, thank you. What time tomorrow?"

"Ah." She thought for a moment. "I'll ask."

There aren't many facts a receptionist should definitely know, but surely that's one of them. Maybe she was new.

As it turned out, my adventure outside was soon abandoned after reaching the limits of what looked structurally safe. With all plans of exploration tossed to the not insignificant wind, I instead dived into a snack bar and bought a sandwich full of *merguez* – thin and red spiced mutton sausages – and then treated myself to two pots of mint tea and a spell of quiet reflection at a café across the road. I'd come to love these moments, full of nothing but relaxation and contemplation. While sitting there, two or three beggars came up to me, and me alone, just because I was white, the racists.

On my way back to the hotel I stopped at a shop and bought water and some buns. The shopkeeper gave me a bag to carry them. Morocco's replacement, in the light of its plastic bag ban, is one made from a thinly woven material that presumably biodegrades. Today's biodegraded a little too quickly. It couldn't handle the overbearing weight of a 1.5 litre bottle of water and a couple of Mars Bars. It split, spilling my stuff all over the town's broken pavement. As I scrambled to pick up my shopping, a hand appeared from nowhere, a passing man offering me a replacement bag. The town may not have been up to much, but at least its people were.

*

Riding past yet another police roadblock – so far I was averaging about two a day – I skirted Casablanca's surrounding shanty towns. It was from such desperate places that the city's 2007 suicide bombers came. These must have been the most inept terrorists in the whole of history. At the end of three days of bombing, just one unfortunate was killed along with seven idiot terrorists. Surely you must receive fewer virgins in the afterlife for such a shoddy performance. But this came on the back of a far deadlier attack four years earlier that claimed the lives of 33. I haven't included the terrorists in this total. They don't deserve to be counted.

It was dangerous such places still existed. If some snake oil-selling mullah can convince you your happiest future involves strapping Semtex to your nipples, things must be tough. Morocco's authorities, knowing that tourism and terrorism don't mix, came down hard on those left standing in 2007. In the end, 45 people were arrested for their part in the fiasco and sentenced to between two and thirty years in jail. I doubt they found any virgins in prison, but I bet they got their fair share of sex.

The city centre approached. Traffic lights in Casablanca

seemed to be there just to brighten the place up a bit. Or perhaps they performed some advisory function. On the whole, though, they were ignored. Several people ran them while on red, often in spectacular fashion, a couple of cars nearly smashing head on right before my eyes. It was like a front row seat at a demolition derby.

It started to rain, my first mild soaking since the beginning, and I ducked into a *salon de thé* to dry off. In case you're wondering, a salon de thé is the same as your bog standard Moroccan café but believes itself to be superior. I ordered a mint tea. The waiter asked me if I'd like a, well, I don't know, because I missed what he said. But in these situations, "yes" is always the correct answer.

I took a table on the salon's covered terrace. My tea arrived as usual but accompanying it was another glass, full of hot water and a twig full of leaves. I fished out the plant and gave it a nibble. It was extremely bitter but reminded me of an unplaceable taste I'd had a long time before. And then something came back to me, a detail I'd read, that in some parts of Morocco additional herbs are supplied with mint tea and one of those was quite surprising, because it's poisonous. I now remembered what the twig reminded me of. Back in the late nineties, while living in the Austrian city of Graz, I'd melted a sugar cube over a candle and added the resulting magma to a thick, foul-tasting green liquid, one that left a scuzzy white residue on my glass when I swirled it around. That drink was absinthe and this herb wormwood, the poison it's traditionally made from.

The online advice about how much was safe to eat was sketchy since there are no official guidelines. All the website said was that a side effect of taking an excess of it was death, but in reality that's true of anything. That's what "too much" means. According to Freddie Mercury, even too much love can kill you, and he should know.

I looked to my waiter for guidance and he mimed popping the plant into the little silver pot that contained my mint tea. The resulting Brew of Death was bloody wonderful. I already loved mint tea, but the addition of a deadly poison took it to a different level of flavourful complexity. It also made me feel like I was dancing as close to the edge of danger as tea-drinking would allow. This was the sort of cuppa you'd get at Andy McNab's gaff.

The rain eventually eased and I continued on my way. A final Highway Code challenge presented itself in the form of a large, chaotic roundabout. Traffic pinged in and out of it without stopping or anyone looking to see what other drivers might be doing. It was impossible to work out who *really* had the right of way and so, having cheated death once this morning, I took my chances and cycled blindly into the mix. I became the Moses of the cycling world as the traffic parted like the Red Sea and I arrived in the centre of Casablanca.

The city has some impressive statistics. While it has never been the official capital of Morocco, it's undoubtedly its economic powerhouse. It has been here in one form or another since at least the seventh century BCE, it's the second largest port in North Africa and home to nearly 3.5 million people. More importantly, it's home to the world's largest swimming pool – almost half a kilometre long – as well as the world's biggest mattress. At sixteen by twelve metres, changing its duvet cover must be a challenge.

I found a hotel – fortunately, the bed was normal sized – dumped the bike and went out to do a little shopping. Once through Casablanca's disappointingly tiny medina, I fell upon the most famous bar in town, possibly the most famous bar in the whole of Africa. Rick's Café, the star of *Casablanca* the movie, never actually existed until 2004. This was the year an astute businessman, understanding that tourists with a dollar in their pockets will buy any old shite, opened it up. At this time of day, however, it was closed. But I couldn't have got in anyway because I wasn't correctly attired. A fake, tourist-conning joint has standards, don't you know?

But what do you think would be appropriate dress to enter such a novelty pub? From the notice on the door, the following garments weren't allowed: flip flops, torn or ragged clothes, shorts, tank tops, low-cut necklines, logo t-shirts, mini skirts, cargo pants and track suits. Backpacks and bare midriffs were also verboten. I fancied seeing if I'd be admitted in moon boots and a mankini.

Reading the reviews, the place takes itself a bit too seriously. While expensive, the food is apparently mediocre, the cocktails likewise, but at least there's a numpty bashing out *As Time Goes By* on a piano and so it probably recreates the joys of a 1940s film studio adequately well.

Being in a city, and since there was one near Rick's, I investigated what a Moroccan mall was like. Once inside, I slipped into another dimension. All the shops looked suitably glossy, but they were brands I'd never heard of. Perhaps these stores were better known in Africa or the Middle East, but, whatever the truth, *Colin's* really isn't a great name for a cool fashion chain. The food court included a handful of recognisables but also present were *Chicking*, a chain from the UAE, which just sounds illiterate, and *Smashburger*, which to British ears suggests unappetising reconstituted potato on a bun.

Unknown corporations aside, it was tough to imagine this opulence coexisting in the same city as those terrible slums on the way in. Of course, many places have inequality but, in Europe at least, the biggest gap is mostly between the rich and those just about managing. I'm sure that same gap exists here, but there's also a stratum beneath, a long, long way beneath, where exploding your innards is preferable to carrying on with life as it is.

Near the shiny shopping mall was the Hassan Mosque, the largest one in Africa and the third largest in the world. It has a laser atop its minaret that's aimed directly at Mecca, although I'm assuming not in a threatening way like that one on the Death Star.

The mosque was beautiful, very grand and ornate albeit in that tediously symmetrical, patterned way so beloved of Islamic architecture. Gimme a Christian cathedral with its frequent depictions of torture and murder any day.

The call to prayer kicked off while I was sitting in the mosque's not insignificant shadow and, yet again, it was another ropey vocal artist. Surely, for such a prestigious gig, they could have employed a sweet-voiced angel. I know it can be done. I've heard it, once only though, in Albania.

The Islamic yelling ended and a man of about thirty came to sit beside me. We got talking. He told me his name was Samuel.

"It's a Christian name," he said. "Not Islamic." He was a Syrian refugee. His wife and children were already in the UK. "I need to get there," he continued. "And the only way is illegally."

His original plan had been to reach Belgium and then steal away on board a truck crossing to Britain. But his progress to Belgium had been thwarted. His plane from Bulgaria, organised by Afghanis, had stopped here en route.

"One of the other refugees was causing problems and as punishment we were all kicked out here."

He'd already seen the inside of a lot of camps, fourteen in total, in Turkey and Greece.

"They were bad. One person had a problem with his head," he said, tapping his temple, "and pushed a guard. He was beaten until he was blue."

But there'd also been some kindness along the way.

"In Athens I was put in police cells. We were only

supposed to be kept for 48 hours, but I was there for months. It was better than the camps though. People came to visit other prisoners but then would come back to give me food."

"Where in Syria did you live?"

"I was a primary school teacher in Aleppo. And I'm a writer. Did you know a lot of writers came to Morocco?"

In the fifties and sixties, the country had lured Europe and America's literary types. Jack Kerouac, Tennessee Williams, Allen Ginsberg and William Burroughs had all ended up here. Some say they came for the easily available drugs but – who knows? – maybe they simply adored badly seasoned tagines.

"Yes, I was in Tangier..." I started.

He finished my sentence for me.

"Yes, Paul Bowles," he said, naming an American author whose exhibition is there. I'd never heard of him before seeing signs for it in Tangier. Samuel was clearly a well-educated fella.

He talked about Britain as a promised land.

"But you need to be careful in England. It's not perfect," I said. "Racism has been rising recently."

"No," he replied. "There's no racism in an intelligent mind."

"Exactly."

"The British are intelligent. Not like Morocco. Here everyone is stupid."

"And what's your plan for the future? To return eventually to Syria?"

"Yes, after the war. But as long as Putin helps Assad, that can't happen."

"So what now?"

"A tanker leaves here tonight."

It came as no surprise when he asked for money. He needed food. Otherwise he'd steal it while aboard, he told me, but then he might get caught.

If none of this were true, if he was just another Moroccan bullshit artist, he'd worked hard for the twenty minutes I talked to him, building such a convincing story that he deserved what I gave him. But I believed him totally. I hope he's now reunited with his wife and kids. And I hope he found a Britain that didn't disappoint him.

I walked back through the medina and saw an intriguing sight, a small stall grilling a row of weird-looking brown-black organs. They looked like little leathery purses. Could that be spleen? I asked the cook. Yes, it was.

"*Chameau?*"

"*Non, mouton.*"

So what if it was sheep spleen rather than camel, this was exciting. I'd previously had spleen as part of *beuschel*, a mixed offal stew in Austria, but with everything chopped up, it was impossible to tell what individual bits tasted of. But unlike liver and kidneys and very occasionally heart, no one eats spleen in the UK. I assumed it must be awful.

I entered the little one-seater room behind the grill and was treated to a tasty merguez sausage while I waited. And then came the main event, a spleen sandwich. And what a surprise! It was superb. It reminded me a little of black pudding the way it's served in Austria, soft and creamy. The bread was also laden with a salad heavy on olives. The whole lot was fantastic. Spleen was easily my new favourite organ.

*

For breakfast, I popped to the café around the corner from my hotel for a mint tea and a couple of croissants. I went inside to pay and realised the place doubled as a bar. Beer sat in the fridge, assorted spirits on shelves. This was my first Moroccan pub. After nearly a month without, it seemed strange to see alcohol for sale again. It suddenly felt naughty, like the stolen glimpse of a top-shelf porn mag back in the eighties.

Although it was only eleven in the morning, one Moroccan was in the corner, already several beers into today's adventure. Maybe if you drink at all in this country, you drink hard. After all, you've abandoned your god, and the devil makes the best cocktails.

I strolled the city's streets. Casablanca wasn't going to win any beauty competitions, but it had a certain industrious charm. Traffic was thick, every driver leaning heavily on his horn. No one stood still. Everyone had something to do.

I reached the city's new medina, but it felt sanitized, like it had been built solely for tourists and filled with the trinkets they'd buy, such as embroidered slippers and teapots and blankets. It lacked the fire, the dirt, the death and twisted limbs of Rabat or Tetouan.

I'd aimed to see the Royal Palace, but I couldn't even glimpse it over its huge guarded fences. What was King Mohammed VI scared of? The starving millions in their shanty towns wanting a slice of his extravagant cake? Maybe he'd good reason to protect himself.

I headed to the city's cathedral, a tall, white building that was entirely fenced off. I could see through a gap that its front door was wide open. Perhaps there was a way inside. In the distance, I noticed a young Moroccan sneakily exiting the cathedral grounds. Then he went back in again. Maybe I could too. I caught him up.

"Can I come in?"

He looked at me suspiciously.

"Where are you from?"

Was that important? But before I could answer, he opened a makeshift door and let me in.

"Come on," he said.

We walked side by side towards the cathedral. I heard a noise behind me and turned around to see a couple of other fellas squatting in a corner. Entering a dark building under these circumstances might not have been my wisest decision. I told my guide my name to humanise myself – he was called Selim – hoping that what had worked with stone-throwing children might also with potentially murderous adults.

We entered the cathedral, but it was entirely empty except for scaffolding at its far end. The building's awe-inspiring majesty had been removed now it was reduced to a shell. It had ceased its religious function in 1956, on Morocco's independence, but was supposed to be open to visitors. I'm fairly sure Selim wasn't there in any official capacity.

We left the building and I attempted to go out the way I'd come in. No, mimed Selim, there were security cameras that way. Instead, he sneaked me out of another door, a secret one through a load of overgrown plants that carried me into a magical world of, erm, heavy traffic.

It was lunchtime and so I walked to the central market. As I approached its restaurants, a tout came out to lure me in.

"Are you a vegetable?" he asked. That confused me. Maybe he thought I was a Swede.

"No, I'm not a vegetable."

"Sorry, sorry. I mean vegetarian."

"No," I replied. "I'm looking for oysters."

A few tens of miles along the coast is Oualidia, Morocco's centre for these usually expensive shellfish. I'd never eaten one before.

I sat down and a scruffy man pounced on my table. He smiled madly.

"You want to buy?" he said, showing me a watch. "It's Rolex."

"Of course it is."

He looked smug, like I should be impressed. This was obviously Rolex's new sales strategy, to hawk stuff around Moroccan markets by a man with teeth the colour of chocolate.

My food arrived, five raw oysters. They were served on ice and a bed of seaweed. I added a squeeze of lemon juice and a drop or two of the accompanying chimichurri-like hot sauce and had a slurp. I'd expected not to like them, either being snottily slimy or like a large mussel, the only seafood I'm not fond of, but they were neither. Instead, they were exceptionally easy to eat and very refreshing. In fact, they were *too* easy to eat. They disappeared in no time at all and not a dent had been made in my hunger. But would they be worth it? Around a hundred people die each year of vibriosis, the disease you can contract from contaminated oysters. After these, and yesterday's poisonous tea, I'd probably be necking hemlock tomorrow.

There was still one item on my To Do list although there was a good reason not to visit it: It'd been closed down. Casablanca's former abattoirs, housed in a large, architecturally interesting Art Deco building, were abandoned in 2002, but they were then unofficially repurposed as a contemporary art space. Just a year before I was in town, this all came to an end when the authorities moved in and no one knew why. It was strongly suspected to be connected to the nation's clampdown on people saying things the state didn't like. By 2015, Morocco had fallen to 130th out of 180 countries for the freedom of its speech. It had previously been much higher. This project was one of the few places such expression had still been possible.

I arrived at yet another fenced-off building but found its main entrance. A chubby guy decked out as a fancy-dress policeman was patrolling inside and wanted to know why I was there. His inability to speak English or French hindered his interrogation.

"Abattoirs," I said.

He hadn't a clue what I was saying.

I mimed painting a picture. That didn't help. So I just pointed forward and walked and he didn't stop me. The outside walls were full of graffiti reminiscent of Berlin and eastern Europe. Most of it was a lot better, more powerful and definitely more subversive than Tetouan's crappy art gallery. I tried to look inside the abattoir building itself – through an open door I could see steel hooks hanging from its ceiling – but the security guard wouldn't let me in. Still, I was glad I'd had a peek at what had once been a symbol of Morocco's fight for liberty and freedom of expression, even if nowadays attempting the latter is likely to end the former.

Back in my room and late in the afternoon I realised I'd missed somewhere, one last place I had to see in Casablanca and, luckily, it was literally around the corner from my hotel. Le Petit Pouchet was a bar that had once been the haunt of Antoine de Saint-Exupéry, the author of *The Little Prince*, French singer-songwriter Édith Piaf but, most importantly for me, philosopher and author Albert Camus.

Despite warnings that Le Petit Pouchet was now a rough dive, I paid a visit. Coming at it from one direction, it looked old and knackered, but from the front, with its outward-facing chairs, it could've been any other Moroccan café. Inside, it was a lot smaller than I was expecting, about the size of a single car garage, but its rogue Muslim, day-time drinkers were making a well-oiled racket. All romantic notions of being infused with the wisdom of Camus were removed. I was more likely to get my face infused with shards of beer bottle.

Just as Camus wouldn't have done, I ordered a tea and took a seat outside. Le Petit Pouchet wasn't cashing in on its genuine claim to fame, the polar opposite of Rick's Café's fraudulence. Its only nod to former glories was etched on to an outer wall, what looked like an original, now faded menu in French offering prawns and oysters and snails all the way from Burgundy.

I sat and people-watched for half an hour. There were far fewer djellabas worn here and only a handful of the older women wore traditional dress. Casablanca and its youngsters were moving with the times. One reviewer of Rick's Café had even complained he couldn't get in wearing a djellaba. The owners were probably nervous he wasn't a proper tourist, the type happy to spaff twenty quid on a cocktail someone had forgotten to put alcohol into. He should have turned up in that mankini.

*

The world was slowly taking notice of the problems in China, especially as Wuhan, a city of eleven million, had been put into quarantine. Over 2,000 people had already contracted the virus and 56 had died. For the rest of the world, the media was taking great pleasure in delivering misery and panic to mailboxes and inboxes, but the disease hadn't even properly started yet.

I, on the other hand, was blissfully unaware of any of this and still had more of the country's Atlantic coast to discover.

Chapter 6: The Pearl of the Atlantic

Oualidia and Essaouira

I rolled out of town, past a huge "destination mall", a term I hadn't heard before, a place presumably so spectacular that even if there's nothing we need, we turn up regardless just to gawp at the glorious consumerism and blow a fortune on clothes we'll never wear and gadgets we'll never use. I wonder what those poor sods living in shacks on the edge of town do for *their* entertainment.

Today's sixty odd miles were uneventful. Around the halfway stage, I saw a man sitting under a tree. At first I thought he was waving, but I looked more closely and saw he had two fingers up. Was that a very British up yours? But then he raised them to his lips and mime-smoked a cigarette. I didn't know if he was selling or requesting and, in any case, it didn't matter. To my refusal he gave me a comedy "Oh, you utter monster!" dismissal.

But not everyone was so disappointed with me today. A row of kids lined up at the side of the road to high-five me in turn, each one squealing like a happy hamster as we connected.

As I reached El Jadida, a coastal town you have absolutely no need to commit to memory, I stopped for a drink of water. A woman of about fifty wound down her car window and talked to me in French. I struggled to understand everything but played along anyway. This was the first conversation I'd had with *any* non-service sector Moroccan woman and what made it even more unusual was how flirtatiously she acted. Maybe it didn't happen. Perhaps I'd fallen off and bumped my head.

As I cycled around the centre of town, an old bloke on a bicycle followed me.

"You need somewhere to stay? I have a riad. You stay with me. My name is Habib."

"No, thank you," I replied. "I've got a room already."

I hadn't, but I would soon enough. I was just sick of chancers. This was the most unfortunate aspect of Morocco. There were so many people who only approached me because they assumed, incorrectly, I was a source of great wealth, that I possibly dismissed those genuine ones who had no such intentions. On my travels throughout the whole of Europe, I'd never adopted this stance. If someone offered kindness, in whatever form, I'd accept it and afterwards think the world a better place. Morocco was testing the limits of my faith in humanity.

I went for a stroll, stopping for a snack and getting lost in the medina. I'd seen photos of an interesting-looking sea fortress and headed for that. On the way a large group of school kids started to follow me and chant things. I'd no idea what they were saying. Hopefully they were lauding me as a new messiah rather than shouting, "Burn the paedo!"

I reached the fort, but it hadn't been looked after. Its cannons were all bashed up and splashed with graffiti. It was sad Morocco let its history be treated like this. The surrounding beach was full of litter, its pebbles covered with cans, bottles, milk cartons, nappy bags and a plastic sack that appeared to contain someone's liver.

Walking back to town, I passed a bunch of guys playing football on a concrete pitch. Either because they were short of players or because no one wanted to hurl their fragile human bodies repeatedly on to such a hard surface, there were no goalkeepers. In their place were a couple of concrete-filled tubs on each goal line to act as obstacles. If the manager of

Blackburn Rovers is reading, maybe it's something to consider.

El Jadida is the Moroccan town that, from all the ones I'd already seen or would visit in the coming weeks, I struggle the most to form any mental image of. However, it did provide at least one positive. Returning to my hotel, I saw a stand selling sweet pastries and it was here I fell in love. I'll describe *chebakia* as faithfully as I can, but I doubt I'll convince you how special they are. After all, they are merely strips of pastry folded into the shape of a small flower, deep-fried and covered in syrup and toasted sesame seeds. Each piece contains the calories of a wedding cake. A bag of those and you skip straight to Type 5 Diabetes.

*

Goodbye forgettable El Jadida, whoever you were.

I cycled out of town, the traffic doing whatever it wanted. On one roundabout a van went the opposite way around to save itself a few metres. Maybe he wasn't reckless. Perhaps he was just thinking of the environment.

Someone who certainly wasn't thinking about the environment had been stalking the outskirts of El Jadida. Morocco holds 75% of the world's phosphates, and here a lot of it is converted into fertilisers and whatever the hell else phosphates are turned into. Serious chemical plants appeared on both sides of the road, their waste products billowing out of tall stacks, reducing visibility. The place smelled of burning plastic, and when I brought my teeth together the air was crunchy, and not in a fun way. Imagine eating a mouthful of sand.

Cycling through, any sane person would feel like weeping at the mess we're making of the planet, but unfortunately Morocco's environment is taking a hit for the sake of humanity in general. Without phosphate fertilizers, researchers say we could only produce 50% of the food that we do. And, like everything we dig out of the ground, it's a finite resource. One day, some say in just a few decades, it'll be gone, along with half of our food. I suppose that could at least be a solution to obesity.

Fortunately, the ugliness didn't last long and then the country presented its most beautiful stretch of coastline yet, uninhabited, wide, wave-battered bays and not a plastic bottle in sight. Was this really Morocco?

With plenty of distance still to cover, I saw the first evidence of this region's seafood industry. Along the coastline stretched miles and miles of low, shallow pools. Today's destination, Oualidia, is the oyster capital of Morocco. As I was distracted by the prettiness of my surroundings, I suddenly swerved off the narrow coastal road as a lorry overtook an oncoming car, forcing me off the tarmac. As he passed me, I caught a glimpse of the driver and he wasn't even looking where he was going. After all, it was only forty tonnes of metal barrelling down a hill at sixty miles an hour. How much damage could it do?

Pulling myself together, I continued beside fields full of carrots and pumpkins. Roadside shacks sold nothing but hundreds, maybe thousands, of different shaped gourds. In huge piles out the front or hanging from its ceiling, every squash was covered in a thick layer of dust. Each shack looked like a museum for antique vegetables.

As Oualidia approached, the real beauty of this area became apparent. The bay on which it sits is wide and shallow, with a natural protective shelf out to sea that stretches almost the length of the town, calming the angry waves outside and rendering them harmless once within. Thick green vegetation and copious palm trees covered the shoreline. This was unlike anywhere else I'd seen in Morocco. The country felt tropical. Maybe I should swap this evening's tea for an Um Bongo. But probably not. It turns out they don't drink it in the Congo. It comes from Milnthorpe in the Lake District, and you can't get much less tropical than that.

After finding somewhere to stay and dump the bike, I wandered down to the sea. Over the last few tens of miles, Morocco had changed. Where was all the rubbish? And why wasn't there someone to hassle me for money? The calm inner bay was full of little boats bobbing about merrily. A sandy island contained a thousand gulls, all standing in the same direction, staring into the sun, like Donald Trump during an eclipse.

After saying goodbye to the glorious Rif Mountains and merely enduring the northern Atlantic coast – Rabat and Casablanca aside – I felt like I'd found the beginnings of a country I could fall in love with. Who knows, maybe one day we'd get married and have a couple of kids.

Feeling peckish, I stopped at a restaurant and ordered a burger that was stacked so tall it would've been more manageable to eat a walrus sandwich. And the accompanying tea was weird. I poured a glassful from the little silver teapot but that's all there was inside. Normally there'd be at least two or three cupfuls. I gave it a sip. It was cold and tasted of – I mulled the flavour over in my mouth – mmm, yummy, cigarette ash.

"Sorry," said the waiter, reappearing. He scooped up my teapot and replaced it with one that was full of hot tea and thankfully hadn't just been used as a makeshift ashtray.

I returned to my hotel and sat at a café table outside, sipping yet another mint tea – this time minus the dog ends – as the sun collapsed into the Atlantic. I liked the vibe of this place. The town itself had little to commend it, but its reputation was built on its natural beauty. And it was the first spot in Morocco that felt chilled, with the sort of vibe that attracted those pot-smoking hippies who headed this way in the sixties. Some still remain, now pot-bellied and in *their* sixties, and you could understand why they stayed.

*

I left the main coastal road and took a route through little hills and saw two shepherdesses. I wonder if, in addition to looking after the livestock all day, they still wash all their families' clothes, clean the house and cook all the food. I bet they do.

After forty miles, I approached another forgettable town, a large one called Safi. As I screamed towards the centre on a long hill, a bloke flagged me down. I stopped for him. He put his phone to his ear. I thought perhaps he wanted me to say something in English to a friend on the other end. Instead, he coughed expressively into his right hand and then, before I had the speed to react, shook mine with it.

"*Bonne chance!*" he said.

Is that good luck not catching whatever diseases you're riddled with, you filthy toad?

After finding an eight euro, electrically challenged hotel, I hit the town. In Morocco's least hectic market, a bloke came up to me and stuck his hand out. No please, no reason, just the expectation I'd give him something.

There wasn't much to commend Safi. That said, it was once the location of the world's largest ever tagine. In 1999, 200 women knocked one up using twelve tons of sardines and 500 kilos of animal fat. And probably absolutely no salt. But, however big their portions, chilled Morocco had once again retreated. It didn't matter. I was looking forward to what lay ahead. Tomorrow was a town famous for its fish, its beauty and its madness-inducing wind and I had a premonition I'd like it.

*

Today was going to be a long one, and hilly. I'd already booked a hotel in Essaouira to cut down on the likelihood of hunting for a room in a dark and confusing medina. A few miles out of town, the phosphate-processing destruction returned, huge plants pumping out thick plumes of smoke. Given the eventual use these phosphates are put to, it was ironic that, compared to other countries, much of Morocco's food is grown without artificial fertilisers. Even so, the authorities have found it valuable enough to kill for in a resource war in Western Sahara, the otherwise worthless desert land to the south that Morocco claims as its own while the rest of the world disagrees. Since 1988, the UN has suggested Western Sahara hold a referendum so that locals can decide who they'd like in charge. Morocco agreed, but it still hasn't happened. It's worth too much to lose.

Forty miles into today's slog I entered the province of Essaouira. I stopped for a self-assembled peanut butter sandwich. My legs were already buggered and really didn't want to do the same distance again. A tortoise crawled towards me to say hello, and then another one. I think they were challenging me to a race. The way I was feeling, they'd have comfortably won.

While the road hugged the beach, the hills weren't too bad. In the far distance, I could see the breakers rolling in, and strange, little walled villages built almost up to the water's edge. The roadside was still very green, which contrasted nicely with the dunes on the beach. I saw my first camel, at least one that wasn't in the form of a burger or roasted as street food. It felt impossibly exotic.

The roads became hillier and I knew a big one lay ahead. With fifteen miles to go, the challenge appeared and the only way was over it. Even though we were still in January, I'd lost a lot of latitude since Tangier and the air was hot and sticky, the hill steep and exhausting. For some people, hyperhidrosis, or excessive sweating, can be a sign of serious underlying health problems. For me, it was simply because I was a fat lump trying to do too much.

And then it was all alright again, as it always is. The top of the hill arrived and I found myself above today's destination, which I could see way, way down beneath me. I freewheeled joyously into town. See, I told you it was easy.

It was immediately clear Essaouira wasn't like the rest of Morocco's Atlantic coast. Fortunately, if it was similar to anywhere I'd seen so far, it was laid-back Oualidia, but Essaouira was far, far larger. The seafront was clean, the beach massive and backed by handsome hotels. None of the buildings looked like they were about to fall down.

I wheeled my bike into the tidiest medina in Morocco and a tout offered me a room.

"I already have one," I said, truthfully this time.

"Which one?" he asked.

I told him.

"It's that way," he added. It wasn't. He'd pointed me off in the wrong direction on purpose.

After locating my hotel, I disappeared into Essaouira's medina and noticed one drawback to a town that tried hard to provide a sanitised version of Morocco, especially when it came to the gastronomic treats squeamish tourists might find disturbing. Unlike elsewhere, the snack bars' display cabinets were entirely free of the more interesting lumps of animal. There were no brains or spleens here. Even liver had been safely excised. I satisfied myself instead with a kefta sandwich. If Essaouira had more interesting foodie options, hopefully I'd find them tomorrow.

*

I woke up with bright sunshine streaming through my curtains and a rumbling stomach crying out for sustenance. I jumped out of bed, ready to face a day of exploration. I hoped I wasn't too late for my hotel breakfast. What time was it? I looked at my phone. It took my brain a moment to take in what I was seeing. Can the clock on a phone stop in the middle of the night, just like old analogue ones used to do? It was quarter past three in the morning. And yet it was so sunny. I pulled back my curtains to reveal not a view, but a street light – an absolutely humungous street light – one that hadn't been on when I'd fallen asleep. Just another six hours till breakfast. Back to bed.

When morning finally arrived, I was ravenous. I went downstairs and took the last table in the little dining room. At the other three tables sat French couples. Visitors from France form nearly a third of all tourists in Morocco, one of the few countries that provides them a safe exoticism while evading the English language's global tyranny.

Along with the usual breakfast staples came *amlou*, a nutty spread, perfect for loading on to the accompanying freshly prepared msemen pancakes. It's made by grinding roasted almonds, honey and argan oil, the oil from the kernels of the argan tree. Amlou tastes like an almond-flavoured peanut butter. A lot of spurious claims are made for its health benefits, the most unlikely being its anti-ageing properties. I turned my phone's camera to selfie mode and watched my face as I ate a mouthful. Nope, the crow's feet remained.

I took myself outside, under bright sunlight rather than street lights, with a list of stuff to see. Cemeteries are usually good places to level your head and give you a sense of your own unimportance and ultimate destiny. Apparently here there were both Christian and Jewish cemeteries, but like similar sites in other Moroccan towns, they were hidden away behind huge walls. This was a shame as someone slightly famous was buried here. It's the final resting place of Leslie Hore-Belisha, a British politician, who lent part of his name to the pedestrian crossing lights that were introduced on his watch as Minister of Transport. I can't help thinking that Hore beacons would've been much snappier.

Because it was on my way to somewhere else, I wandered

past the town's prison. As you'd expect, and just like the cemetery, it was surrounded by more high walls, this time to keep people in rather than out, and topped with thick rolls of barbed wire. Essaouira may be a Disneyfied version of the country, but a Moroccan prison here must be pretty bloody grim. The shared toilets in a cheap hotel were bad enough. And they do like to lock up folk. Using figures from 2019, while the EU averaged 116 prisoners per 100,000 people, Morocco had 222, nearly twice as many. If you're going to visit this country, you'd better be on your best behaviour.

"Do you want a shave?"

It was the third time someone had yelled this at me from the doorway of a barber's in Essaouira. Was I looking that dishevelled? Possibly not. In this country, the touts would shout the same thing at Sinead O'Connor.

I'd found a website that gave the lowdown on how a man should dress in Morocco. Luckily for local sensibilities, I was sporting neither tattoos nor piercings, these adornments being considered, according to the website, "gay". Unkempt hair, which was currently my preferred style, is apparently sneered at because its owner would be unable to get a "proper" job. I have in the past successfully held down several "proper" jobs and they ain't what they're cracked up to be. But the most damning comments were reserved for my style of facial hair. These days, full beards – and mine was definitely in that category – are "associated with religious fundamentalism and liable to arouse suspicion". So, in summary, the blokes I passed in the street would assume I was almost certainly an unemployed jihadist, but I probably wouldn't touch them up.

I kept walking. I wasn't sure what was causing my fascination with Christian churches in Morocco – maybe they just seemed out of place – but Essaouira had one too. It was strange Morocco should allow Christian churches at all given how little confidence they appeared to have in their own religion. After all, Arabic translations of the Bible are banned here. Perhaps they're worried the locals would read about talking snakes, Jonah and the whale and the virgin birth and go, "Yes, that makes much more sense!"

Essaouira's church was small, but its walled yard held an oddly large amount of security guards, especially as the building itself was entirely empty of people until I arrived. There wasn't much to see and I was in and out in seconds. Leaving the yard, I could hear a voice on one of the security guys' walkie talkies.

"Isis operative now exiting the area," it probably said.

Out of the church and as yet unarrested, I made for the beach, a beautiful sweep of empty golden sand. Essaouira doesn't attract the sunbed brigade, at least not the ones who've done any research. This area is renowned for its strong winds, the sort that whip up sand and blast it right into your eyeballs. And that's when they're in a good mood. When they're angry, they knock you down, fling a jellyfish at your head and roll you into the sea. Today, though, was utterly calm and the quality of the light infused everything with richer colours. There was something mesmerising about Essaouira.

What I most wanted to see here was the fishing port. At this time of day, hundreds of sky-blue wooden boats were tied up as the fishermen traded what they'd landed. This part of town had been left untouched by the Disneyfiers. Through a heavy smell of diesel, I walked the harbour's stone jetties, careful not to slip on casually discarded sardines and the mud created when fish-preserving ice mixed with ground dirt. Flocks of gulls wheeled about the sky above, screeching aggressively, like a scene from *The Birds*, while cats stalked any that were stupid enough to land.

After the madness of the port, the medina seemed a little

too sane. But it was here I climbed the next rung up my Moroccan pastilla ladder. The insides of my *pigeon* pastilla, a thick disc of filo-like pastry the size of a small plate, were darker, gamier and more complex than the chicken one I'd had back in Rabat. At times, it seemed drier, at others juicier. It was definitely an improvement and a shame most Moroccan menus were opting for easier-to-obtain chicken nowadays. This pastilla ladder had only one more rung to go. Once I'd found the holy quail, my quest would be complete.

After lunch, I climbed the town's ramparts. Large openings in its crenelated walls looked out on to waves crashing on to the rocks below while providing shelter from both a hot sun and a strengthening breeze. It was the perfect place just to sit and wallow. I could happily have lived there, on that spot in the wall, forever.

Evening came around and my thoughts turned to food once again. As I wandered the medina, a little stall caught my eye. I went to look what they were selling. In a glass cabinet were some breadcrumbed objects. They looked like something as yet unsampled on my list of Moroccan food to try.

"Are they sardine balls?" I asked. That's fried orbs of sardines rather than fishy testicles. But you probably knew that.

"No, they're *maakouda*," replied the stallholder.

This was also good news. Maakouda are fried mashed potato balls, another item on my list.

"But these ones are sardine," he added, pointing at some balls beside them that looked identical.

I opted for a mixture. For six dirham he handed me a half loaf stuffed full of balls and smothered in a spicy tomato sauce. The sardine variety tasted almost meaty and the whole sandwich was heavenly.

Later on, to complete a gastronomically successful day, I

popped to a bakery and got some authentic Moroccan pastries rather than the wannabe French rubbish I'd been sampling throughout the country. Each piece was sweet and sticky. Some were nutty little tubes of joy but the ones I'd been most looking forward to, the much talked about "gazelle horns", just tasted like lumps of marzipan. I decided this would signify the end of my patisserie experiments. The French cakes were rubbish, these poncey Moroccan ones better, but the first prize still went to the cheap and oh so sweet chebakia, those syrup-laden pastry flowers of loveliness I'd had in otherwise forgettable El Jadida.

*

I'd given myself another day off in Essaouira, although I'd already exhausted its sights. This didn't matter because today I'd an important job, the fixing of a spoke. I'd noticed one missing all the way back in Tetouan but hadn't come across a bicycle repair shop since then. But here, while wandering the medina's alleys, I'd finally seen one, a dark cave, its inner walls lined with oil-covered boxes of spares. Online sources warned of low-quality repairs in Morocco. Maybe I'd hand over my beloved bike and the mechanic would hammer the new spoke in place with a nine-inch nail through my tyre.

I was about to find out. A middle-aged fella worked in the alleyway outside. As he spoke neither English nor French, I simply pointed at the gap in my back wheel. He popped inside, got two new spokes – he'd noticed a second failure on his subsequent inspection – removed the tyre, bent the spokes alarmingly – I didn't think that was a thing – before screwing them into place, and tightened each of the wheel's other spokes with a turn or two of his spoke key. Three minutes' work, two replaced spokes and three more to take away in case future repair shops didn't have my size came to three euros. In the past, every other broken spoke I've suffered has meant the slow but inevitable death of my back wheel, with additional spokes usually dying within a week. Not this one. It's still going strong, the best three euros I've spent on my bike and not a nail to be seen anywhere.

I'd expected the repair to take a while and so, with my schedule suddenly open, I wandered aimlessly and joyfully before sitting in that lovely spot on the ramparts some more, with the wind ruffling my unemployable hair, my mad mullah beard and my uninked heterosexual arms. Then I went to get a fishy lunch from one of the stalls near the port gate. Choosing from a vast array of seafood – large baskets of prawns and squid, and crayfish were strewn clumsily over a multitude of fish, both round and flat – I opted for a plump red mullet and six sardines. With a salad they arrived, grilled and stickily delicious.

Morocco is the sardine capital of the world, and the centre of this capital is right here in Essaouira. Nationwide, the fishing industry employs 110,000 fishermen as well as countless thousands in its food processing plants, and fish accounts for 7% of the country's exports. They're a big deal to Morocco. Their sardines might arrive in Britain packed tightly into little tins, but you've not eaten one until you've had it freshly plucked from the briny sea and seared over hot coals.

In the evening I hit the medina again, its streets having been converted into a night market with people selling small piles of fish, fruit and other goods while thousands of others squeezed through its narrow lanes. Young men pushing carts forced their wheels against the crowds, as did lads on bikes and pram-wielding mums using their babies' chariots as battering rams.

I eventually smashed my way through the heaving masses and popped out the other side, landing in a dark, out-of-the-way café, one that aimed itself squarely at locals. As the sun set on the horizon, I could see a thousand gulls circling the port, dancing in the sky. I'd fallen for Essaouira, its light and space and food. It was such a joy to walk around and I could imagine coming back for longer, a pleasant place to live cheaply for a while, with balmy temperatures even in the middle of winter. I'd be sad to leave in the morning, but at least it'd be on a fully functioning bike and with the distinct feeling it wouldn't be long before I'd return. This coastline, famous for its oysters, had provided limited beauty, but I'd finally found a pearl.

Chapter 7: The Ghosts of Agadir

Sidi Kaouki, Imsouane and Agadir

I may have been sad to leave Essaouira, but I was consoled by a lazy start, knowing today was the shortest of days. My next destination, surfing town Sidi Kaouki, was only fifteen miles down the road. A splendid coastal ride eventually gave way to an unmade stretch under construction whose workers pleaded for cigarettes as I passed. The final miles were back on tarmac as I rolled into a pleasant little resort, home to 4,000. What wasn't small was its beach, an enormous expanse with rolling breakers, although more people seemed to be in their hotel rooms surfing the web rather than out there surfing the waves today.

The village is named after a nineteenth century saint whose tomb sits on the coast here. The internet was surprisingly reluctant to offer up any details about the fella and what conjuring tricks led to his canonisation, although I read that women make pilgrimages here when they want to get pregnant. But maybe that's just surfers for you.

Sexy times come in other forms too. Sidi Kaouki made the headlines in 2018 when a 36-year-old British tourist, already off his nut on drugs, tried to get lucky with a stray dog. Possibly offended at not being taken out for dinner first, the dog turned on the man and bit off his penis. I think the mutt would've preferred a different sort of bone.

Hotel prices were inflated. A bed in a dorm here cost the same as an individual room elsewhere, a room that wouldn't also contain five other blokes snoring and farting. But all wasn't lost. There was a campsite, and so far I'd cycled a thousand miles with a tent and used it only once. But even this was over-priced. I'd already found a handful of hotel rooms in Morocco cheaper than what I paid here to sleep on a patch of gravel.

After setting up, I cycled back to a cluster of restaurants I'd seen as I entered the village. While I was lunching, a couple of young women walked past in tiny bikinis to go surfing. A group of young Moroccan men sitting at a nearby table were transfixed, ogling them very much like I imagine our dog lover viewed his target. If these fellas were unmarried, this might have been the only time they'd seen a sexually mature woman in the flesh. Maybe this was why they'd come to Sidi Kaouki in the first place.

Back at the campsite, I got speaking to a young French fella who was carrying a thick wooden pole.

"We're driving to South Africa," he told me.

"What's your car?" I was expecting him to tell me the name of a 4x4. Well, it *did* have a four in it.

"A Renault 4."

That was brave. They stopped making the boxy Renault 4s in 1994. It's got an engine the size of a small motorbike's.

"Is that even possible? I've seen photos of West Africa where the roads are all mud."

"Mmm," he replied. "It could be a problem. We've raised the car to give it more clearance."

"And how long is it going to take?"

"In a perfect world, six months. We'll camp beside the car each night. It'll be alright."

"What's the pole for?"

"We've a problem with the chassis. Gonna use it as a lever to tip the car up."

"Er, well, good luck then."

But they'd probably need a lot more than that.

The sun was sinking along with the temperatures. I threw

on my fleece and walked back to the beach, sat on a large rock and watched the pink-orange ball of fire melt slowly into the Atlantic. On the sand, a single runner, a lone horse person charging about and a seemingly abandoned camel, still loaded with its saddle for tourist rides, danced silhouettes in the distance.

Morocco was odd. At times, it could be nothing but hassle, touts lying to your face as you fight your way through crowded medinas, but at others it feels like the most peaceful place on Earth, the calm only punctuated by the lapping waves, the distant hooves of a galloping horse and the terrified screams of a drug-addled idiot having his genitals bitten off.

*

The first hour of today was ideal cycling. A gorgeous temperature, zero wind, a cloudless blue sky, absolutely no traffic and almost flat. I even composed a song about how perfect it was. The gods don't like such complacency.

I arrived at a junction. I could turn left, entirely in the wrong direction, and join the main road with all the hills that this would bring but remain on tarmac, or I could turn right and relegate myself to a stony lane for a while. How long could such a crappy track really go on for? Effing forever, that's how long.

Sometimes I was presented with sand, other times pebbles and occasionally huge rocks. None of these surfaces were ideal for my thin tyres. As soon as any hill appeared, and they appeared really quite often, I pushed. And I wasn't near civilisation now. I turned a corner and before me was a gang of dogs, the sort that carry flick knives. They walked slowly towards me, but I growled and flapped my arms, and presumably because they've received such awful treatment from humans in the past, they scarpered.

I passed several camels at the roadside, just munching on

some trees. This made me wonder. Are dromedaries dangerous? Subsequent research says yes, they can be. A sixty-year-old Australian woman was apparently knocked to the ground by her pet camel – yes, her *pet* camel – which then climbed on top of her and, from the news report, "exhibited what police suspect was mating behaviour". It killed her. With love. Anyway, my camels weren't dangerous nor amorous. Their front feet were tied closely together. They had to hop about to move at all.

On and on my stony path went and the sun's heat increased. Fifteen miles of bumping later, I knew I was due to join another road, one I strongly suspected and even more strongly hoped had an actual surface. I decided I'd lunch at the junction, a celebratory or commiseratory one, depending on what I found. After several hours of weary pedalling, I hit the road and – praise be! – it was tarmac. I was so excited I didn't stop for lunch. I just wanted to get some proper miles under my belt. I was now near the sea and the coastal views were gorgeous. I flew downhill on a surface as smooth as Barry White when the road disappeared again. More bloody rocks, and this time there were no new roads between me and my destination, Imsouane. It might be this slow-going the whole way.

I hadn't done anything close to half the miles I'd hoped today and it was already three in the afternoon. There was no way I could get to where I wanted before sunset. After a few more miles of bobbling over rocky surfaces I came to a lone business at the side of a silent lane that connected Nowhere with Oblivion. It called itself a "boutique". Being honest, it didn't *look* like a boutique. A more appropriate word would have been "shack". Better still, "hovel".

Its owner was sitting outside. He babbled some words at me. One of them sounded like "room". I'd already been travelling for six hours, not at any great speed admittedly, but it'd been a wearying day. I'd see what he had to offer. It turned out to be a cheap, enormous apartment with a kitchen and a roof terrace overlooking the distant sea, too good an opportunity to pass. There was no hot water for a shower, but you can't have everything.

The owner locked my bike in an attached building and then I visited his "boutique", where all I could find to eat were some very dry biscuits. Still, I had a roof over my head and, in the unlikely event of rain, if it wasn't watertight, the biscuits would go a long way to soak up any leaks.

It was a pity that, in attempting, and often failing, to keep my bike upright today, I hadn't been able to appreciate the scenery. But I could now, sitting on my terrace, drinking tea I'd brewed myself. About two miles away, across yellow-green fields, a bundle of low, brown, shrub-speckled hills fell into the Atlantic on a wide bay filled with white crests. There wasn't a sound.

The living room had a huge window that looked out on to the same ocean scene as the terrace. As I ate some emergency noodles alone, watching the darkening sky, I felt sad, a long way from the people I loved, and, with no WiFi here, disconnected from them and the rest of the world. Through this melancholia I thought more about Morocco. If you asked someone who'd never visited to describe it, they'd probably mention deserts and not much else. But, in reality, the country was constantly presenting new faces. Not *all* of them were great – the faltering Atlantic property developments were particularly rubbish – but *almost all* of them were amazingly beautiful. Through my window I could see the edges of two distant, dirt-poor villages. Despite the lack of money, everyone I'd met today, or who I could see right now through my window, looked happy enough, the women colourfully dressed, the kids playful and inquisitive. Despite being only thirty miles away as the crow flew from Essaouira, this latest face Morocco had presented felt more like a million.

I fell asleep in the living room and woke up about three in the morning to a skyful of stars. Through the panoramic window, they looked spectacular. I climbed the concrete stairs to the roof terrace and gazed at them properly, lying on my back on the cold tiles to take them in. The air was clear, the sky cloudless and the night as dark as it was possible to be, no artificial lights to pollute it. The constellations were all there, close enough to touch. I reached out my hand as a meteor tore across the Milky Way and burnt up in the Earth's atmosphere.

As I pondered the mysteries of the universe, a profound thought hit me. Yes, of course! That's why those camels' feet were tied together. Sidi Kaouki's dog perv was back in town, his bits reattached, and he wasn't taking any chances this time.

*

I left the apartment to find my bike already outside and with another packet of dust biscuits as a gift, balanced on my saddle. That was nice of him. Or perhaps he'd had trouble shifting them and was making way for new stock.

Yesterday's bumpy roads continued and got even worse. Twice, one of my front panniers threw itself loose. I longed for tarmac.

The views over the sea were great, but once again I couldn't look at them while moving. The road climbed high up a hill above the cliffs. The rocks became bigger, shaking my bike to bits. And then, for no reason I could fathom, tarmac suddenly reappeared. It was like a gift from the gods, albeit gods that hadn't put any effort into an integrated and well-surfaced road network.

Eventually came the final turn-off for Imsouane, the place I'd been aiming to reach yesterday, followed by a steep downhill. Three ten-year-old boys were walking up. One applauded me and the other two joined in. I yelled them a hearty *merci*. They should have seen me half an hour ago. God knows what appreciation I'd have received for thirty miles of boulders. Probably a handshake and a box of Quality Street.

And then, finally, the town appeared. Within what felt like seconds, I was washing away two days of thick, orange dust. Examining the shower tray afterwards, you'd have thought it'd been used to hose down a team of Oompa Loompas.

I found a restaurant and sat in the shade. As I'd moved farther south, the temperatures had been steadily climbing. Although now only early February, it already felt like Spain in June or the UK in, well, inside your house and next to a radiator.

"I'll have a meat pizza, please," I said. No need for specifics on this menu. Chicken, beef, ferret, I'll have whatever you've got.

"Any drugs?" asked the waiter.

"No, thanks."

My, this *was* a casual town.

After lunch, I explored the rest of this little place, another fishing centre, although not in the same league as Essaouira. A concrete slipway hosted fifty or so tiny, sky-blue wooden boats. Nearby was a beach where the surfers hung out, literally hundreds of them. They paddled out to the larger waves beyond a stone breakwater that acted as a viewing platform for us mere mortals. Some of them were excellent, twisting 360 degrees, deftly swerving and skilfully avoiding the front teeth of the less able surfers in their way.

The beachside was full of stalls, their owners grilling fish, sending delicious clouds of sardine essence over those walking by. Surfers aside, Imsouane felt like a Greek island village, although here the Hellenic blues and whites were extended with the rainbow colours of graffitied surf shops, which made up the vast majority of businesses in town. There were plenty of places to eat but nothing else to do here except surf or relax, which was all the assembled crowd wanted anyway.

Later on, back in my room, I felt peckish enough to open that gifted packet of biscuits. I drank a pint of water to get just one of them down. Perhaps they were dog biscuits. I only managed to eat two and then hopped on to the bed, scratched my ear with my foot and fell asleep.

*

I left town with a thick blanket of mist covering the place. The first 45 minutes involved a steep push up the hillside that overlooked Imsouane and its spooky low cloud. It was a lung-busting way to start the day.

The cycling today was pleasant but uneventful. The plethora of roadblocks made me realise the only days I hadn't seen one was on these last two off-road sections. If you're driving the length of Morocco with a dead body in the back of your car, you've good reason to be nervous.

I came through clouds of grilled meat smoke to the town of Tamri, set back a little from the coast. As well as being known for banana cultivation, this area is big on pioneering animals. Tamri is the epicentre of Morocco's argan tree-climbing goats.

Argan oil, made from the nut of the tree, has near magical properties claimed for it. As well as tasting nice, it's supposedly great for your hair and skin, reduces the effects of ageing, and even cures diabetes and cancer. Let's close down Big Pharma and just drink a pint of argan oil each morning.

But if argan oil is so saleable, why do local farmers let goats climb into their trees' branches and munch down all their fruit? The answer is because between its flesh and its inner nut is a tough skin. The goats eat the fruit and their digestive juices strip away this protective layer, rendering the nut accessible to anyone motivated enough to sort through a massive pile of goat poop.

The locals have found a second source of income using the goats and their trees. Given how much tourists love to coo over these daredevil billies and nannies, argan farmers have taken to placing any reluctant creatures in the trees themselves and tying them into position. They then charge any tourist who attempts to capture the image. It's probably not so photogenic when you see a poor bleating goat dangling by its hoof.

The day continued, past the fishing village of Aghroud, looking like the location of a children's TV programme, every building painted a different colour. I even spent a night in Taghazout, a place my five-year-old guide book promised was another laid back surfing town like Imsouane. Presumably in the time since publication, success had gone to the local tourist industry's head and they'd swamped a fairly ugly and crumbling old dump of a town with even more hideous developments. Let's scream right past and pretend it never happened.

My destination was the city of Agadir. On the way, two blokes in a car got my attention and relayed a banana to me while I cycled. It was tricky riding, facing forward so as not to crash into the kerb, while reaching left and blindly taking the fruit like a baton.

Upon first viewing, Agadir seemed like nothing more than a grimly industrial port, but, continuing onwards, the cranes and warehouses gave way to a huge crescent of palm-lined beach. I headed for the promenade, full of jazzy-looking bars and restaurants, the likes of which I hadn't seen in Morocco before. This area was so lacking in character, it could've been absolutely any Mediterranean resort. But if you came here for sunshine and seaside, I'm sure it'd do its job.

Agadir can perhaps be excused its anodyne appearance. In

1960 it suffered a devastating earthquake and had to be rebuilt from scratch and, looking at the results, as cheaply as possible. How the authorities dealt with other aspects of the aftermath, however, was unusual. After finding a hotel, I schlepped towards the site of Agadir's erstwhile medina to discover more.

On approaching the area that my map told me was *Ancienne Malborjt*, I saw a lot of cars parked up. Maybe this modern history really lured the tourists, I thought wrongly. The vehicles were actually here because this area was now essentially wasteland and a good place for learner drivers to practise their manoeuvres, safely away from Morocco's more dangerous qualified motorists.

And they *are* dangerous. The country's number of road deaths per head of population is almost six times higher than the UK's. But a lot of Moroccans don't own a car. If instead you look at fatalities per number of road vehicles, Morocco is a whopping 36 times more deathly than Britain. I was lucky to have made it this far.

A few metres above the cars was a raised area with a flat top, a scrubby patch of land, several acres in size. I scrambled up and on to it. All alone, I surveyed the scene. There was nothing there but tufts of yellow grass and low shrubs ruffled by the blast furnace breeze. In the gaps between them, on the dusty, salmon-pink earth, were the usual scatterings of litter and broken glass. In the distance, up on a high hill, was what looked like a castle, the town's kasbah, which, after standing for centuries, had suffered badly during the earthquake. But not as badly as here, where I now stood, Ancienne Malborjt, the old medina of Agadir.

The quake hit close to midnight on February 29th 1960. Only a malevolent god would wreak such havoc in a town of shoddily constructed houses at a hour when everyone was sure to be indoors. To compound the issue for anyone questioning their faith, it occurred on the third day of Ramadan, the Islamic holy month.

Matters weren't helped by the weather. At around 40°C, it was unusually hot for February. Many of those pulled from the rubble refused medical treatment, fearing it'd mean breaking their fast and disobeying the entity who'd smashed them up and killed their children in the first place. In the heat, the bodies of the dead still trapped within the ruins quickly festered.

The town's sewerage system had been ripped apart and what was left of the medina became infested with rats and stray dogs looking for a meal. These weren't the only scavengers. Opportunist looters turned up too. The command was given to shoot them on sight and, once dispatched, they too were tossed into the same mass grave as those bodies that had been pulled lifeless from the rubble.

Overwhelmed, the authorities covered the entire area in disinfectant, DDT and quicklime to destroy the cadavers but also anyone still trapped alive. Throughout the whole of Agadir, there were 15,000 casualties. Here in the old medina, 5,000 people had once lived. Fewer than ten survived.

Newspaper headlines from the period reported the earthquake had lasted just ten seconds. Imagine that, everyone you know, all your family and friends, and everything you own, destroyed in the time it takes to tie your shoes.

I walked back to where the cars were parked. There was no memorial on this site, but there was a flat, white, concreted area a metre or two wide whose purpose wasn't entirely clear. A man was there, amidst the ghosts of Agadir, in an act of worship. He didn't see any irony in kneeling beside a mass grave and praying to, if his beliefs were correct, the author of this modern Pompeii.

Nearby, there was a garden, as littered as the scrubland. I

wandered around to see if there was any mention of this history, but I found nothing. Thinking about it, why should these poor sods have a memorial? Whoever we are, we're all forgotten within a couple of generations. We all disappear. Our dreams and fears, our greatest achievements and most embarrassing failures, are all ultimately vanquished, and in a depressingly short period of time. It's probably best we enjoy ourselves while we can and stop worrying what people think about us, now or in the future, because in the end they won't think about us at all.

Bloody hell, sorry about that. The gloomy history of this place had brought me down a tad.

*

The next morning I walked a mile to see the city's enormous El Had souk. Unlike the vast majority of Moroccan markets, the grid layout of this one, with twelve huge gateways into it, made it easy to navigate. Its inner lanes were wide enough for you not to feel like a salmon swimming upstream. It reminded me of Blackburn's old indoor market, but with more dates, olives and annoying touts. Blackburn's souk had been remarkably light on people offering to guide you around for money.

Inside the market, I stopped for food, tucking into two of those pepper-flavoured msemens and a pot of mint tea. Recently, the tea had been arriving at the table unsweetened in contrast to how it was further north. Instead, a huge brick of rock-hard sugar accompanied the teapot. For the last few days I'd spent considerable effort in trying to break the sugar into pieces, first with my hands, unsuccessfully, and then with my teeth. Any shards I cracked were dropped into my tea cup. Today came the realisation I was just supposed to plop the entire brick into the teapot. I'd nearly been forced to the dentist's before I'd worked that out, idiot that I am.

I left the market and walked to the beach via another royal

palace, complete with hundreds of guards, many carrying machine guns. He's doing alright for himself, that King Mohammed VI, isn't he? The amount blown on Morocco's Royal Family is five times that of Britain's.

Strolling back to my room, I saw a group of teenage Moroccan girls ambling along the street with a blonde girl the same age. I didn't see her face but it just *had* to be Madeleine McCann. There was no other likely explanation in the entire universe. After all, there were rumours she'd been sneaked away to Morocco, and she would've been that age by now. Maybe I should say something, I thought. But Madeleine had suffered enough, hadn't she? By now, she almost certainly had no memory of her real parents. It'd be wrong to disrupt her life all over again. Better to leave her in peace and not run to the tabloids. So what if I was forgoing a six-figure cheque from Rupert Murdoch. It was only money.

Although I'd seen a couple of interesting things here, I'd no real love for Agadir. It was a soulless place, choosing same-old same-old, run-to-the-sun tourist appeal over developing any personality of its own. I was more than happy to be changing direction. After almost a month of moving south, I'd now head east into Morocco's interior, where its gorges and deserts lay, where the country could show its true colours rather than offering what it thought tourists might desire. *Real* Morocco, here I come.

*

That strange virus was leaking out of Asia and spreading fast, having already reached Britain, the USA, Germany, Spain and Australia. By now, anyone paying attention had heard about it, but because of the media's previous attempts to portray every new disease – SARS, Ebola, bird flu and the rest – as the end of the world, it was still easy to dismiss them as yet again crying wolf. For most people, myself included, it was just something happening a long, long way away.

Chapter 8: Long Live King Steven

Taroudant and Tafraoute

The cycle out of Agadir was under an uncharacteristically grey sky, but at least I had no chance of overheating. The rough route passed first through suburbs and then villages that seemed poorer than most of the places I'd seen so far, all breeze blocks and crumbling houses that looked like a strong wind would blow them over.

From one village, I bought a couple of loaves. They were still warm and so I had one for breakfast. As I sat at the roadside, Josef came up to me, a bloke of about twenty with a sharp haircut and a strong smell of aftershave. We chatted for a while.

"Are you married?" he eventually asked.

"No."

"Why not?"

I chuckled.

"Why would I want to?"

Well, because in Morocco sex outside of marriage lands you in prison. For whatever reason, he found this all highly amusing and wanted a selfie. Tradition is so strong here that perhaps not to get married isn't even an option. Or maybe life's simply too hard for any man without a wife. How could he possibly spend all day in the café without his personal in-house slave catering for his every whim?

The road eventually improved and the villages became less poverty-stricken. In one of them I saw some children ahead. One of them nodded in my direction to his mate and they both bent down to pick up stones. I cycled as close as I could to them and performed my repeated and deranged "Bonjour!" trick. They looked at me like I was crazy, but at least they didn't throw anything.

Eventually, after what had felt like a flat day but actually involved a 600-metre climb over fifty-odd miles, I arrived in Taroudant, a town of 80,000, famed for its well-preserved walls and its nickname of Mini Marrakesh.

My room cost 160 dirham, exactly what my five-year-old guide book said it would. Then I noticed the price list on the back of my hotel room door. Its charge hadn't increased since at least 2008. This seemed weird until I learnt Morocco has had an average of just over 1% annual inflation in the last ten years, one of the lowest rates and one of the most stable economies in the whole of Africa. For a comparison, in 2019, South Sudan's inflation was 36%, Sudan's 71% and Zimbabwe a whopping 676%. Worrying for different reasons, Eritrea's was –28%. Morocco is doing some things right.

For its relatively small size, Taroudant felt a bit mad. Bicycles and mopeds whizzed around everywhere. The narrow streets were full of business, not all of them what you might have expected. One guy sat on the pavement peddling pieces of bread in various states of decomposition, right up to fully green and mouldy. Is there a market for that?

Everyone was selling to everyone else. It was capitalism in action. As long as there was a big enough difference between the price that sellers paid for their stock and the price at which they sold it, and provided there were sufficient customers, everything was fine. They could spend the difference they made on whatever they needed to survive. But what if this system temporarily failed, if no one bought anything for, say, a week or two or more? The fruit and veg man's stock would rot and become unsellable and then he'd have no money to buy curtains and cushions. The soft furnishings shop owner would then have no cash to buy bread. The baker...you get the picture. The whole edifice would collapse. It's scary how fragile these systems are. Hopefully, no such business-halting calamity was on its way.

I bought myself a tea opposite the main square. Taroudant well earned its nickname of Mini Marrakesh. I'd yet to see that famous city, but this one here certainly matched what I'd read about it. Hundreds of people were jostling about the square. Taxis and bikes pushed their way through the crowds on the surrounding streets. Groups of locals gathered around to watch an old guy telling a story. Another mob watched an acrobat doing the splits.

More interesting for a former maths student like me was a fella with a wooden board containing hundreds of numbered circles. From a short distance away, punters threw a one dirham piece at the target. If it landed entirely within a circle they received back the number of coins specified. Big, tempting numbers like seventeen and fourteen were surrounded by twos and threes. The highest numbers of all were on the top edge of the board, teasing players to throw harder and miss the target entirely.

Looking at a photo I took, I did the maths and the numbers were perfectly chosen. Whether you were a safe player who aimed for low-scoring but easier to hit groups of fours, fives and sixes, or whether you were a glory hunter hoping to win big, you were virtually guaranteed to lose if you played more than a few coins. Visually, your chances of getting a dirham entirely inside a circle looked easy enough. In reality, it would happen fewer than one in five attempts, provided you hit the board at all. If you watched for a couple of minutes there were frequent winners, but because more than two-thirds of the prizes were twos, threes and fours, payouts were almost always low. Still, seeing money returned kept a steady stream of willing victims queueing for a go. UK and European roulette tables, with a single green 0 slot, make

2.7% profit, while US ones, with their additional 00 slot, collect 5.3%. This guy was making at least 15%. Gambling is completely forbidden by Islam, but nevertheless God was willing.

Not everyone was coining it in though. A scrawny fella walked past a neighbouring table and pointed to the spare sugar lump sitting upon it, next to an empty glass of tea. The customer nodded. The skinny bloke picked it up and popped it into his mouth, desperate for calories.

With a craving for satsumas I went a-hunting and, although eventually successful, my head had been turned during my search. A man was selling sweet treats from a cart, including chebakia, those delicious, flower-shaped, syrup-covered pastries. I put fifteen dirham on his counter and mimed that I'd like a selection. In addition to the flowers, there were miniature spring roll- and samosa-shaped pastries full of nuts and dates and other tasty things. I walked away with what felt like an unfeasibly large collection of goodies. I took them back to my room and had every intention of making them last a day or two, but who was I kidding? The entire bag was gone before bedtime. It was just as well I had some tough cycling coming up in the next few weeks. A 3,000 calorie night-time snack isn't ideal.

*

Today I had an appointment with Taroudant's outdoor Sunday morning market. On my way, I passed through this little city's most famous landmark, the walls that entirely surround it. Being a fan of such structures, Donald Trump would love it here. And the walls were orange. He'd love that too. They were also as thick as several bricks. I'm sure you can provide your own punchline.

If yesterday's town centre was madness, the market was whatever is the next insanity level beyond that. It covered a large sandy area the size of a couple of football pitches, jammed with uncountable makeshift stalls of wood and canvas selling mostly fruit, vegetables, piles of clothes and live animals. The legitimacy of some of their products was suspect. One stall had a pyramid of saffron so huge and so red that it had to be fake. Saffron is more expensive by weight than gold. If that stack of pretend crocus stamens had been genuine, the salesman could've retired to his own Caribbean island rather than scratching an existence at what was essentially a provincial car boot sale.

The track in and out of the market field wasn't quite two cars wide and yet had to handle masses of traffic attempting to travel in both directions as well as accommodating bicycles, mopeds, tuk-tuk style contraptions, donkeys, lads pushing carts and thousands of shoulder to shoulder pedestrians. Everyone with a horn was using it. To add to the cacophony from the people, the animals, the hooters and the engines, many of the stalls had their own PA systems to announce their latest special offers. These were always loud and distorted and often included short blasts of lively music. It sounded like a thousand Bollywood movie soundtracks playing at once.

Back at my hotel, I got chatting to a lovely English couple, tandem-riding John and Nicole from the Isle of Wight. There was something beautifully gentle and heart-warming about them. After this morning's market, they induced in me a much needed sense of calm. Mentally, I was slowly transformed from a cocaine-addled Taz of Tazmania to a Dalai Lama on diazepam.

My new friends tipped me off about somewhere on my route in a couple of days' time. There was a long stretch of dusty road ahead, full of mountains and pain, entirely lacking in accommodation, except for one very bizarre hotel I'd never heard of. Price-wise, it was way beyond what I'd been paying, but it looked like one of those special places that shouldn't be passed over. But I'd one more stop before I'd reach it.

*

I woke up at around half six to the painful wailing of another muezzin. If God was great, this guy was grating.

Today's ride hinted at my immediate future. The roadside greenery of the country's north had given way to orange dust and low shrubs. Everything looked parched. A row of low, round, thirsty mountains forced me and the road southwards. The desert lay ahead.

Thankfully, the tarmac remained flat for the first part of the day. It took me past a village school. Outside, dozens of kids stood around joyfully banging things and making a racket. Several of them shouted me a bonjour. I didn't need to worry about a rock-based assault from this happy bunch.

The final quarter of today's forty miles presented some proper little hills. I was going to have to get used to this again. The Atlantic coast had been mostly flat. This wouldn't be the case for the next few days. I pushed the bike and realised I'd also have to pay close attention to my water supply. There were few places to refuel and running out far from civilisation could be fatal. That said, I was currently on about five litres a day, apparently enough to cause water poisoning, which could also be a bit deathy. Oh well.

The 5,000-strong town of Ait Baha appeared over a small hill, its modern-looking tower blocks coloured to match the exact salmon-pink tone of the earth around it. If you looked at this place from afar, it was camouflaged.

I cycled down Ait Baha's single main street and located its one hotel, a disproportionally large affair for a town of this size. Presumably it only comes close to being full when some popular local marries an even more beloved out-of-towner here and drags everyone they've ever met to the ceremony. The rest of the time it just sits empty in echoey silence, waiting for smelly cyclists to turn up. But today, my luggage and I were going to be far from malodorous. In fact, we were destined to be fragrant beyond belief.

I was about to have a wash when I realised my almost new bottle of shower gel felt emptier than expected. In fact, it was *completely* empty. I looked at it closely and noticed a small hole near its base. Something must have rubbed against it. I reached my hand into my pannier, inside the carrier bag holding my mobile bathroom, and felt a sudden gloopiness accompanied by an overpowering tang of chemically-induced summer meadows. Everything was covered in thick goo.

I removed the bags, washed them out, cleaned the soap from my razor and my nail clippers and, more distressingly, from my toothbrush and hung everything to dry. The bathroom smelled like someone had taken a baseball bat to a Debenham's perfume counter. It burnt my eyes.

With the taste of shower gel in my mouth, I escaped into the streets, well, the street. I wandered for five minutes before realising I'd seen it all. I assumed this place wasn't much of a tourist draw, given the number of stares I was receiving – or maybe it was my overpowering floral aroma – but at least this felt like "real" Morocco again.

I threw myself on to the small terrace of a café full of fellas and ordered tea. The guys here weren't speaking Arabic or French but a Berber language, one that sounded like they were talking backwards. I watched the street. There were a few little shops and cafés but that was all. And while daytime temperatures were gradually increasing with each passing day, now approaching those of a Costa del Sol summer, the evening still rapidly chilled, especially as I was now around 600 metres above sea level. Every man sitting at the café wore a thick winter djellaba. And tomorrow I would double my altitude.

Just as Casablanca's salon du thé had provided absinthe to accompany my mint tea, today's watering hole gave me lemon verbena and nice it was too, but I needed calories and so, with few other options in town, I headed to my hotel's restaurant.

"Can I have a menu please?" I asked hopefully.

"No."

"Ah, OK."

"Would you like a salad and a tagine?"

"Is there anything else?"

"No."

"Then yes, I'd *love* a salad and a tagine."

My lack of taginic success was set to continue. The salad was fine, but the main dish had been assembled from all the things hanging around the kitchen. The tagine lid was removed to reveal lentils, olives, prunes, a hard-boiled egg, two lumps of creature and some chips on top. Only one piece of the animal – I'm guessing it was goat – was edible. The other was, as far as I could determine, half a hoof.

I returned to my room having forgotten about the earlier incident with the shower gel. I opened the door and almost instantly passed out.

*

Today's climb started immediately. It was going to set the tone for the day. Not long out of Ait Baha, I saw my first oasis, a ramshackle collection of sand-coloured buildings gathered around a small lake. It made a nice change. The last freshwater body I'd seen was that turd-filled river back in Kenitra.

The road became steeper but my surroundings more beautiful. Shrub-covered hills marched off into the Anti Atlas mountains further away. Occasionally, a tiny Berber village would nestle in a distant fold, a sprinkle of blocky houses of muted tones from beige to terracotta with a dwindling population scratching out a meagre existence.

After a day of climbing, I reached its highest point and

then enjoyed a long and glorious descent. In the distance I could see the hotel that lovely John and Nicole had told me about. In the centre of a dusty plain, several miles wide, atop a high volcanic mound of rock, sat Tizourgane kasbah, a thirteenth century hill fort and granary that had now been restored. All day long I'd seen hilltop buildings but none were as impressive as this one. Its location must have taunted passing armies. I felt like Monty Python's King Arthur approaching that French castle.

I cycled towards the kasbah, pushing up the steep final section. Just as I arrived, a young couple were exiting the huge entranceway accompanied by a Moroccan fella. I asked if he had a room, which confused him. Maybe, out here on this lonely plain, they didn't get many people turning up on spec. But a room was available. In fact, there was only one other couple staying here. I'd almost have the fortress to myself.

The bloke walked me around the back of the building, to a hidden car park and a room where I could leave my bike. Carrying my luggage up to the heights of the hotel rooms looked a daunting task. I picked up my bags and set off stairwards. He stopped me.

"We have a crane."

A steel basket was lowered from on high and all my luggage was loaded into it before being winched skyward. Why can't all hotels have a crane?

This amazing place, while too rich for my daily budget, was only 56 euros a night, cheaper than most Premier Inns. Although clean and pretty, the room itself wasn't anything special, but I'd have happily paid double to experience the view from the hotel restaurant's terrace. A wall of mountains encircled the vast plain with me, King Steven, in my castle high in its centre, a thousand metres above sea level. I imagined the armies and tribes in bygone centuries down below, looking upward with jealousy in their eyes and murder on their minds. But for now at least everything was peaceful. The only sound was the gentle hiss of the warming breeze and the occasional avian tweet. I stood there for a good twenty minutes just taking in my surroundings, enjoying my temporary royal promotion. This was the real magic of Morocco and, after a few false starts, it was finally seeping into my bones.

Unless you've brought your own entertainment, there were only two things to do here, and one of them was simply to be. The other, luckily, was to eat.

I shared the comfortable dining room with an English couple who'd come here to climb the surrounding mountains. She was a nurse and he was, well, I'm not sure of his job title, but he told me he worked in Yemen digging toilets and then locals would throw a knackered camel into the hole, claim it was a *racing* camel and try to get suitable compensation, so whatever job that is.

"Is this a good place to climb?" I asked.

"Oh yes. It's quartzite, better than the limestone back home. Lots of natural holes."

"And do many people come here to climb?"

"Not really."

"Does that bother you?"

He thought for a second.

"Well, it's a little disconcerting to think we're the only climbers for miles."

"And is there a local mountain rescue service?"

He laughed.

"Absolutely not."

The fish soup starter was fine, but the star of the meal was a tagine that was actually tasty, full of sardine balls and vegetables, the whole thing raised by the inclusion of pickled lemons. It was easily the best tagine so far, and there wasn't a hoof in sight.

*

It was another stunning day. I'd long since taken this weather for granted, but I shouldn't have. If you're going to suffer with rain and cold in Morocco, it'd come during these early months. But this year was a lucky one for winter cyclists, if not for the country's farmers, who badly needed some rain.

Today the scenery continued to blow my mind. On several occasions I pulled over to the side of the road simply to comprehend what I was seeing. Huge distant crags offered nothing but dramatic nature until I peered hard enough at them and discovered a tiny village the same colour hidden within. It was like a large-scale, geographic Where's Wally?

I watched a huge hawk dancing on thermals above my head. It wasn't the only creature affected by moving air. The wind got up, sometimes in my favour, and pushed me along, but because such assistance isn't allowed, it would then turn around again and spend longer blasting me in the face.

I reached today's high point, a wild pass at 1,500 metres above sea level. Cute, stripy Barbary ground squirrels darted repeatedly across the road. I rolled down the other side of the mountain and witnessed the reason why I'd come here to Tafraoute. The town is surrounded by the weirdest rock formations. The globular stone looks like it was formed by lava oozing out of the earth.

I found a room and went for a stroll. A bloke came up to me. We should all be used to this by now, especially in a town that manages to attract a fair share of tourists.

"Hello, my friend," he said, shaking my hand like a brother. "How did you arrive here? By coach?"

"No."

"By camper van?"

"Nope."

"By car?" he offered, running out of options.

"No, by bike."

"Ah! Very good," he lied and then pointed to a nearby business. "That's my bicycle hire shop over there."

And with that he walked away, our profound friendship severed, because clearly someone who'd cycled here wasn't going to rent one of his bikes.

In the evening I went looking for something interesting to eat. I found a restaurant with a little roadside terrace. My main dish had me ascend yet another rung of the tagine ladder. This time I'd chosen a different animal. The menu sold it as "Beef and vegetables with prunes and almonds" and no one could sue them under the Trade Descriptions Act. There were definitely prunes – plural – but only two of them. They tried to compensate for this with an overabundance of nuts, but in the end decided on just five.

Still, the food tasted alright and, despite being 1,200 metres above sea level, it was warm enough to sit outside as darkness descended. The shops and street were lit with fairy lights and people, locals and a smattering of tourists, milled about. Like Imsouane, the whole experience had the feel of a Greek island. I sipped my tea happily while deciding if it'd be appropriate to smash my crockery and dance on top of it.

*

Morocco has great cities, scenery to rival anywhere in the world and, most tagines aside, some delicious food, but there's one thing the country doesn't do, something abundant in Europe, particularly in the continent's less over-polished corners. Inverness has its tiny, half-arsed, one man band of a Titanic museum, where you can see a 1/12th scale model of the doomed liner constructed out of caravans. Zagreb has its Museum of Broken Relationships, each exhibit – a suspender belt, a dog light, a decapitated toy bear – and each tragi-comic story a testament to a pairing that might have been. Former

Soviet locations have bonkers bits of military hardware lying about the place and enormous Brutalist concrete hotel monstrosities that defy physics. Europe thrives on quirkiness. This country has no idea what it is. Look at a Moroccan guide book and it sends you to medinas, souks, mosques you can rarely enter, kasbahs and areas of scenic beauty. These places are all interesting, but lack oddness, that undefinable quality when you look at something and just ask, "Why?" But today, I was going to visit Morocco's one stab at quirk, and it was very telling that it'd been created by a Belgian artist.

I cycled out of town, past more bizarre orange rock formations. Huge boulders lay on either side of the road. They looked like those polystyrene ones the 1980's Incredible Hulk used to throw around. Some individual stones were the size of a large house.

One tall geological structure that towers over the edge of Tafraoute is called Napoleon's Hat, a name that makes no sense as it doesn't look like any headgear the general would have worn. It's tall and tapered and leans to one side. It was more like Jamiroquai's Hat.

A few miles further, I came to what I was looking for. A simple, tombstone-like sign simply said "Painted Rocks" with a translation in French and Arabic. I followed it, heading into the desert. A little way down the dusty lane, I could see in the distance a coloured blob or two, one painted red and the other blue. I headed towards them. I'd been expecting more than just a couple of colourful stones, but then I came to a cliff edge and looked down upon the main feature.

Jean Verame visited Tafraoute in 1984 and, as a tribute to his late wife, painted some rocks. But does it still count as painting when it's carried out by a team of firemen and their hoses and you use eighteen tonnes of paint?

Rising from the desert floor were several large piles, each the size of a hospital, painted in primary blues, reds and yellows. Occasionally a stray boulder had been sprayed orange or black. The sight was surreal and, from this distance, looked like the world's largest blob of plasticine. It was, uniquely for Morocco, quirky.

I left the cliff edge and cycled along the path and down to the rocks. Up close, the colours were incredibly rich and vivid. Someone told me the locals repainted the stones every year, but that would've been a time-consuming job even for a large team and cost a fortune. Besides, this clearly isn't true if you search for photos on the internet. In many, the rich cobalts I saw were faded to pale sky blues. But, luckily for me, they'd definitely been repainted recently, probably around 2018 if Google Images is a reliable detective tool. I doubt it'd stand up in court. See them now before they fade away again.

Back at my hotel I went online to find out what the world thought of today's painted rocks. I shouldn't really have been surprised at the outrage. These days, taking offence is a well-established hobby. You can probably buy how-to periodicals about it at WH Smith.

Yes, the primary colours jarred with the muted tones of the natural landscape and I understand the argument that it's simply vandalism, but it's all hidden from the road that passes this way. You'll only find it if you go looking for it, but that's the case with most offence.

I was less sympathetic towards whiners like TripAdvisor reviewer Mpampi who said it was "pointless". Of course it is. It's art. Besides, hadn't he examined reality lately, the insignificance of our drifting through the void on a ball of rock destined soon to die? *Everything* is pointless. Your life is pointless. Your partner's life is pointless. Your kids' lives are pointless, even your favourite one. The whole stupid universe is pointless. But that doesn't mean you can't dance around, get drunk or spray-paint a bunch of rocks from time to time.

They have at least as much point as Love Island, adult colouring books and organised religion, which is to say none at all.

Albert Camus, the philosopher we met in that bar in Casablanca, had something to say about this:

"The literal meaning of life is whatever you're doing that prevents you from killing yourself."

So c'mon, Mpampi, buy a box of paints and cheer the hell up!

Chapter 9: Stains and Desert Lanes

Tata and Zagora

Roads in this part of Morocco were sparse. Originally I'd planned to stick to well-established routes and cycle sixty miles north-east to Igherm and then eighty miles south-east to Tata, but I found a recently paved shortcut over the mountains. This shaved forty miles off the journey but, on the downside, I would climb to 1,800 metres to cross this lumpy bit of Morocco. Additionally, there were no hotels en route and so tonight, Valentine's Day, I'd be wild camping. Hidden away somewhere in my lonely tent, there'd be no one to cuddle up to lovingly, and so my Valentine experience would be the same as that of most married men.

Just a few miles out of Tafraoute, I stopped to buy water. Outside the shack was a man in beautiful blue robes. We chatted about my ride and where I'd been in Morocco.

"And where do you go next?"

"To Tata."

"On a bicycle?" he asked, bemused.

"Yes. I'm going everywhere by bike."

"Tata is great," he said. "Is that where your car is waiting?"

He really hadn't got his head around this cycle touring thing.

With the hills I had to climb today, it was thankfully a cool morning. I soon reached the pass I'd crossed a couple of days before and started down the other side. There must have been strong winds here recently. Two bus shelters had been blown over and left lying on their sides. I guess they hadn't provided much shelter.

And then I turned on to the loneliest road, my shortcut. All day long I saw only five vehicles. It was wild and barren with dramatic scenery around every twist of the tarmac. The day's second and final climb came, and I reached 1,800 metres after a long, steep, wearying push. The views back down were worth it though. I stopped and stared at them for ages, but to be honest I'd have done the same if the area looked like Luton. I just wanted to get my breath back.

The road at the top of the hill was desolate. I'd expected some compensatory downhill, but for hours I kept regaining any height I lost. The ground around me was covered with small rocks and a single species of low shrub for miles on end. But looking beyond, the world was beautiful, the mountains folded into bizarre shapes. I felt like the last man.

The landscape tilted and I finally headed downwards. The scenery changed again. There was a glass souvenir you could buy from the Isle of Wight filled with distinct bands of its different sands. The mountains around here were similarly banded, dozens of multi-coloured horizontal strips stretching for miles. Some local could chisel away and make a comparable tourist product, except there weren't any tourists here. There probably weren't any locals either.

After what had already felt like a decent day's ride, I arrived at the bottom of the hill and into an oasis thick with palm trees, the land all green and fertile, particularly noticeable after the increasingly desert-like landscapes of late. I'd reached the end of my shortcut and was now back on the main road to Tata, not that I'd have noticed. Traffic was still almost non-existent. Maybe, as I tooled around happily in those mountains, mankind had finally annihilated itself.

Near the junction was the tiny village of Issafn, a potential resting place for a cup of tea. But as I cycled in, I noticed the sign for a combined hotel and café. Maybe I wouldn't have to wild camp after all. I walked inside and asked if they had a room.

"We're not a hotel," came the reply. The sign outside was obviously just there for a laugh or to honour a time when people used to come this way. The man took me on to the road and pointed to a building further up. "Try there."

So I did, and exactly the same exchange occurred there too. The guy in the second place pointed me back to the first. In a town with a population of seven, didn't these people ever talk?

After the slightly ropey surfaces of today, the main road was beautifully smooth. Attractive mountains glowed warmly in the evening sun. Now resigned to wild camping, there weren't many places to pitch a tent that wouldn't be immediately visible from the road. After an hour, I saw a little house, partially collapsed and lacking a roof, set back a hundred metres or so from the roadside. I pushed my bike to it over rough, stony ground and wondered what I'd find. Luckily, its concrete floor was flat and quickly cleared of stones. It was just big enough to hide my tent inside. Should a convoy of Valentine's Day revellers come this way – unlikely admittedly – I'd be completely invisible.

As I sat in my tent eating a congratulatory tuna sandwich, I heard a noise. I leapt outside to investigate. On a nearby hill I could see a man leaning on a stick and looking in my direction. From his viewpoint, he could easily spy my tent over the collapsed sides of the house. Two wild camps and busted twice. I had all the stealth of a hippo in a fridge.

But then I heard the noise again, a clopping sound, and turned to see a donkey, stamping its hooves on the rocks. Presumably he belonged to the fella giving me the evil eye. I looked back towards the figure on the hillside. Let's be friendly, I thought. Out here in the dust, surely there was no need to move me on. I gave him a little wave, but he remained impassive, staring, commanding me to leave without needing to raise his voice.

No, if I had to go, then he'd have to come and tell me himself. And if he couldn't be arsed to walk all the way over here, then I couldn't be arsed to pack up and leave. I waited for a while and then looked back at the hill. He was still there, leaning on his stick. That wasn't a particularly comfortable pose to hold for so long, and yet he hadn't budged an inch. I waited some more. Oh, you silly sod. Either my angry landowner had died up there or he was just a weird-shaped tree.

Darkness fell around eight but by then, after a physically demanding day, I'd already fallen asleep. I woke up twelve hours later, completely refreshed and ready to continue on my way to Tata. I climbed out of my tent. That silly old bugger was still staring at me.

I wondered what would've happened if I hadn't stopped early at the abandoned house. Nowhere over the next twenty miles of pedalling was suitable for camping. You'd think in such a deserted location any place would be as good as anywhere else. But everywhere the ground was rocky and open, exposed to passing traffic. Yes, there was only one car every twenty minutes, but that in itself could be as much a danger as a busy road. An opportunist would know he was unlikely to be seen doing whatever heinous act he'd dreamt up. Hidden was the only way. I would've had to push my bike a couple of miles over rocks before clearing the ground and setting up, and that would've been less fun than trying to house-train Jedward.

None of this mattered now. I wouldn't need a camping spot today. It was another spectacular road, flat and with beautiful, dawn-lit mountains on both sides. The landscape was parched. I crossed several fords, each as dry as the last. I'm not sure how passable this stretch would have been in a wet winter. Given the predictions regarding climate change, maybe no one has to worry about that ever again.

At today's halfway point, I hit unglamorous Imitek, a shabby village whose name sounds more like an evil eighties sci-fi corporation that manufactures human-looking robots to take over the world. Perhaps the ramshackle houses were just a front.

I saw a makeshift outdoor café with three old dudes sitting outside and stopped for a cuppa. The café building could best be described as a concrete shed. I went inside to order my tea and found a friendly bloke, who told me to sit down and rest. I looked around the old place. There was a knackered sink and a pile of old kettles. The crumbling walls were decorated with a few pictures, the previous King and a faded photo of a local football team. If the fella had gone around the joint with a Glade Air Freshener, the fragrance he'd chosen was dust.

The owner set up a rusty table outside with a wobbly chair and a few strips of cardboard as a cushion. He patted it to welcome my arse aboard. My tea came and I sat there, sipping it with the others. They smiled and raised their glasses like we were all on the vodka.

Then the gas men arrived, three of them in a large truck. I think my café owner must have been the local distributor based on the number of empty canisters that were brought out of the place. As each spent drum was launched on to the truck, a gas-filled replacement was tossed off its back, crashing on to the concrete pavement with a loud metallic clank. Surely this wasn't best practice.

The two young black guys worked like dogs while the older Moroccan boss yabbered to the café owner and basically found fault in everything the two lads did. The only thing he didn't complain about was the collision of concrete and steel and the likelihood of any impending explosion.

My tea was finished even if the delivery wasn't. I went to collect my bike, parked near their truck. There was an overwhelming stench of gas. I thought it best to get away before someone lit a cigarette. Imitek was supposedly my farthest point south on this entire trip. I didn't want to be blown another hundred miles into the Sahara.

I continued on my way, the landscape almost completely flat within a few miles of the road but with small, pointed mountains off to either side. Only rarely would I see a village hiding in the distance. Somewhere along the way, the gas truck passed me and parped its horn. It still stank of fumes.

I finally arrived in Tata. After such a lonely couple of days I was excited to be visiting a metropolis of 40,000. I felt like I'd made it to New York City.

I quickly found a hotel and had a shower. The head wasn't attached as it should've been and water squirted unhelpfully out of the hose. I unscrewed it all and fastened it back together properly. Now, with a decent seal, pressure built up inside the plastic until the entire shower head fired off like a rocket. I re-screwed it and the same thing happened again. Presumably, that was why it hadn't been fastened together properly in the first place. I just removed the head entirely and hosed myself down. Such is life in a cheap Moroccan hotel.

Tata was an odd bird. Unusually for this country, the whole town – or at least the parts I saw – was constructed of arcades. Each archway contained a lock-up, most of them seemingly unused. Now, at five in the afternoon, I felt like I'd stumbled upon somewhere with a huge secret, the setting for an American B-movie. It had the aura of a ghost town. The few operational businesses had their signs caked in sand, some so thickly they were completely illegible.

There was an army base near my hotel. Three bored soldiers stood outside. I kept walking, looking further afield.

As we passed six o'clock, the streets became busier. One road in particular was full of life. In one lock-up, a guy was welding, looking right at his work without any goggles.

"Hey! Where you from?" shouted a guy in his twenties, materialising from a shop.

I told him. I was expecting the worst, but he wasn't selling.

"Do you like Tata?" he asked, his eyes dancing wildly in his head.

"Yes, it's, er, very nice," I lied unconvincingly.

"Yes, it is better than London," he said with a wonky grin and disappeared as quickly as he'd arrived.

I'd enjoyed the desolation of the last two days, and especially the lack of traffic, but I'm not sure long-term lonely cycling would be for me. I doubt I'd like it for much more than a handful of days. I needed humans, even crazy ones.

*

For the next few days, I wobbled through the desert. This wasn't your classic Lawrence of Arabia dune country. It wasn't as romantic as that, but it was still desert. The scenery wouldn't change much. The roads were flat, the ground parched and low hills added a little distant interest. This might all sound as dull as a wet weekend in Swindon, but it was beautiful in its own way. Traffic was sparse. The sun shone a warming rather than stifling heat. The air was still bar a gentle breeze. Silence reigned except for the conversations in my head.

On this lonely road, the majority of traffic consisted of camper vans, usually French or Dutch. Every hour or so would see a small convoy of three or four, trundling together as though nervous of dealing with Morocco individually.

My cycling continued without drama. This region clearly didn't see many cyclists, which sometimes gave the locals cause for concern. While I rested at the side of the road to eat a peanut butter sandwich, a Moroccan slowed his motorbike and checked if everything was alright. That was nice, and he didn't even have a tour to sell.

Twenty miles before Tissint, today's destination, a strange incident occurred. In the middle of the desert, not a building to be seen in any direction, a truck stopped and offloaded four kids, probably aged about ten, on bicycles a little way in front of me. It drove off, leaving them there. With a gentle tailwind, I'd built up decent momentum and screamed past. They called out after me, but so did everyone in Morocco. I didn't think anything of it until a little later. Were they left behind *because* I was there? Was I supposed to guide them into town, bringing back the rats like a reverse Pied Piper? I don't particularly like kids, but I didn't want to see them all desiccated and bleach-boned because of something I didn't do. But if that *was* the case, maybe it would've been better if he'd cleared it with me first before abandoning his kids in the desert.

Eventually I arrived in Tissint. Given its supposed population of 10,000, I was hoping for more than its one street. And it had odd geology too. On one side of the road, set a little back, was a steep, stony slope that looked to be made of volcanic rock, globules of lava that had cooled and solidified. Even in the expansive setting of the desert, it gave the place a claustrophobic, oppressive air.

A large motorbike sidled past me, calling out a friendly hello. As I pedalled into town, the bike returned and slowed to ride beside me.

"Can I invite you to a tea?" came an unexpectedly Scottish accent.

So, before the usual formalities of organising a hotel, Steve from Falkirk and I found a café and had a chat. He was coming up to the end of the first year of a decade-long round-the-world adventure. He'd saved up a pot of cash that'd hopefully last the distance, but his budget was tight, twenty euros a day for fuel and just three for food. There was no money for hotels. Steve was wild camping most nights.

He'd had an interesting and frequently complicated life over his 52 years. An engineer by education, he was working for a corporation in Nicaragua when he decided to set up a T-shirt printing business. He was successful, despite being repeatedly held up at gunpoint. The final time it happened, a receipt book was stolen and some of these receipts turned up in an important case of fraud. When the finger of blame pointed in his direction, he was forced to leave the country.

He moved back to Scotland where he went from whisky tester to an international diplomat for the Johnny Walker distillery, making presentations to top-end clients at luxury resorts in the Caribbean. It was a glamorous life. Unfortunately, it also involved drinking a lot of his own product. After worrying symptoms, a doctor told him if he didn't change his ways, he'd be dead within six months.

A diagnosis like that has a way of focussing the mind. He stopped drinking, moved to Spain and coached people on how to present. In his spare time, he ran a self-sufficient farm, breeding chickens, rabbits and pigeons for his personal consumption. He also grew various crops and, for a while at least, made his own wine.

But he wanted to move around, and so his most recent change was to set off on this world tour, initially with his Colombian girlfriend, but they'd fallen out and split up. Steve was now pining for his most recent love interest, a married Turkish woman.

See, I told you it was complicated.

Time was passing and I needed to find a hotel. Steve said he'd enjoyed our chat – I think it'd been a while since he'd spoken English to anyone – and was interested in a room too if it was cheap enough, and so I went in search of a bed. I walked the unmade and sand-filled lanes. This was a desperately poor place. The two hotels listed by MAPS.ME simply didn't exist, but then I spotted a tiny sign above the town's only other café.

I went inside. It was a scruffy den, full of blokes watching football. The owner was surprised I might want a room there, but he showed me a poky hole with an unmade bed. Skanky shared bathrooms and a dirty sink in the hallway completed the package. It cost six euros and was probably a little overpriced.

I told Steve there was a second room available. We gave it a once-over. Lacking a window, it was even crummier than mine.

"I've had worse," he said.

Having dumped our belongings, we had a look around town, but there was nothing to see and so we headed back to the hotel's café and ordered dinner. Steve's French was better than mine and he negotiated a cheap vegetable tagine. As even my chicken tagines had been entirely flavourless, a vegetable one sounded unappealing and so I asked the café owner what meat options he had.

"We go to the butcher's," he said.

Across the lane was a hole in the wall, a stench of death emanating from it. The guy behind the counter looked into his cupboard and pulled out a handful of floppy organs. It was goat's liver or nothing.

"Yep, that'll do."

A goat's head, possibly the liver's previous owner, stared at me blankly from the counter.

We took a table outside, just across from the butcher, and chatted some more. After a while, a little truck pulled up with a docile sheep on its back. The animal disappeared inside the meat shop.

"He's just killed the sheep," Steve said, a while later. "I can smell it."

It was dark by the time dinner arrived. Now, you've probably never had goat's liver and there's a reason for that. After all, it has a fairly strong and earthy flavour, but it wasn't terrible, and it was certainly better than those boring chicken tagines. It did, however, have a smell and aftertaste that lingered for hours, a musty, sour odour of goat urine. I don't think I'm selling this very well.

Later, lying in my cell, I received a WhatsApp message. Gary, a good friend from Cómpeta, had booked us – me, him and a trio of mates – into a shiny, all-inclusive hotel in Marrakesh for three nights in three weeks' time. He'd told me ages ago that he might come over, but I hadn't expected him to. Now I had a deadline.

I checked out the hotel's website. It certainly wasn't my usual sort of slum. I looked at my plaster-peeling wall. At least I was going to experience the full gamut of Morocco's visitor accommodation. I bet you couldn't get goat liver there though.

*

Before I left in the morning, the taste of goat liver still lingering in my mouth, I said goodbye to Steve, arranging to meet up in Foum Zguid, today's target. Power-assisted, he was setting off later than me. I would only manage six miles in the time he'd take to rattle off the whole forty.

The desert continued and I valued the peace it brought, especially when I saw a family of camels, two brown adults and a cute, entirely white baby. Other people weren't feeling so happy. A dog came running across the road with what looked like animal innards in its mouth, chased by an angry, fist-shaking shepherd, or maybe just someone who enjoyed re-enacting scenes reminiscent of Punch and Judy.

I arrived in Foum Zguid about half one, having expected Steve to pass me on the way. I was welcomed with a large arch over the road, and the town, at least to begin with, seemed strangely neat and tidy after the tatty poverty of Tissint. The roads were wide and the buildings distinctly uncrumbly, everything constructed from an attractive pink stone. It also had a large, flashier than normal mosque. Further into town, its beauty retreated, but here was the usual bustle of businesses and cafés. Overall, though, the place had a sense of space, which, thinking about it, should be a given for anywhere built in the desert.

The town's focal point was a small roundabout. Several restaurants bordered its fringe, grilled meats sending up clouds of deliciousness. I stopped to get my bearings. A bloke approached me and asked if I wanted food. I told him I was looking for a hotel. He said he had one that matched my meagre asking price. I followed his moped, struggling to keep up at times as he took me down lanes deep in dust. We arrived at a place calling itself a *riad*, although that meant a house with an internal garden – something that bumped up the price – and this had no such feature. It didn't matter. For a tenner I'd found my bed.

"Do you want my passport?" I asked, the first requirement of every hotel owner so far.

"No, later," he replied.

"Do I pay now?"

"No."

This was very odd, especially for a money-obsessed country like Morocco.

That earlier waft of grilled meat was calling my name. I returned to the roundabout for food, but it was also the ideal place to keep an eye out for Steve since he'd have no choice but to come this way.

It turned out to be a good call. Two dishes of olives followed by spice-marinated chicken brochettes, bread, water, a large glass of fresh orange juice and tea came to little more than a fiver.

The cook worked at the grill, wafting its coals, just in front of me. While I ate, Steve's motorbike approached the roundabout and he looked in my direction, but it was also the direction of the cook and a smokey lunch option. I gave him a wave, but I think his concentration was elsewhere and he set off up the road. Either that or he was utterly sick of me. Whatever the reason, I never saw him again. Such fleeting friendships travel provides.

Even though the hotel's beds were made up and a sign outside proudly displayed its name, there was the strong sense this place wasn't finished. Workers were on its roof, hammering away until darkness arrived at eight.

I heard voices in the lobby area and went to settle up.

"Pay in the morning," said the person who I took to be in charge.

"I'm leaving early."

"OK. Pay now then," he replied grudgingly.

This reluctance to take money wasn't very Moroccan. Maybe I'd just paid one of the builders. Anyway, they gathered their tools and skedaddled, leaving me in the building all alone.

Tomorrow was a long day. Although flat, it was eighty empty miles to Zagora. John and Nicole, the tandem cyclists I'd met in Taroudant, had done this leg years ago. They'd described how awful it was against a strong headwind, and tomorrow the forecast was for...well, you can guess.

I needed sleep and pulled back the tightly made bedclothes.

Ah.

On the sky-blue sheets were – how can I put this delicately? – evidence of male excitement. Three excitements in fact. Was this the result of one fun-filled evening of solo play or one emission each from the room's previous three occupants? Only a DNA specialist could provide that answer but I wasn't sure it really mattered.

My room had a strange curtain-less window that looked out on to a corridor, like the observation pane in a cell for the criminally insane. This made the stains on my bottom sheet all the weirder. Maybe he'd liked an audience.

I removed the soiled bedding and slept in my sleeping bag. After all, with a potentially tricky ride tomorrow, the last thing I needed was to wake up pregnant.

*

Morning had arrived and I headed for the main door. Before reaching the dusty lane outside, I could already hear the wind. Out in the alleyway, I fastened my panniers in place as mini-tornados of sand swirled around me. This wasn't a good start.

I renegotiated the dusty tracks back to the main road, imagining twelve hours of grinding into a gale with my eyes full of grit. But as soon as I reached the tarmac and faced the bike towards Zagora, the wind died completely, and it stayed dead for the rest of the day. Thank you, Wind God!

Although today wasn't fundamentally different to any of my previous desert rides, it *was* longer and eventually grew tedious. I bungeed a portable Bluetooth speaker to my handlebars and matched the desolation of my surroundings with a soundtrack provided by Radiohead. I wailed along mournfully with Thom.

Considering today's tarmac was only about five years old, it was bloody rough. As the sand around me became finer, more of it had been blown on to the asphalt, reducing the width of where I could cycle to a narrow lane. One big storm and the road could disappear entirely.

With 25 miles to go, for a few minutes at least, the desert retreated as I hit an oasis, a forest of palms and the thickest, greenest grass outside of Ireland. A 4x4 drove by, its passenger window down, and slowed beside me.

"*Ça va?*" said the young Moroccan.

"*Très bien.*"

My Lancashire accent had obviously impressed him. Or more likely, he couldn't hear me properly over the roar of his own engine.

"*Français?*" he asked incredibly.

"*Non, anglais.*"

He cleared his throat dramatically.

"Lovely jubbly!" he announced.

I smiled at his unlikely knowledge of British sitcoms. He put down his foot and zoomed ahead.

Weary, I finally arrived in Zagora. The town has a famous sign, a cartoonish camel and the words "*Timbuktu 52 jours*", indicating the number of days it'd take to reach this end of nowhere location. While I looked at it, a hawker came up and tried to sell a desert tour. I declined. I really didn't need to see any more sand.

After finding a pleasant hotel with a pretty garden, I headed out to see the town. I picked a direction at random, which took me down Car Mechanic street. Every bloke I passed tried to sell me something.

"Where are you from?"

"England."

"Ah, lovely jubbly!"

This exchange happened several times. When I'd visited the hole that is Turkey's Marmaris in the late nineties, every salesman there was flaunting his knowledge of British commercials with his cheeky bum slap, cheesy grin and an "Asda Price!" Today's "lovely jubbly" was the local equivalent. I could imagine them at the AGM of the Moroccan Institute of Rubbish Guides and Annoying Touts, all huddled up, sharing sales tips.

I wandered on to Zagora's main thoroughfare. Although the town was less populated than Tata, there was far more life here and loads of people asking me for money. With a proper high street full of cafés and restaurants and a very pretty mosque, it felt more like a little city, albeit one for which I was apparently financially responsible for absolutely everyone in it.

*

Here's a tip: If you're coming to Morocco and you're going to spend a lot of time in the sun, bring sun cream with you. Unless you've the wealth of Elon Musk, don't buy it here. A tiny tube from a pharmacy in Zagora cost me an eye-watering nineteen euros. It would've been cheaper to pay for the skin cancer treatment.

Today I went in search of this trip's first museum. I wanted to learn about the Draa Valley Berbers, the Draa being Morocco's longest river, around 700 miles from its source in the High Atlas Mountains to the Atlantic, beside which I'd cycle tomorrow.

The main road through and out of Zagora lasted forever and had clearly been designed lazily by someone on a computer overusing copy 'n' paste – café, café, barber's shop, petrol and repeat! – each section identical to the one before and after.

As the town's buildings grew sparser and then disappeared completely, a mud-walled kasbah appeared, looking like the sort of sandcastle that'd win an award. Excitingly, the museum was within this old fortress. I followed its signs and ended up peering into a barely lit tunnel. I walked slowly inside. After the bright sunshine, I was unable to see anything, including my own feet or where they were going. A dim orange light gave a hint at a turning up ahead and, like a genie, a man in elegant robes appeared, greeted me and welcomed me into his museum.

The dimly lit interior held a collection of objects, signed in English and French, and covered in a thick layer of dust, as you might expect from a mud-walled building. Less expected was the dust inside all the display cabinets. An intense incense assaulted my nose but, I suspect, probably masked a less pleasant whiff of damp.

The museum housed agricultural tools and old musical instruments, water jugs and carpets, prayer beads and wedding garments. Its highlights included a birthing room which, for reasons left unexplained, had only a two-foot-high doorway. Maybe the Draa women were tiny.

The traditional wedding ceremony was also explained. Before the young pups are joined in matrimony, the bride must ride a donkey three times around the wedding tent. If the beast stops, then the woman is clearly not a virgin – donkeys know these things – and proceedings can be halted. There's always one ass that spoils every wedding.

The museum filled a fun half hour. I re-emerged into the sunlight to be greeted by a load of little kids. Then some slightly older ones came along with their usual chant.

"One dirham! One dirham!"

Are they taught to beg from infancy?

The evening came around and I needed my ritual cup of mint tea. I returned to the café of this morning's breakfast to be greeted like an old friend. The waiter wanted to get to know me better.

"Isle o' Man?" he asked.

My, that was spooky. I mean, I'm not Manx, but I've spent a lot of time there. Most of my family lives on the island. But how could he tell that just by looking at me? Maybe it was my third leg. But then the penny dropped. I'd misheard him. He was asking if I was German, which in French is *Allemand*.

I was now roughly halfway through Morocco's desert regions. Goat liver aside, this wasn't proving to be happy hunting ground for original and interesting food, but hopefully this would change as I continued eastwards.

*

The disease kept on spreading, with now well over a thousand cases outside China. Deaths had occurred as far away as Iran and, more alarmingly for the West, in France. And we finally had a name for our serial killer: Covid-19.

Chapter 10: Digging for Dinosaurs

Nkob and Erfoud

After the beautiful but repetitive desert of the last few days, cycling along the Draa valley provided a welcome distraction. Lining the river were date palms, dangling their sweet treasure. If your only experience of these fruits is from an oblong box of dry, tasteless, brown Yuletide lumps whose label ironically screams Eat Me, then you could be forgiven for dismissing them. Real dates are something else. The non-processed, Eat Me-sized one are stickily delicious, but if you spend a bit more and try the *medjool* variety, each fruit is like a mouthful of caramel.

It was interesting to see the villages, usually a little way in the distance, predominantly built of mud but, with their crenellations, looking like something from *Game of Thrones*. Over time, some buildings had been partially worn away, revealing their underlying wooden frame. Surely dried mud isn't ideal in torrential rain. But maybe that just never happens around here. I particularly liked the mismatch of these primitive, ancient-looking mud houses and their attached satellite dishes.

After an hour or so, I stopped for breakfast, sitting on a wall and marvelling at a verdant oasis. This was yet another beautiful face of Morocco. I was suddenly overcome with a sense of extreme happiness. Such bliss is usually only seen in retrospect, when you look back fondly on some rose-tinted time in your life. In the moment, you rarely notice just how happy you are. But today I was happy, joyously happy. It wasn't the smooth tarmac or the gentle tailwind or the unexpected cycle lane that gave me safety even in the face of slightly increased traffic. It was something more than these fleeting positives, grateful though I was for them. It was the trip as a whole. Yes, Morocco was full of minor annoyances – the touts, the begging and the general grubbiness – but these paled when you looked at the complete picture. My elation may also have been fuelled by my complete lack of alcohol, given its well-known depressive qualities. I was into my eighth drinkless week and that alone sounded like a cause for celebration. It was just a pity, without alcohol, I'd no idea how to.

With a smile on my face, it was time to leave the Draa Valley and turn eastwards towards the comedy anagram town of Nkob. Unfortunately, this meant turning into the wind. At the junction was yet another police roadblock, this a 21st century variety, with one of the coppers sitting at the roadside, tip-tapping on a laptop. It was a slow day. He was probably playing Candy Crush.

This modernity contrasted with what appeared a little further down the road, a dozen or so makeshift stands, a man behind each, selling dates by the boxload stacked all around him. I passed them by and cycled on to a bridge over the wide river Draa. While I took a photo, one of the date salesmen, or in this case a salesboy, took the initiative. He approached me on his bicycle.

"Dates?" he asked, thrusting a box at me.

"How much?"

"Thirty."

That seemed like good value for a kilo.

"Do you have change?"

He did, and so I gave him a hundred dirham note. He handed me back a fifty.

"You said thirty."

"Ah, yes," he replied as innocently as he could before

handing me the rest of my change.

I continued on my way, dates bungeed to my back pannier rack. The tarmac deteriorated, the cycle lane vanished but so did the traffic. I was obviously heading somewhere deeply unpopular. As a Blackburn lad, I was used to that.

After the morning's lushness, the route had once again returned to desolation. Only the occasional tuft of rough grass grew around here. A series of grey elevations appeared to my right, too low to be mountains, but too sharp and angry-looking to be hills, the Tommy Robinson of geographical features except, like I said, they were sharp.

Suddenly, a convoy of little cars came in the opposite direction, each bearing a Uniraid sticker. Uniraid is a six-day orientation event for students driving jalopies at least twenty years old. Partially through the desert, they navigate between points using only paper maps, y'know, just like in th'olden days, well, the nineties. Orientation was clearly having a bad day, as today's leg was supposed to finish in Nkob and yet all these fellas were driving away from it. One of them was also waiting for help as his car lay gasping for breath with a smashed and steaming bonnet.

I reached Nkob. Tonight would be spent at only my second campsite. I set myself up and, within minutes, the owner had come out with a very welcome and complimentary pot of tea.

"Moroccan whisky," he said, handing me the tea. They're obviously taught this at tourist school.

I cycled into the centre of today's 7,000-inhabitant town, basically built around a single junction. Several dozen Uniraiders were sitting at the handful of restaurants there, using their compasses to find their way to the bathroom.

Nkob's claim to fame – apart from its silly name – were the 45 kasbahs supposedly here. This confused me. I'd always thought a kasbah was a large fortress. All the ones I'd seen so far fitted this description. The one housing that Berber museum in Zagora had the dimensions of a sizeable village. And it was hard to believe that one small town, half the size of Oswaldtwistle, could possibly hold 45 fortresses. I followed *La Route de 45 Kasbahs*, and it seemed someone had used a very loose definition, a kasbah here being any three-bedroomed detached house with a faux-battlement-effect rooftop.

Back at the junction I found a restaurant and ordered chicken brochettes and tea. The young waiter attempted to pour the boiling liquid from an extravagant height, resulting in half of it being splashed all over the table. He grinned like a man who'd overdone his medication.

"How much?" I asked, when it was eventually time to pay.

"Eighty."

I gave him a hundred dirham note.

"Thank you," he said, handing me back a ten.

On the way home to my tent, I stopped to buy a couple of bottles of water at six dirham each. The shopkeeper needed a calculator to solve this diabolical numerical conundrum. Maybe all of today's miscalculations weren't down to scamming. Perhaps Moroccans are just terrible at maths.

*

Today's scenery became tedious, with none of the earlier background mountains or stray villages to add interest. Nothing changed for hours on end except for an increasing headwind, which made every mile an effort, despite the route being as flat as a roadkill hedgehog.

And then came a quick bout of weirdness. Over the course of five minutes of desert road I was asked for water by ten separate individuals, one a handsomely blue-robed nomad and the rest happily dancing schoolkids in groups of twos and threes, either waiting for a bus or just delivered by one. Plenty of cars passed by and these weren't being flagged down by dehydrated nippers. I was merely an easy target, one the kids could chase enthusiastically. If I'd watered even half of them, my own bottles would have been empty and I'd now be a shrivelled husk, having my bones picked over by a bearded vulture.

At two in the afternoon, I reached Alnif, a small but important junction town. Here you could turn north to Morocco's famous gorges, the movie city of Ouarzazate and eventually Marrakesh, all places I still had to look forward to. My route, however, would continue eastwards. Twelve miles of orange-brown hills and wandering camels later, I arrived at Addi's Campsite, although Addi's Car Park with Toilet would have been a better description. Still, it only cost two euros to stick my tent up, use the facilities and get a free tea and chat with friendly Addi himself. He told me just ten cyclists a year come this way.

Addi was fifty and had eight kids, aged between four and 25. He seemed impressed he'd managed to create such a large brood with only one wife, but I'm guessing she did most of the work. The missus and kids all lived in the next town, while he dossed here, in a little shack on a campsite that needed no maintenance and which his mates frequently visited.

"Are you married?" he asked.

"No."

"Children?"

I shook my head.

"Liberty," he said and then repeated it dreamily several times. "Wake up when you want. Sleep when you want."

He was managing to do that himself pretty well.

Addi turned his attention skywards.

"Look," he said. "A plane."

I'd spent too many of my days in the desert looking towards the horizon rather than upwards. It hadn't occurred to me how few planes were in the sky. These weren't the criss-crossed contrails of Europe. South Africa was the only sizeable tourist destination south of here.

Darkness fell. Dim yellow lights glowed lazily in a far distant village, presumably the one housing Addi's clan. I crawled into my tent and clambered into my sleeping bag.

"Have you locked your bicycle?" came Addi's voice.

"No."

"You should."

I got dressed again and climbed out. Addi watched me to make sure I fastened my bike properly, chaining it to an external pipe on his little shack. I looked into the surrounding darkness. This area didn't feel like a hotbed of criminal activity, but maybe this was the Caracas of Morocco. The last thing I wanted was some gun-toting mafia boss wobbling off on my bike.

*

The number of photographs I snap on any given day indicates how stimulating its views were. Today I didn't take a single one. Still, you don't need amazing vistas to enjoy a ride. An astounding sense of space and all-encompassing feeling of peace cannot be captured in a picture. For such a dead place, I'd never felt more alive.

With the need for a calorific injection, I stopped for a date break. Although I was miles from any town, the roadside verge contained countless tiny shards of green glass, the remnants of beer bottles. This had been the case on absolutely every road in Morocco and I only mention it here because of the total absence of other features, natural or otherwise, on which to focus. But it was interesting just how much evidence of drinking there was in a country in which it was religiously taboo. Judging by the verges, everyone was at it.

Islamic hell, or *jahannam*, is a place where your scorched skin is constantly renewed so you can experience the burn all over again before having boiling water poured on your head to melt your insides. Such a punishment seemed a bit extreme just for indulging in a pint or two, even if you're going to be selfish enough to throw the empties out of your car window afterwards. But that's a loving God for you.

Five hundred years ago, Rissani was a big deal, the location of a famed desert city, trading in gold and slaves. Now, the only reason you'd come here would be to go somewhere else. Those in 4x4s head south to Erg Chebbi and its field of dunes. I'd had enough sand and so I was going the other direction, north to Erfoud.

I crossed over a large dry river bed surrounded by palms, thirsty and wilted. Under the right conditions, these trees could each produce a hundred kilos of fruit a year, but the ones here were struggling even to retain a hint of greenness. It was a pitiful sight.

The road to Erfoud was straight and flat and in the process of being widened to something approaching a motorway, despite minimal traffic. The area had money and it came from underground. I passed two or three large warehouses claiming to be fossil museums, but really just elaborate ruses to flog the many trilobites and goniatites dug up around here. These were the source of the local wealth.

I found a room in town. It was nice enough, but its walls were decorated in brown, swirly paint not dissimilar to what could be achieved in a prison cell and a very motivated dirty protest. All the walls were done, top to bottom, as were both the door and the flush-to-the-wall cupboard. Any incarcerated artist hoping to recreate such an effect would need to gorge himself plentifully the day before.

After several days in the desert, gastronomically speaking, there was a particular restaurant I needed to find here in Erfoud, one that specialised in *medfouna* or Berber stuffed pizza. I hit the town to hunt it down. Many of the cafés looked a lot snazzier than those in Zagora, a similar sized place. The fossil industry was clearly bringing in Tyrannosaurus cheques.

I found the eatery I was looking for, Des Dunes. From its outside it could've passed for a decent Indian restaurant on any British high street. Although nearly seven o'clock, there were no other customers, just five staff members sitting around a table, looking bored. Maybe things got busier later in Erfoud, or perhaps they never got busy.

I grabbed a seat and ordered the star attraction, a meat medfouna. If you want to recreate it at home, roll out some pizza dough, put your filling in the middle, pull the dough up and over the filling, roll it to a thickness of about an inch and then bake it. Mine was full of minced lamb and onions. The medfouna is very similar to the countryside around Erfoud. Both are pleasant enough, if a little repetitive, and crying out for some moisture. A spicy sauce would've made it sing. That's the medfouna, by the way, not the countryside.

*

My plan had been to visit the real fossil museum, not the ones flogging souvenirs, but unfortunately it was closed. Instead, and with no other obvious attractions in Erfoud, I was limited to wandering. At the edge of town was what looked like a slum, makeshift shelters of wooden poles and tattered tarpaulin. This though was a large workshop. Everything around here was covered in a fine white dust. The air screamed with the sound of grinding stone. Here, rocks were smashed in the hunt for evidence of prehistoric death.

Fossils are big business in these parts. Marine deposits from the Devonian Period, 400 million years ago, are exposed. Stone is cut from one of several quarries and then transported here to be cut, carved and polished. In many ways, it's like the Gold Rush. Your rock might contain something rare and expensive, but it's more likely to be yet another low quality ammonite or nothing at all.

But, as in every commercial pursuit, man can't stop himself. The sites are being over-excavated and the fossils illegally traded. Even though UNESCO-protected, these valuable remnants of old sea creatures end up in bazaars in Marrakesh or sneak their way into European museums. And if you're thinking of coming here to pick up a stegosaurus for your mantelpiece, a few words of warning: Many of the fossils on sale, even those at high prices, are plaster cast replicas. Who'd have thought Moroccans would use deceit to earn a tourist dollar?

"Where are you from?"

I was caught off guard. Avoiding the fossil touts on one side of the street, a young fella had jumped into my face.

"Er...England," I replied distractedly.

"Do you like Morocco?"

I turned to talk to him properly, but he wasn't looking at me, clearly not interested in any answer I might give and so he carried on regardless.

"I have a shop."

"Good."

"I sell Berber clothes and jewellery."

"Nice."

"It's here, in the market. Come with me."

"No, thanks."

"No, come with me!" he said insistently, grabbing my arm and trying to drag me in the direction of his cash register.

"No, I'm going this way."

I started to walk away.

"Excuse me? Excuse me?" he said in that "Oh, Jeremy, you absolute monster, how your indifference doth offend me so" tone that touts here have perfected. It used to bring out the apologetic Brit in me. Two months of Moroccan salesmen's games had long since done for that.

I left him behind and climbed a nearby hill, one offering great views over the town and the plain on which it sits. As the sun set and cast a low light on Erfoud, the scene became a painting by an artist limiting her palette to just beige and chestnut, each cuboid building half-illuminated, half in darkness. It had a surreal, dream-like quality. I moved my foot with a crunch of broken glass. It was green. The boozers had been up here too. Morocco has a way of holding up great beauty and then immediately bringing you back down to earth.

After a final cake test to see if pastries in the south-east of the country were an improvement on the other areas of Morocco – they aren't – I went for dinner. It was just a simple café and, lacking more interesting options, I chose a harissa-smeared kefta sandwich. But it wasn't the food that was noteworthy about this visit.

The café's evening bread was being delivered by hand, by which I mean a dozen or so discs of bread were stacked and carried in the sweaty mitts of a young delivery boy. He couldn't have been older than thirteen. Just before the café's terrace, he stumbled and dropped his wares all over the floor. At least one loaf wheeled into the road. He scooped them all up, brushed away any gravel and carried them inside. No damage done. *Bon appetite!*

Chapter 11: Gorging on Gorges

Todra and Dades Gorges

My journey had gone as far east as it could. In that direction, beyond Erfoud lay only desert and the Algerian border, sealed tightly since 1994. I turned west again, to take a road that, 200 miles from now, would deliver me to Ouarzazate, the closest thing Morocco had to Hollywood.

Some villages around here felt like they were at least keeping their heads above water. Others, such as today's Jorf, were an absolute mess. Its 12,000 residents were stretched out along an ugly main road that crumbled beneath me like one of those platforms on Manic Miner.

MAPS.ME had labelled a curious attraction on the lonely road ahead. It merely said "Historic waterworks". I wasn't expecting much. As I approached, hundreds of large molehills appeared in the desert, each several metres tall with a crater in the top. There was also a little house. I stopped to look, perplexed.

I turned my head and there was Abdul, an older man in a funky blue turban with the skin of an alligator and teeth that practised social distancing. He tried to entice me into the building. I'd grown so distrustful of anyone who approached me that my automatic response was to decline, or, in this case, lie that I'd hundreds of miles to do before bedtime and so I couldn't possibly spare the time. Maybe I missed a treat, but I doubt it.

I kept cycling, but slowly. The molehills remained. What was curious was that in a country with few public toilets, there were several here, just in this one stretch, out in the middle of the desert. One of the larger molehills had a none too safe wooden ladder constructed around it. Tourists from a parked minibus were heaving themselves up it to look inside the crater. Or maybe they were being hurled into it. I wasn't really paying attention.

I cycled further down the road, away from the touts, and scrambled up the sides of one of the larger craters. Looking inside, it appeared to be a bottomless pit. Nearby was a sign that said "Underground Canal". These piles of earth had been removed during the construction of a series of subterranean channels, *khettaras*. They'd been started here back in the seventh century but were borrowed from a 3,000-year-old Persian idea. The molehills were important because they enabled access to maintain the canal. The water comes from the mountains miles away and is used for agricultural irrigation. But it begged the question, and one with a fairly obvious answer, where was the outflow from all those toilets going?

I kept heading across the wasteland. After a slog, I approached Melaab, a sizeable town of such insignificance it didn't warrant even a single-line Wikipedia entry. From a distance, it was attractive enough, a wide oasis with tiny houses of various shades of pink and brown, but something about it seemed unreal, like I was viewing cheap CGI from a nineties movie.

The town looked better from afar. In reality, once I'd penetrated a shell of grand but half-built houses, I was welcomed on to a drab main road of shops aimed at no one but foreigners, most of their signs in badly spelled English or Spanish. People called out as I cycled past. It was obvious this otherwise forgettable town was on the main route from Marrakesh to the desert. The only thing going for it was the possibility of snaring a passing tourist. I don't know why they didn't just put out massive nets and do a proper job of it.

Eventually I reached today's supposed destination, Tinejdad, and it felt, well, apocalyptic, "a post-Corona virus nightmare" as I wrote in my notes at the time, my first acknowledgement of the coming turmoil. All the businesses were closed. Dust covered everything. A trench, presumably some uncompleted roadworks, had been carved near the edge of the main street, rendering the shops on that side inaccessible, even if they'd been open, which they weren't.

At the far end of town I found the hotel and restaurant where I'd hoped to stay tonight. I went inside and was told it no longer offered rooms. There was no need for accommodation in a town that was closing down.

I kept on cycling. A customer at the restaurant had mentioned a campsite ahead. A few miles along the road, I saw a sign for the fella's recommendation but with no hint of any camping facilities. If anything, it looked like a posh hotel, one out of my league. Regardless, I went in to investigate.

Luckily for me, there were no other guests staying here. This may have been the reason the friendly owner said I could camp anywhere I liked. There was a covered terrace near an outdoor Bedouin-style lounge and a large herb garden. I was taking the piss when I suggested I set up right there on the terrace, but the owner was fine with it. I think he was just glad of a paying customer.

Evening was approaching as I took my place in the hotel's empty rooftop restaurant. A wide but dry river away was a mud-walled kasbah – a proper one this time, a small fortified town rather than a glorified house – all bathed in sunset gold. The palms around it marched off until they met the mountains in the distance. It all felt so exotic that I should probably have been eating a Fry's Turkish Delight or something.

My starter was a large *briouat*, a real version of what that yacky, fishy, noodle-filled pastry was trying to be, all the way back on my ride towards Tetouan. It contained the same ingredients in its filo-like wrapper – pasta and seafood – but was delicious rather than stomach-churning.

The main course though was yet another variety of tagine, this one full of great juicy chunks of braised camel, huge and sticky medjool dates and topped with a hard-boiled egg. The meat was as soft as marshmallow, not an attribute usually associated with camel. Maybe they were fibbing and I'd just paid over the odds for beef.

Full of dromedary, probably, I left the restaurant and walked back to my tent.

"Mr Stevens! Mr Stevens!" called the hotel owner. I didn't bother correcting him. "Do you want to see peacocks?"

He gave me a little tour of his facility, its various birds and its herb garden, where he pointed out his wormwood.

"See how all the other plants have weeds around them," he said, patting the soil. "Not wormwood. It kills all the plants near it."

"How much of it do you put into tea?" I asked him.

"Ah, little. Very little."

He broke off a piece no bigger than a fingernail. It was a lot smaller than the entire branch I'd stuck into my teapot back in Casablanca. Maybe I was already dead and this was the afterlife. It'd explain the endless perfect sunny weather.

Then a young fella appeared.

"This here is the youngest son of the hotel," said the owner. "He cooked your meal tonight."

"Thank you," I replied. "It was delicious."

"Yes," came back the owner. "He's good, but he's stupid."

I laughed. That had seemed a little cruel, but the cook clearly didn't mind. He smiled gormlessly. Or maybe he couldn't speak English.

"Why is he stupid?" I asked.

"I don't know. He just is."

*

After a wonderful breakfast of orange juice, coffee, omelette, msemen, honey, jam and cheese – well, Dairylea – the owner appeared.

"You should see the kasbah. It has a museum."

"Is there a path to it?"

He pointed across the dry river bed.

"A man will meet you," he said. "Whatever you do, don't give him any money!"

The museum was similar to the one in Zagora but without the thick layer of dust. In addition to English, French and Spanish, its exhibits were also labelled in the Tifinagh script, the one used for Berber languages. It's a fun-looking alphabet, full of circles and right-angles. There has been a lot of wrangling in Morocco over its use, and it's only recently Tamazight, the most widely spoken Berber language, and Tifinagh, the script used to write it, have been officially supported. If you come to Morocco and see graffiti depicting what looks like a headless stick man with his arms raised, this is the Yaz character in Tifinagh and a symbol of Amazigh liberation.

It was time to move gorge-ward. My route continued, mostly flat. The land was scrub all day long, but I glimpsed my first snowy peaks of the High Atlas in the distance. In a week or so, I'd be crossing that range's highest road pass.

I arrived in Tinghir, the stopping off point for an exploration of the Todra Gorge, and found a cheap hotel with an attached café. I was accosted on its terrace by a twenty-something English-speaking local, who invited me for tea and "Moroccan hospitality" despite dark eyes that moved shiftily.

I asked if he lived here and what he did.

"I work in the silver mine."

"Wow. Is that tough?"

He nodded.

"Six days a week, eight hours a day. For 200 euros a month." For a miner he looked slight. And clean. Maybe he'd just had a shower. "Only day off is Sunday," he added.

I didn't mention it was now the middle of Tuesday. Besides, perhaps today's shift was already finished.

"Are you married?" I asked.

He thought for a second and took slightly too long to answer.

"I have two children, a boy and a girl."

Did a statement like that in Morocco imply he'd tied the knot? Before I could ask, a guy he was sitting with jumped in.

"By the way, my name is Mohammed."

"And yours?" I asked the first guy.

Once again, his eyes gave the impression his brain was cooking something up.

"I'm Marco."

Who knows? Maybe his mum was Italian. We continued to chat, but I couldn't shake the feeling everything he said was a fib. He asked why I was there.

"That's good," he said. "You are not a tourist."

"Why not?"

"Because you have your bicycle. You are a traveller. Tourist arrive on bus, take a photo and leave. They have no time."

I had a look around the bustling town, its thriving little market entirely free of hassle. There was a sense that people were too busy with life to be distracted by someone like me. They'd better things to do. But not everyone ignored me. A little kid came up to me, said "Bonjour" and offered me a tiny hand to shake.

I had my usual evening tea and grabbed a cheap and cheerful kefta sandwich. On my way back to my room, I resupplied for the hills that I knew I'd suffer tomorrow in search of the famous gorge. I popped to a shop, a little place hidden around the back of my hotel and bought provisions.

"There you go, mate," the shopkeeper said, handing me my change, his voice straight out of Essex.

"Are you British?" I asked.

"Nope."

"Then how come you have such an amazing accent?"

"From you."

"Me?"

"Tourists like you."

Hang on, I've just been told I'm not a...oh, it didn't matter.

"What, a tourist taught you?"

"No, I just picked it up."

I scooped up my purchases and left. That all seemed very unlikely. I mean, yes, you could learn the odd word from a customer, but this guy was speaking English like a native. But if he'd studied the language at university, or while living in Britain, or via a girlfriend from Southend, or in some other innocent manner, why wouldn't he have admitted it? His English lessons might not have been so guiltless. Maybe he'd learnt on the job, one he shouldn't have been doing, working with a Londoner or two in Syria. Perhaps he'd had linguistic guidance from someone like Jihadi John.

I looked at the water bottles I'd bought. Neither had labels on. Maybe he'd filled them himself, and from where? I hadn't thought very highly of this afternoon's perfectly friendly silver miner either. Was Morocco making me paranoid?

Of course, it was. The water was fine. And there were endless innocent explanations for my Thames Estuary accented shopkeeper. In Morocco it was equally too dangerous for him to admit he'd picked up his incredible English by Skyping the blokes he'd met on Grindr.

*

Today I'd see Todra Gorge, the huge limestone canyon carved into the High Atlas Mountains. I set off early and the road climbed immediately, twisting repeatedly. One turn would see me and the surrounding orange rocks bathed in warming sunshine while the next plunged me into icy shadow. At turns, it was too cold for a t-shirt and too hot for a fleece. The clothing hadn't been invented for these conditions.

A mile or two across the valley, the mountains were climbing too, villages hidden within their folds, constructed in materials the same shade and composition as the hills. Where the slim river Todra fed the valley floors, the rich greenery there contrasted with the barren dustiness beyond. Water was life.

A dark passageway lay ahead. After eight miles of climbing, the sides of the gorge shot skywards, 400 metres high. The walls closed in claustrophobically. Sunlight was removed, except for a thin sliver overhead. At this time of day, few tourists were around, but the stalls hawking trinkets were already set up to exploit those who would arrive later.

I continued onwards for a few miles, but the gorge opened outwards and it was clear its best bits were behind me. Then, seemingly a long way from humanity, I heard a dog bark high up the rocky mountainside. I looked up to see the hound was guarding its owners, a family living in a cave up there, a real life Fred and Wilma Flintstone. No rent, no rates, no problem neighbours but a hell of a schlepp to the nearest supermarket.

I freewheeled back towards the narrow gorge, passing some German rock climbers on the way. Amidst all this scenic beauty, they'd spend their entire day staring in the one direction without any.

I descended into the narrowest part of the gorge again. In my absence, tourist numbers had increased massively, but the little humans were dwarfed by this natural cathedral. Unlike the main streets of Venice and Barcelona, Todra could handle them with ease. And when it'd had enough of them, it could do what it did in 2014 and flood them out. In that year, 47 people died in flash floods throughout Morocco. In 1995, it was a massive 730.

By midday, with a rumbling stomach, I was back down the hill. I headed to my hotel's café for a late breakfast. On the way in I said hello to "Marco", who was still sitting there, still not mining silver.

*

Cycling through and out of Tinghir this morning, I'd been expecting some ugliness, but it never came. I was confused by the guidebook's description of the place as a charmless mining town. Yes, it was no Chefchaouen, but it was no worse than anywhere else I'd seen. Only when "Marco" had mentioned his job did any of it make sense, but the mine wasn't even in Tinghir. It was twenty miles along my route today in Imider.

At the time, I was unaware of all of this, but if I'd passed through Imider five months earlier, this village of 4,000 might have made more of an impression upon me, because before October 2019 there was a huge and perpetual protest here.

Imider's is the largest silver mine in Africa and the seventh largest in the entire world. By rights, this should make the area rich, but it's had the opposite effect. The protesters accused the mining company of stealing the village's water – the mine needs over 1,500 cubic metres every single day – leaving this desert region even drier and the land unfarmable. It's made earning a living here beyond difficult. As reported in 2015, half of the villagers were surviving on less than a dollar a day.

Given that the mine brings so much wealth into Morocco, perhaps you'd think that one benefit of an autocratic country would be that the King could step in and ensure a little fairness, that the profits could be made to trickle down to the villagers, even if the water couldn't. Unfortunately, the King himself is one of the mining company's major shareowners and the state has taken a more dubious approach, framing the most vocal protesters and imprisoning them for crimes they didn't commit.

"There is no relationship between the mine's water exploitation and the decrease of groundwater in the region," said Youseff el-Hajam, a spokesperson for the mining organisation. This statement sounded highly unlikely, but he added it was based on a hydrological study. Unfortunately, he wouldn't tell anyone which study or where they could find it. And now it didn't matter. The protesters had given up.

Boumalne Dades seemed neat and tidy as I entered, but then the road went downhill, as did the look of the place, and the usual Moroccan scruffiness appeared. The town here was basically one main street lined with broken pavements and squalid cafés.

I found a cheap hotel with an attached restaurant. Possibly because he could speak French, some bloke who I later discovered wasn't the owner, negotiated the price with me and then suggested I have lunch on the hotel's roof terrace. This seemed like a pleasant enough idea, but the real reason for enticing me on to the terrace, which contained me and me alone, was so he could later bum money off me without an audience.

After lunch I went out to explore Boumalne, but it was the slimmest of pickings. I found a place with aspirations to be a mall, but it was tiny and neglected, containing a few clothes shops, a barber and a butcher. It was certainly no Bluewater.

And then in a country that knows how to put on an outdoor market, I found its weakest, a large patch of wasteland containing about ten stalls, each so far apart it looked like the stallholders hated one another.

I wanted some crisps from a supermarket near my hotel. The most appealing variety was a single bag of chilli flavoured ones. They cost fifteen dirham. I picked the bag up and the owner appeared from nowhere.

"You can't buy them," he said, taking the bag from me and placing it back on the shelf. I was intrigued. Were they going to be too spicy for a pasty little European like me?

"Why not?" I asked.

"They are out of date."

He removed the bag once again and showed me the sell-by date. They'd expired a month earlier. He'd obviously returned them to the shelf for someone else not to buy.

"Or," he said, with a glint of mercantile mischief in his eyes, "you can have them for ten dirham."

Ah, now I understood. He wasn't prepared to throw away his manky stock, even if legally he couldn't sell it any longer, but he could at least make a deal. Everything in Morocco is a negotiation.

*

Today was probably Morocco's most famous geological feature, the Dades Gorge. Many a visitor, holidaying in Marrakesh, gets driven through it on their way to the Sahara, but it lacks the immediate drama of Todra's high-sided narrow slit but generally feels a lot wilder.

Leaving my heavy panniers at the hotel, I headed towards the gorge. A legend says the wind has a son in Boumalne, one he likes to visit in winter. It was hard to think of my last two months as anything other than summertime, but the old bugger was certainly coming to see his offspring today and was already whistling towards me.

The road twisted and turned for mile after mile. Each bend revealed another amazing view, ancient Berber villages full of crumbling mud fortresses, seemingly one thunderstorm away from completely dissolving, overseen by jagged rocks and surrounded by lush fertility. This was the Morocco of postcards, if postcards still exist these days.

Halfway along, there was a curious rock formation known

as the Monkey Fingers, eroded digit-like protrusions that covered the mountainside. Nearby was a sign for Monkey Fingers House and my mind was flooded with simian pornography and a very uncomfortable-looking Hugh Laurie.

But the photographic star of the gorge, the one that appears first on any Google Image Search for Dades, is a series of hairpins. As the road climbs breathlessly towards the Dades Gorge Hotel, snaking like Shakira's hips, the Dades river cuts a slim channel through the rock below. And when you arrive at said establishment, with your heart pumping wildly and forehead leaking profusely, you too might find a lone motorcyclist standing outside, ostensibly admiring the view over the valley below but also sneakily having a piss.

And then it was time to turn around. The wind had clearly finished visiting his son in Boumalne, because he was now on his way back home again. At least it was mostly downhill.

Along the way, a number of kids appeared from nearby villages to give me a series of high-fives. One little girl came out of her house when she saw me approaching, rushed over to my side of the road and said something softly to me. I couldn't understand her. She repeated it. It wasn't her volume that was the problem but the language. I still didn't know what she was saying. She seemed heartbroken at this lack of communication. Maybe she wanted me to take her away from all this. I mean, these stone-coloured villages that vanish chameleon-like into the rocks look sexily exotic, but what future does anyone have here? The menfolk might be able to find work mining or fleecing tourists in any way they can, but what about the women? Their futures, one of repeated child production and domestic servitude, must stretch out before the more ambitious and imaginative like a predestined prison sentence.

Today's ride had been a beautiful one that'd linger in the memory for a long time. But now I had to leave Morocco's dramatic Gorgeland and head towards Marrakesh. But before then, we first had some movies to see.

*

The world was succumbing to Covid-19 one nation at a time. By the end of February, it'd infected every continent bar Antarctica. But one country was noticeably absent from the roll call of disease. Morocco still hadn't logged its first case. Maybe it never would. Some reports suggested the virus was foiled by warm weather, and sunshine was Morocco's speciality.

The countries already recording deaths – China obviously, but also South Korea, Italy, France, Iran, Japan and now, for the first time today, the United States – were still few enough that this thing could be contained. They'd get their acts together, stamp out the virus and everything would be alright. Surely?

Chapter 12: Moroccywood

Ouarzazate and Ait Benhaddou

Today was about small towns and villages with only the occasional desert stretch to separate them. My route was close to a region known as the Valley of Roses, such is the quantity of flowers grown here, although this wasn't the time of year to see them. Almost every business along the roadside advertised rose-related products. There was rose water and rose-scented perfumes and signed photos of Rose West. Only kidding.

A little down the road I got an interesting high-five from a kid dressed like a forty-year-old Artful Dodger. It was odd to see an eight-year-old in a trench coat, a flat cap and with gold rings on his little fingers. He didn't ask for money but then again perhaps he'd already picked my pocket.

Not far from Skoura, today's target, I could see the huge oasis that surrounded the little town, its palms stretching for miles. It used to be a lot bigger than this. Here was another place not having an easy time of it.

Thirty years earlier, apple and pomegranate trees grew here amongst the palms. People moved to Skoura specifically to farm. But with climate change and over-exploitation of resources, it's a different story now. Back then, wells only needed to be sunk to a depth of around ten metres. Now, the water is forty metres beneath the surface. When water pumps became cheaply available, they abandoned the old system of khettarats, the channels under those large molehills I saw a few days ago. Now the apples and pomegranates are gone, the earth dry and cracked. Droughts, which used to visit twice a decade, are now here every other year. It looked like 2020 would be another.

Skoura itself was only home to around 3,000, and its shops and other roadside businesses felt more rundown than in most towns I'd seen recently. It had nothing obvious to sell to tourists, unlike the places coming up and the gorge towns I'd just passed. It's difficult to turn drought into an asset.

A couple of miles down the road, the gateway to my campsite promised a swimming pool and WiFi, but this seemed like clever marketing or just outright lies. The site was simply a large gravel car park and my phone failed to find the outside world. I later discovered that next door, hidden behind a mud wall, was a hotel, and if you crept assassin-like into its garden, there was indeed a pool and functioning internet. Whether or not I'd have been arrested if I'd flung my pale torso into its watery depths, we'll never know.

Now unloaded, I cycled back to Skoura's desperate-looking main street and its least desperate-looking restaurant, La Vallee des Fleurs. Food away from Morocco's big cities had only rarely offered anything noteworthy – the goat liver in Tissint, that Berber pizza in Erfoud and the chunky camel tagine had been exceptions – but Skoura was going to surprise me.

I started with the best salad Morocco had thrown at me since Tangier, with tomato, potato, apple, beetroot, onions, a hard-boiled egg and a dollop of fresh, cloud-like goats' cheese. But that wasn't all. Because it was usually a decent enough fall back on a menu that didn't otherwise inspire, I went for another kefta tagine. And this one was the best ever. The meaty balls were how I had imagined all Moroccan food would taste, loaded with layer upon layer of spice. Sitting on top was a zinger of a chilli, long and fruity, raising the heat to something that would give even Speedy Gonzales the sweats.

The night fell on my little tent and the desert around it. At four in the morning I woke to see starlight streaming through the ventilation mesh in my roof, a patch normally obscured by a rain cover. There hadn't been much point putting it on in a place as dry as a Weetabix. I crawled outside to take a proper look at the constellations. With few street lights to pollute the atmosphere, the Milky Way was painted across the heavens. Maybe little Skoura could reinvent itself as a Dark Sky location, attracting amateur astronomers. Then they could stick on a spacesuit to explore the surrounding area. It already looked like Mars.

*

I packed away my tent and, while doing so, a worker came past pushing a wheelbarrow and sneezing violently into the air. There was a time when this would have passed unnoticed, but not any more. The media was still reporting Covid-19's global takeover as something like the flu. Maybe the bloke with the wheelbarrow was Morocco's first case. But there was an easier explanation.

From the constant clearing of throats in cafés to the ever-present hacking up of something unpleasant while walking in the streets, everyone in Morocco seemed to have a perpetual cold. Or perhaps a new one arrived the moment the last one faded away. I'd had two myself while I'd been here. Cups, glasses and cutlery are rinsed rather than properly washed. As I've already mentioned, your daily bread has been mauled by many hands, if not simply dropped on the floor and scooped up, before it touches your lips. The marketplaces and medinas are thick with people, breathing into each other's faces. If Covid-19 *did* reach Morocco, there was a good chance it'd bring down everyone within a week.

I cycled away from Skoura on flat roads, with no wind and lovely temperatures as usual. A gentle pootle later, I arrived in Ouarzazate. With its 70,000 people, the place felt like a properly modern little city. Each business had a manufactured sign rather than its name scrawled on a wall by its owner's wonky hand. We'd left behind the thrown-together world of Berber villages.

Such a gentle entry wasn't in keeping with the place. Ouarzazate is the starting point for what has been called the planet's toughest footrace, the Marathon des Sables, a seven-day, 150-odd mile slog through the Sahara. It's run in the middle of April when midday temperatures can push a brain-melting 50°C. Billed as "An Extraordinary Race for Extraordinary People in an Extraordinary Place", you carry all your food for the week, a daily water ration as well as a compulsory kit list that includes dozens of items, some obvious, like a sleeping bag, and more worrying ones such as an anti-venom pump in case you're set upon by a herd of angry scorpions. A fun run it ain't.

I reached the centre of town and found a hotel, one with a large but shallow pool in its reception, something that can only exist in a location that doesn't attract British stag weekends. Imagine the death otherwise.

I'd arrived early and so had plenty of time to explore Ouarzazate. This town might be the starting point for the Marathon des Sables, but Ouarzazate is more famous for its Atlas film studio, the largest in the world, by size rather than the general quality of its output. But it *is* responsible for a handful of big hitters. Parts of *Gladiator, The Living Daylights* and *The Jewel of the Nile* were filmed there.

In its time, the landscape has doubled-up as Egypt, Iraq, Syria, Afghanistan and every other politically unstable cabbage of a country. Most movie budgets won't stretch to cover even the crew insurance for a shoot in somewhere like Baghdad. Here, on the other hand, you can fly 'em in on Easyjet.

The Atlas studio was way out west though and online opinions about it were none too glowing, slating it for being disorganised and pricey. So rather than see the well-known, expensive but badly-reviewed studio a few miles *out of* town, I would visit the barely known, cheap and badly-reviewed one *in* town.

It was hopeless really, but fun. Nothing was labelled and so I made up my own stories as I moved from scene to scene. In each set, most of which tended to be throne rooms, a pinned sheet of A4 told you the films made within it, mostly involving Jesus and utterly unfamiliar even to the online movie know-it-all IMDb. In fact, in one of the throne rooms, of the eleven films that had been shot there, IMDb recognized only one, a 1994 TV movie called *Solomon and Sheba*. An online reviewer described it as "one of the most hilariously dreadful films I have seen in a very long time." And that was the most successful one.

Along with an obsession for throne rooms, there were plenty of comically painted hieroglyphics as well as posters of other desert-based films that were definitely not filmed here. Outside there was a smashed up plane, and two boats in a similar condition, lots of plastic Roman columns and a fibreglass cave. The studio also doubled-up as a museum of the movies. There was a room full of knackered old cameras and mixing desks, many with their knobs fallen off. If you find yourself in Ouarzazate, I highly recommend it. But take along your imagination and a sense of humour.

There was something I was after, and I hoped it could be found in my first ever large European-style supermarket in Morocco. On entry to the French chain Carrefour, I noticed bread was twice the street price and therefore no one bought it. It sat on the shelf, untouched by human hand, the only loaves in Morocco with this quality.

What I needed was booze, something not available from

smaller supermarkets here. This wasn't meant to torment me in my current teetotaldom, but I wanted to see if they sold *mahia*, the only spirit produced in Morocco, a clear grappa-like drink traditionally made by the country's Jewish community using figs. It'd make a good present when I met my mates in Marrakesh. And while you could buy local Moroccan beers, wines and spirits for the same price you'd pay for a more recognisable international alternative in the UK, mahia wasn't one of them.

Abandoning my search, I walked around the town's shops and its tiny souk and then found the Moroccan equivalent of an off licence (or liquor store if you're American), the first I'd seen in the country. Perhaps I'd have more luck here.

"Do you have mahia?" I asked.

The guy behind the counter frowned and then looked at his boss, standing a little distance away. Quick, make something up, his superior's expression seemed to say.

"Err...we have this," he chirped, reaching for a bottle of clear liquid. "It's the same."

He handed it to me. Weirdly for a spirit, its label included its ingredients, none of which were figs.

"Are you sure it's the same?"

"Oh yes."

"But there are no figs in it."

He shrugged his shoulders.

"What does that mean?" I said. "Is it mahia or not?"

"Yes, my friend."

"But mahia is made with figs."

He smiled.

"Not this one."

My hunt would have to continue elsewhere.

As I'd noticed my room had a little kettle, I'd bought myself some tea bags from Carrefour. Back at the hotel, I prepared to make a cuppa. Unfortunately, in a design master stroke, the kettle's little power lead was a good metre short of reaching any of the room's wall-mounted sockets. For this Taskmaster challenge, I constructed a wobbly but functional pannier-based kettle tower. I might not have found my mahia but at least I had tea.

*

I was moving onwards, and today I had a more impressive movie location to visit, the village of Ait Benhaddou. But I had to get there first.

The ride was mostly uneventful except for one lorry, whose driver beeped me from behind for several seconds. I think he expected me, a lowlife on a bicycle rather than a big man important enough to fart copious amounts of life-destroying gases into the atmosphere, to move off the road. There was plenty of room for him to pass, good visibility and no oncoming traffic. When I didn't yield, he squeezed by me as closely as possible. I could almost smell his B.O.

After the essentially westward direction I'd been cycling ever since Erfoud, I now turned north and Marrakeshwards. You don't need me to tell you from which way the wind was now blowing.

It wasn't long though before I could see Ait Benhaddou in the distance, a sand-coloured settlement hugging the side of a sand-coloured hill. What distinguished this from other such villages I'd seen in Morocco was that the hilltop in its centre was covered with colourfully dressed people who were clearly not from around here. Ait Benhaddou was popular with tourists, something that brings out the worst in Moroccans. Stories abounded of scammers guarding the entrances to the old town and charging visitors to go inside. They'd steal your underpants if you told 'em they contained your crown jewels.

A visit to Ait Benhaddou was popular enough when it was only famous for having been used as a location for *Gladiator*,

The Man Who Would Be King and *Jesus of Nazareth*, for which the town was completely reformed. But there's no fan like a *Game of Thrones* fan, many of whom base their entire holiday schedule around visiting its various filming locations. Ait Benhaddou played the part of Yunkai, the slave city freed by Daenerys in season three. If you're planning on coming here for this association alone, you should probably lower your expectations. Much of what you saw of the city on telly was added by computer. TV's Yunkai is to Ait Benhaddou what a *Jurassic Park* T-Rex is to a terrapin.

I rolled into the newer part of Haddou as a minibus passed me with its holiday company logo painted on the side, the very appropriate named BS Tours.

After finding the campsite and setting up my tent – not easy in today's wind – I waddled to the old town. Even before I reached it, various hordes of tourists were being shepherded in my direction, each one led by a young Moroccan in a blue turban and flowing robes, just like the locals around here *never* wear. Since authenticity clearly didn't matter, why choose the outfit of a desert nomad? They should have gone the whole hog and thrown on a Donald Duck costume.

Filtering through the crowds, I crossed a bridge over what I imagine, under the right conditions, could be a mighty river but whose flow today was sadly reduced to that of a garden hosepipe.

And then I hit the town. All the streets were lined with shops selling plastic ornaments and crap paintings, and this was a shame. I passed by the stalls, their salesmen shouting after me, and scrambled up the village's steep lanes. Stripped of its money-grubbing tackiness, it would've been beautiful and invitingly atmospheric. As it was, it was just a very dusty theme park.

After a surprisingly short amount of time, I reached the top of the village, a little plateau containing a solitary stone building, an old granary rather than the golden Aztec-inspired pyramids of television's Yunkai. For all its fakery, the views from the top were gorgeous, looking down on the palms and the nearby villages and the other, more modern half of Haddou, where all the town's residents really live. One of those villages, somewhere in the distant hills, had actually been a real-life slave town.

I climbed back down and saw an information board. In parts of Morocco, history can be amusingly fuzzy. Whether or not Jesus ever existed, I'd have bet good money his contemporaries walked the streets of ancient Haddou. That's how old it feels, plastic camels aside. But since Berber history was oral rather than written, no one knows. The current best guess was that the whole place was built in the eighteenth century, making it roughly the same age as St. Andrew's Golf Club, and I'd never imagine Jesus there. Just think how he'd struggle to hold his golf balls with those stigmata.

I had time to kill and a hole in my stomach. We've already established that Morocco's Chinese restaurants only appear in locations frequented by tourists. Even so, it seemed unusual that, on a stretch of road with about ten eateries to choose from, two of them were Chinese. They may have been overpriced, but this country's non-city food had rarely thrilled and I needed a change. On the menu, the only nod to Moroccanity was beef with cumin.

"We have no beef," the waitress said a bit too happily.

With a substitute ordered, I looked around the completely empty restaurant. This was an establishment aimed squarely at tourists in a town full of them. Why weren't there any...oh yes...Covid-19. Chinese food outlets were apparently suffering the world over. The virus may have originated in that Wuhan wet market, but it wasn't as though this place was selling bat soup. I wish it had. And if the tourists in these parts were scared of everything Chinese, they should've been terrified of what the shops here were selling.

My dumplings arrived, doughy and meat-filled, although presumably not pork, in a gingery, garlic broth, followed by chicken noodles, scattered with black beans. This meal didn't represent good value, being five times the cost of a typical Moroccan lunch, but just to eat something both tasty and different made it worth every dirham. So what if I now had Covid.

After my food I needed tea and so I headed to a café across the road. Sitting at a nearby table, one of those Disneyfied blue turban fellas was chatting up a female tourist. I have to admit his outfit made him look rather dashing, which probably wouldn't have been the case if he'd stuck on the Donald Duck one.

I walked back to my campsite, passing loads of freshly arriving minibuses, each one assigned its own cartoon guide by a tit with a whistle, flapping his arms and shooing people off the main road like he'd some sort of authority. It takes a lot of organisation to move the quantity of tourists that come this way, especially when each one has to be individually scammed.

Ait Benhaddou could have been a great little village but its rabid desire to milk its visitors removed most of its charm. Was that also going to apply to where I was now heading, Morocco's Tourism Ground Zero, Marrakesh?

Chapter 13: An Infector Calls

Marrakesh

The plague had arrived. Today, March 4th 2020, I learned Morocco had its first Covid-19 case, a local who'd returned from Italy, a country with over 3,000 cases of its own and already 107 deaths. Disease was on my doorstep, even if that doorstep was 270 miles away in Casablanca. Spain, to where I'd be returning at the end of all this, had also just confirmed its first death.

I assumed last night's camp site was next door to a kennel or dog pound. Every so often, a bark would kick off and then fifty other hounds would join in raucously. Either that or a massive pack of strays had wandered close to my tent. Maybe I'd been lucky not to be eaten. And there was me worrying about Covid.

But let's be positive. I started early into a windless day, the sun continuing to shine. Although I twisted through hills, the first half of the journey passed without any real effort. Dozens of Berber villages nestled in the mountains, hiding from view among rocks that slowly turned from orange to pink. At the half way point was a series of steep switchbacks that slowed me down and raised the heat. At the top of the climb, my world became a moonscape. But even here, a village, seeking shelter from the sun, had been built at the bottom of a gorge, surrounded by lush greenery.

The kids I passed still asked for money, *bonbons* or *un stylo* in that order. When I told one little girl I had no sweets, she looked really quite angry. I thought I was going to get decked by an eight-year-old with early onset diabetes.

I passed the tiny village of Anmiter. In the river that ran by the place, women were washing clothes. Maybe this happens everywhere in Africa, but it was the first time I'd seen it with my own eyes. Had we been born elsewhere, from a less fortunate womb, this too could have been our fate. I wanted to remember this, to recall every time some trivial nonsense annoyed me.

"Yes, Derek, that *is* unfortunate, but we could all be spending hours on end scrubbing our husbands' skiddy underpants, ankle deep in an ice cold river."

"All I said was that we were out of Hob Nobs."

I'd no idea what to expect with today's destination, Telouet, and so I mistakenly believed the hotel I found beside an old kasbah was all there was to the place. Stopping outside drew the attention of the establishment's owner, busy directing operations in the outdoor restaurant on the other side of the road. He'd do me half-board for 400 dirham, he said. Thinking this was the only place I'd get any food between here and a huge climb tomorrow, I succumbed. It was a lot more than I was used to paying. How annoying! Thoughts of being born as a female slave beating clothes against a rock in a chilly river seeped into my head. No, it wasn't annoying. Not at all. I was *delighted* to be paying so much.

The owner invited me into the restaurant for a tea and then asked if I was hungry. Of course I was. He promised a Berber omelette and some brochettes of unspecified species. I was particularly excited by the forthcoming eggy component of my lunch, having not yet tried a Berber omelette, but I can now conclude that, in this context, Berber just means tomato.

"When you are finished, I'll give you a tour of the kasbah," the fella said.

"Very good," I lied.

Luckily, in the meantime, a group of tourists arrived in a

car and he disappeared with them.

I ate my fill and asked a young waiter if this meal was included in the price of my room.

"Oh, I don't know," he replied. "How much did you pay?"

I told him.

"Oh yes," he said, nodding his head violently. "Definitely."

Clearly, I'd been robbed. He even brought me a dessert.

With lunch done and the hotel owner still absent, I went to the kasbah without him. Apart from one staircase leading to a single smartly tiled room, the whole place was falling down. It was a mud and straw affair that looked ancient but was in reality about the same age as Mary Berry.

Whatever the state of the building, it would've been nice if the locals hadn't used the whole site as a rubbish tip. At least it gave the family who lived in a shack there somewhere to graze their chickens. A beaky life picking over old packets of crisps and discarded water bottles had one advantage though. Upon plucking their feathers you'd probably find them ready shrink-wrapped.

It wasn't long since lunch but I needed calories for tomorrow, and so my evening meal couldn't come soon enough. Unfortunately, it was the blandest of chicken tagines. That's how poultry tastes when you feed them exclusively on old Coke bottles.

Tomorrow I would cross Tizi n'Tichka – at 2,260 metres above sea level, it's the highest major road pass in North Africa – a day that'd see me ascend a total of 1,800 metres. It was on evenings like these that my thoughts turned to e-bikes. There was no way I could arrange one of those in time, but what I *could* arrange was to eat early in the morning to enable me to reach the summit before the sun hit its peak.

"Can I have my breakfast at half past eight?" I asked the young waiter.

He looked pained.

"It's too cold at that time."

"Is it? I'll wear a jacket."

"No, it's too cold. Breakfast is at nine."

Clearly he didn't want to get up that early.

*

I was sitting on the sunny, already toastily warm restaurant terrace at 08:55. On the stroke of nine my breakfast appeared. It wasn't going to be the later start that held me up this morning but the size of the meal. Henry the Eighth would have struggled to eat half of it.

As I was about to leave, the young waiter muttered that I owed money for water I'd had with yesterday's lunch and dinner. I knew I didn't have any with my evening meal, but I couldn't remember if an unordered bottle had shown up at lunchtime. Besides, it was odd that food was included as part of the hotel package but not water. Was he going to charge me a rental fee for the cutlery too?

"I'll pay for the lunchtime bottle and I'll have one to take with me please," I said to him.

So he fetched me the water and told me the whole lot was twenty dirham, about twice what I'd pay in a shop. I handed him a hundred, but he didn't take it.

"The change is here. Come," he replied, nodding in the direction of the hotel. I followed him inside and the transaction took place there. He took out his wallet, the one that had been in his pocket all along, and gave me my money. I could only think of one explanation for this odd behaviour. There were CCTV cameras outside the building and on the terrace. He was carrying out this dodgy financial transaction somewhere he couldn't be seen by the hotel's security or his colleagues. I seriously doubt I should've been charged for yesterday's water. Money must've been tight if he was prepared to risk his job for a couple of euros.

It was only a few minutes into today's ride that I realised Telouet was more than just yesterday's hotel, a crumbly kasbah and a chicken with a yoghurt pot stuck on its beak. I passed through the little village itself and it felt like a film set on which the director had shouted "Action!" the moment I arrived. It all felt too perfect, like the Morocco of TV commercials, full of people bustling about happily. The market stall owners sold, the café's waiters served and the metalworkers welded, all with smiles on their faces.

"He's gone!" I imagine the village's evil overlord screamed the second I was through. "Back to the Death Machine!"

I swept down the road and out of civilisation, the views improving from an already high standard with each curve. I passed three stray kids who sang out "*un dirham!*" in what sounded like well-practised unison. I'm not sure they didn't actually harmonise.

And then came the climb. It wasn't as bad as I'd thought. Two months on the bike had toughened my legs. I popped out on to the main road that would, in a couple of miles, reach the high Tizi n'Tichka. Standing at the junction, a man sold gaudily dyed geodes, those cracked-open rocks full of crystals.

"You want?" he said, as I waited for a car to pass.

What, did I want some stones to carry to the top of one of Morocco's highest roads?

"No, thank you."

He grabbed my arm roughly as I set off again. Does that approach ever win someone over? Oh yes, thanks for that. Now you've bodily handled me, I'd love to buy a dozen of your crappy ornaments. I growled at him and he let go.

Considering this was Morocco's most important mountain pass, one of the few routes through the middle of the country if you wanted to go from north to south or vice versa, traffic was light, and the 2,260 metre summit came surprisingly easy.

The only thing that slowed me down was stopping constantly to take photos of the scenery. The brown, lifeless landscape folded in upon itself and up above, the highest peaks of the Atlas, maybe even the 4,167 metres of Morocco's highest, Mount Toubkal, stood with only the lightest dusting of snow. I'd been lucky. It wasn't unknown for this pass to be closed and entirely iced up at this time of year. Today's weather was more likely to melt the tarmac.

They say the grass is always greener on the other side, and this was certainly the case today, although, being the northern face of the High Atlas, that shouldn't have come as a surprise. A humongous series of switchbacks carried me downwards on the smoothest of surfaces, but then the roadworks started. For such an important pass, apparently the busiest in North Africa, they could have made the effort to finish it. Every mile brought another construction site, each one attended by precisely zero workers. Morocco suddenly felt like the stereotype of Africa, the one were nothing worked properly and everything was cobbled together.

I knew another hill was approaching, but I wasn't sure of its size. It turned out to be a further 400 metre altitude gain and upward slog. There were roadworks here too, and the construction workers' habit of spraying the dusty road with water meant the dirt eventually became concrete-hard lumps that made for a bumpy ride. My teeth chattered like comedy wind-up gnashers.

The views at the top of this second summit were incredible. In a south-easterly direction, the lush valleys made the landscape look like Switzerland. North-easterly, however, this was clearly the arid Morocco you'd expect of the country. In the distance, the flat plain that Marrakesh calls home was visible through the heat haze.

But I wasn't going there today. It'd been a long day already and just around the corner was a lone hotel. I chose it for its location rather than its ratings. It only had two TripAdvisor reviews, both one star, but I was excited to try its restaurant's tea. One reviewer described it as tasting like slurry and having little animals in it.

I couldn't wait for the morning. I would enjoy an enormous freewheel through some of Morocco's most glorious scenery and then I'd enter the country's most celebrated city, Marrakesh. Nothing could spoil it.

*

Well, one thing could spoil it.

I woke up and looked out of my window. All steamed up, I rubbed the glass before realising the fogginess was on the outside. I was inside a cloud. This was going to take the shine off my descent, a reduced speed and none of the spectacle. All these amazing views were around me but just out of sight. I felt like Warwick Davis at Glastonbury.

After a breakfast that disappointingly contained no little animals swimming in my tea, I set off into the fog. Rather than taking a fairly central position to avoid the tarmac's crinkly edges, as I'd done yesterday, I stuck to the sides and listened for traffic. There wasn't much of it and what there was went slowly, but when a car or truck loomed out of the murk, I could only see it at the last minute. Juggernaut or precipice wasn't a choice I really wanted to make.

After fifteen miles of downhill, the fog lifted, but unfortunately by then the spectacular views had already been left behind. Still, in my favour, the road was now flat and, in contravention of the Universal Laws of Cycling, I had a deliciously strong and tropically warm tailwind. For 25 miles, I sailed like a fully sheeted clipper down a dual carriageway and its beautifully wide cycle lane with barely a spin of the pedals.

A couple of miles before I hit the centre of town, I was offered a gentle introduction to the madness of Marrakesh when a large horse legged it across all four lanes of my busy dual carriageway. The cars slammed on their brakes, but the drivers' nonchalance suggested this was just an everyday event around here.

I arrived in town. After the sleepy backwaters I'd experienced recently, the city felt instantly crazy. I cycled towards its centre and stopped to check the map on my tablet.

"That won't work in the medina," sneered a cocky young Moroccan.

"Oh, won't it?"

"What are you looking for?"

"To be left alone."

But I realised this was a big ask in Marrakesh.

Regardless of what my wannabe guide had said, I found my way through the narrow alleyways to Jemaa el-Fna, the city's huge main square. Even now, early afternoon, it was lively, but only later would it come into its own.

As my pals wouldn't arrive in town for a couple more days, my first job was to locate a bed. I was amazed to find a clean, comfortable if basic room a hundred metres from this, the country's touristic epicentre, for just twenty euros. Imagine what you'd get within a hundred metres of Trafalgar Square for twenty quid. Probably a wee in its public toilets.

I expected the forthcoming all-inclusive hotel to sacrifice gastronomic adventure for customer contentment and so these next 48 hours, alone in Marrakesh, was my time to discover what the place really had to offer food-wise. I'd heard that the best of one of Morocco's most popular meats lay just around the corner and so I headed to Lamb Alley in the central medina. I didn't know it yet, but I was about to eat my tastiest Moroccan meal, possibly my tastiest meal anywhere.

Lamb Alley was just three or four stalls, backed by a restaurant in some cases or nothing more than a hole in the wall in others. Slabs of freshly roasted whole lamb – or *mechoui* – lay on their counters. A board in French and Arabic explained the dining options. There weren't many. You could either have your baby sheep oven-roasted or cooked in a *tangia*, or you could opt for a sheep's head. That was all.

I opted for half a kilo of mechoui and was invited into the stall's back room, a small table surrounded by a continuous bench on which five Moroccan men were already troughing, their faces greasy with lamb fat.

I slithered around the seating, broken in places, and found a space. A tray appeared in front of me containing a pile of meat and a round of bread. A glass of mint tea quickly joined it. In the centre of the table were two or three bowls of a mixed cumin and salt condiment. I'd already seen these in several Moroccan eateries, but today, in a freshly plague-filled world, they flashed a warning. In the past, I'd copied the locals, who'd reached in and taken a large pinch of brown-white powder before sprinkling it on whatever they were eating. If those fingers made it as far as a mouth, and then returned to the bowl, it was no surprise everyone had a cold here. I watched the guy opposite me take a different approach. He dipped chunks of lamb into the mix before stuffing the whole piece in his mouth. That seemed more hygienic, slightly. But the others pinched and sprinkled.

As far as I knew, the virus had only made it as far as Casablanca. These next few days might be the last ones when such condiment bowls were still relatively safe. Besides, at this stage, Covid-19 was being reported as a condition only dangerous to those a good twenty years older than me. I'd take my chances.

I grabbed a chunk of lamb and dipped it in the salt before loading it into my face and grinding my molars slowly. Oh my word! This was, by the most comfortable of margins, the tastiest, juiciest lamb I'd ever eaten. Even better, and something I didn't know was possible, was the lamb crackling, the crispy, chewy skin surrounding it.

This combination of tenderness and chewiness could only be achieved by its method of preparation. The whole lamb had been placed in an underground oven in the floor, the cover of which was occasionally removed to allow gawpers to look inside. There, it bakes for hours.

I made my way through my mound of meat, at times dipping and other times sprinkling the cumin salt. As the pile reduced, I started to feel sad. Yes, I could easily have stuffed down another half kilo, but I knew Marrakesh had a lot more culinary options and I didn't want to explode before I'd found them all.

I said goodbye to Lamb Alley and wandered the medina without a destination. The souk was much more like the markets of Istanbul than the others I'd seen in Morocco, more colourful and tourist-friendly, but not as authentic as in the less visited cities like Tetouan.

I returned to the main square. Water sellers, men dressed in red and black, covered in bells and wearing something approaching a sombrero, goaded visitors.

"You want to take a photo?" they ask.

If you do, they'll chase you down the road for payment.

Also here were snake charmers, their cobras poised and ready to pounce, as well as other animal abuse in the form of little monkeys on chains. Cruel it may be, but they wouldn't be here if it didn't bring in a regular income.

I left the centre and walked in a random direction. A woman was cooking tagines at a stall on the roadside. She removed the lid from one to check its progress just as a gust of wind blew a huge cloud of sand and grit from the road into both her face and her food. Chicken, olives and gravel was a tagine I'd still yet to try.

After half an hour I stopped to check where the hell I was.

Luckily, I wasn't far from an area of Marrakesh with plentiful booze shops. The first one I tried didn't have any mahia, my sought-after fig liquor, but the second one did. As happens in Turkey, the shop assistant placed the bottle into a black bag – the sack of shame – the first of this colour I'd seen in Morocco. They're obviously reserved for sinners.

Around eight I returned to the main square. By now, darkness had descended and Jemaa el-Fna had put on its evening clothes. Gone were the snake charmers and monkeys, and in their place was a mini city of brightly lit, temporary food stalls. Each stand had a number and, disappointingly, its own aggressive tout.

"Remember: number one-one-four gives you more!" sang a hawker as I walked past his counter.

"Number eleven takes you to heaven!" hollered another.

One tout tried a different technique. He put his arm on my shoulder.

"I spoke to you yesterday, didn't I?" he said, like we were mates.

"It wasn't me, but then again, we do all look the same" or "Yes, you said I had beautiful eyes" would have been better responses than what I actually said, which was, "Er, no."

In the distance, I found what I was looking for. Every night in Marrakesh, a few stalls specialise in snail soup. I'd had *escargots* before, cooked the French way in hectares of garlic, but what would Morocco do with them?

Sitting around the edge of the stall, you could order your molluscs in three portion sizes, small, medium or large. For this first attempt, I opted for the smallest. Just five dirham bought me a little stripey bowl and perhaps ten fat snails.

On the counter was a tub of toothpicks. You lance the meat inside its shell, scoop it out in one fluid motion and pop it into your mouth, throwing its former home into a receptacle in front of you. Once all the snails have been dispatched, you take the bowl in two hands and slurp the broth left inside. The snails themselves didn't taste of much, but the liquid was a meaty, umami overload and probably cured some ailment I didn't know I had. The website *theculturetrip.com* lists this dish as one of eleven foods no visitor should ever eat in Morocco. They don't know what they're talking about.

I wasn't done yet. I continued to walk around the stalls. More touts tried to lure me in their direction.

"Number 25 makes you feel alive. You want a nice tagine?"

"No, too boring," I replied. "I want a sheep's head."

The tout stepped back. His stall didn't offer such things.

Eventually I found them, a rack of ovine noggins, skinned and roasted, teeth bared to the sky. I approached the stand and pointed to one.

"You sure?" asked the server.

I looked at the stall's clientele, Moroccan to a man, and sat down, earning a grin and a cheer from one of the other diners. Twenty dirham bought me a quarter head. It wasn't as macabre as it sounds. The roasted flesh was already removed from the skull and sliced up, served with bread and a murky-looking spiced dipping sauce, watery and tinged yellow with unexplained globules resting in it. The grey meat looked unappetisingly gelatinous – and it certainly had that quality in spades – but it was soft and very tasty, especially when dredged in that yellow puddle.

There were still more things to try, but with another night here I'd leave those for later. Instead, I wandered around the acts that had set up elsewhere on this massive square. Some were sub-Grumbleweeds comedy performances. In one, the lead chump was playing with a bra while the audience laughed hysterically, like we'd fallen through a time portal back to the days of Carry On films or we'd somehow found ourselves stuck inside Benny Hill's brain.

Other acts were musical, or wished they were, banging drums or wailing tunelessly. One old blind fella was sitting on a stool, singing quietly, all alone, very near to one of the comedy acts and its multitudes. Every time the crowd roared, he smiled. Did he think they were cheering for him? I suppose he'd find out later when he checked the contents of his begging bowl.

Each audience was four or five people deep, but none of the acts was worth getting to the front for. Those on the crowd's outer edges had to contend with pickpockets, lone Moroccan men, hollow-cheeked and hungry, lurking like hyenas.

I wanted something else to eat, but nothing savoury. I settled for an ice cream and got a scoop each of two flavours I've never tried before. The date was great but the avocado one was particularly nice, a bit like a soapy banana, which sounds awful but honestly wasn't.

Marrakesh was a lot to take in at once, the crowds, the noise, the touts and the new sensory experiences, and I was glad I had another day here. But back in my room, I learnt of a second Moroccan case of Covid, and in a location so utterly stuffed with people, this was the last thing I wanted to read.

*

The ease with which I'd found things yesterday had given me false confidence. Today this would be shattered. The morning's mission was to find the Derb Douria and the photography museum. I got myself so spectacularly lost in the medina, that I was lucky, two hours after setting off, to reappear in the main square right back where I'd started.

While trying to find my way, I'd seen an advertisement on a wall for an escape room. It surprised me that anyone would set one up here. The whole of Marrakesh is an escape room.

I made a second attempt, almost equally long-winded, to find the Derb and just at the point when I was about to give up and get something to eat instead, I stumbled upon it accidentally. It was a little museum with lots of old musical instruments and nice fancy tiling, but, if I'm being honest, the effort to find it meant that if it didn't contain fire-breathing dragons it was always going to disappoint.

But it *was* my first experience of the new reality that was seeping this way from China and mainland Europe. As I handed over the entry fee to the young fella on reception, he instantly used sanitizer to rid himself of the infection I was no doubt carrying. It was a wise move, but suddenly, without such protection, I felt vulnerable. Worse, I walked inside his museum and, in the first room, one visible from his desk, I got an instant tickle in my throat. I coughed, not violently but enough to have him looking over in my direction.

"Security," I could imagine him saying into his lapel microphone. "We have a zombie. Repeat, we have a zombie. Take him down!"

Given that I'd probably need a month to find it, I left the photographic museum until after lunch. I returned to Lamb Alley and popped into the place next door to yesterday's loveliness. This was a joint that specialised in *tangias*, not to be confused with tagines.

Just as the word tangine refers to the pot in which the meal is cooked, so does a tangia. But whereas a tagine has a hole in its conical lid, a chimney to release steam, a tangia is a small pot into which ingredients are put and then the entire thing is sealed shut, ensuring neither flavour nor moisture can escape. This pot is then placed on a source of heat, cooking its inhabitants slowly.

Moroccan men often fill a tangia with dinner ingredients and visit the hamman for a bath. There, they stick the tangia in the hot coals that heats the establishment's water, and collect it later, ready to eat. For this reason it's known as a bachelor's dish, the Moroccan equivalent of Super Noodles.

My tangia arrived at my table and was tipped on to my plate. This still being Lamb Alley, I'd opted for sheep again, this time cooked with preserved lemons, an ingredient I'd expected, and failed, to see all over Morocco. Bread accompanied the meat along with the biggest, sweetest pot of mint tea. The lamb was a little fatty but very tasty, although it couldn't reach the lofty heights of yesterday's.

While finishing off my giant pot of tea, I planned my route to the photo museum with the precision a Field Marshal would be proud of. The last thing I wanted was to get lost in the depths of the souk and only reappear a few days later having missed my friends' visit. When I put my planning into operation, I made just two errors, although one of those did have me mistakenly walk into someone's house.

Later, I headed back to my hotel and read some more grim news about Covid-19. Young people were dying, younger than me at least. I suddenly felt extremely paranoid.

In the evening, I went out again, returning to the bright lights of the main square and its food stalls, looking for brains this time, but the mass of people was overwhelming. What had seemed like a lively explosion of humanity yesterday felt now a very dangerous place. Some say Jemaa el-Fna, the name of the square, means "the assembly of death", after the executions historically carried out here, and that translation had never felt so apt. This place was so in your face, and in your face was precisely what you didn't want during a highly contagious pandemic.

Instead I bought bread and chocolate and retired to the tranquillity and sanctity of my room. With my window open, I could hear the conversations of passers-by. Almost every single one of them was Italian. How was that possible? They had thousands of cases and a couple of hundred deaths. Shouldn't they be in quarantine at home rather than travelling around the world spreading infection?

While I cowered indoors, I was receiving hourly updates from my friends. They'd left Cómpeta early this morning, driven to Algeciras and taken the ferry to Ceuta, the other Spanish enclave in Morocco. They'd hoped to clear customs and reach Rabat by the afternoon, but they'd been waiting for ages.

I found a news report saying, three days earlier, Morocco had installed thermal imagers at its entry points to check and prevent anyone with a fever from entering the country. Presumably this was the cause of their delay.

In the end it took them seven hours to cross the border.

"Did they check your temperatures?" I messaged, once they were on their way to Rabat.

"No, no checks here," came the reply.

Three days in and Morocco had already apparently given up testing incomers, including those from Europe's second most infected nation.

Morocco took on a new and darker feel. Now Covid had arrived, that multi-pawed bread in every shop, which had previously seemed amusingly unhygienic, now felt like the quickest way to an early grave. And could *any* food be trusted if cooked by someone carrying the disease? I didn't want to be unnecessarily paranoid about this, but I also didn't want to die, not yet anyway.

Chapter 14: Dream Sequence

Marrakesh

Today my mates were arriving in Marrakesh. Individually, three sets of friends from Spain had said they'd meet me on my tour of Morocco. After all, it was merely a hop across the narrow Mediterranean. Similar get-togethers had been promised on my previous travels too. But as these plans are usually the result of alcohol-fuelled exuberance, I don't ever expect anyone to turn up, which is just as well because they almost never do.

Of these three groups, I'd thought Gary's party the least likely to make it. He'd ditched his original idea of coming by motorbike and was instead bringing a carful with him, including one person who, for medical reasons, really shouldn't have been travelling at all.

They were scheduled to arrive at the hotel around one in the afternoon. Their journey had already been an ordeal, a three-hour drive to Algeciras, a ferry ride to Ceuta, that seven-hour wait to enter Morocco, and then another 200 miles on the motorway to Rabat, where they arrived close to midnight. And this morning, without a chance to see the city and perhaps sample a delicious camel's head, they were leaving early to cover yet another 200 miles. I really wasn't worth this much effort.

The hotel Gary had chosen was ten miles from the centre of Marrakesh. The handful of photos I'd seen made the place look great, but its reviews were a mixed bag. People talked fondly of its food and the entertainment team, but had been less kind about its reception staff, the bar staff, the quality of the rooms and the location of the hotel, in the middle of a vast and empty wasteland. Since few of the hotels I'd visited in Morocco had bothered with reception staff, and none at all with bar staff, and my rooms had been dodgy enough to include shower head explosions as well as previous occupant explosions, sexually speaking, Gary's choice would be a considerable step up the quality ladder for me and an opportunity to experience the other side of Morocco's hospitality industry.

But I had to get there first. I reloaded my bike and pointed it northwards. Stage One of what would be an excellent computer game was Escape the Medina. Weaving down the narrow alleyways, fingers hovering over the brakes, was exhilarating. I competed with mopeds and donkeys moving in both directions, people walking with and against me, sometimes criss-crossing in front, including at least one old blind man who tap-tapped his stick across my path. I would've gained 200 bonus points for whipping the cane out of his hand and using it to beat an old women to death – this game came from the same stable as Grand Theft Auto – but that seemed a bit mean.

Stage Two was Cheat the Streets. The alleys opened up and faster vehicles were added to the level, larger motorbikes and mini-vans. Stage Three, ramping up the speed even further, was Carriageway Chaos. Two lanes of traffic in either direction saw cars and sixteen-wheel trucks tearing past me but also sometimes blocking my route entirely, forcing me into the fast lane.

Stage Four was You've Arrived Too Early, You Pillock. I'd had so much fun screaming down the variety of Marrakesh's highways that it was all over too soon. I'd wanted to get to the hotel in plenty of time. I hadn't expected to get there an hour early. I couldn't check in without Gary and so I found a shady tree outside the hotel compound, near an abandoned and overgrown crazy golf course, took out my tablet and played a real computer game.

"We are on our way, matey. Should be 1ish," squeaked WhatsApp.

They were still on schedule. At least I'd only have to wait an hour. I returned to my game. A member of the hotel staff walked by me, eyeing me suspiciously. Their car finally turned up at quarter past two.

"Hello, matey! Good to see you," Gary said, crawling out. "Almost on time."

Phil, Mally and Dave climbed out too and all gave me a hug.

"Yep, good going," I said with a smile. "Just an hour and a quarter late."

He laughed.

"No, only fifteen minutes."

I suspected what had happened.

"What time is it with your watch?" I asked.

"Quarter past one."

"No, it's quarter past *two*."

Geographically speaking, the UK, Spain and Morocco are all in the same time zone. But because Spain's favourite fascist, Francisco Franco, wanted everything Hitler had, he changed his time zone to match Germany's, pushing it an hour ahead. This meant, upon arrival in Morocco, you'd set back your watch an hour, as Gary had done, and your food hygiene standards about 300 years.

However, in 2018, Morocco abandoned its twice-yearly clock change. Instead, in order to save electricity, they believed, they'd remain permanently on Summer Time.

None of this mattered. They were here now. And the fact that Dave had come with them was a minor miracle. Older than the rest of us and as thin as a stick, he wasn't a well man. In addition to suffering from asbestosis, he'd had cancer for years. He was due to have an appointment with his doctor the day they returned to Spain, ahead of a major operation in a week or two to remove several lumps from his stomach. He'd taken a lot of painkillers to get this far and keep that smile on his old face.

Riding in tandem, me behind the car, we entered the complex through a huge, salmon-pink archway into lush, tropical gardens. This certainly wasn't your four-euro a night sort of place. I bet they didn't get many visitors turning up on bicycles.

And into the lobby we went, the height of an airport terminal, with Greek columns, Trumpian gold tiling, an enormous chandelier and countless comfy sofas, a sumptuous cavern completely and utterly devoid of jizz stains.

Unlike what its reviewers had said, the staff were courteous and efficient, checking us in and strapping a blue armband to each of our wrists, the gastronomic and alcoholic equivalent of Willy Wonka's Golden Ticket, as much free food and drink as our stomachs and livers could cope with.

Gary had booked two rooms. Phil and Dave were sharing, choosing each other ostensibly because they both smoked and, self-sacrificingly, to save the rest of us the unpleasant odour and inevitable lung cancer. In reality, they knew Gary and Mally snored like adenoidal wildebeests.

We dumped our belongings and took ourselves, blue wristbands an' all, to the bar terrace. An azure swimming pool, the size of a lake, twinkled invitingly in the sunlight. And then, after 68 days without a drink, it began.

The problem with alcohol, especially after such a drought, is that, while social interactions are heightened, memory-forming abilities aren't. In my mind, my three days there merge into a happy, fuzzy-at-the-edges blob of joy, a dream sequence within a bike ride of often gritty Moroccan reality.

It started off with a G and T-fuelled discussion about how

they simply refused to take any money off me for the hotel. I wouldn't have come to a place like this, they said. It was their treat and I now had to shut up about it. So, as the drinks flowed, the discussion moved on in the way it usually did whenever we met up, which is to say overly loaded with bollocks, although its primary topic Brexit had now been usurped by the equally damaging Covid-19.

Our first evening meal was a buffet of gargantuan proportions. There's no point describing all the options. Whatever your imagination can summon was there, unless you're weird and want something like pickled dolphin in custard. Notably, although it was thoroughly international, one of the few nations barely represented was Morocco. Perhaps the local cuisine wasn't considered safe enough.

When it came to wine though, Morocco was here. In fact, the country's red, white and rosé were the only options available. That was fine by me. I wanted to see how the local stuff fared, especially in a country where no one's really supposed to drink it unless they're prepared to burn for all eternity. I adore wine, but not at *that* price.

Morocco has a long tradition of wine production, dating back to the Phoenicians, although it never had any real reputation. When the French left in the 1950s, output fell, with lots of viticultural land being repurposed. The industry was rebooted in the nineties under the rule of the current king's old dad, Hassan II – the lad clearly liked a tipple – and they now produce over fifty million bottles a year, employing 20,000 folk, almost exclusively for local consumption and, so the official website says, mainly to tourists. The vast majority of output is red and rosé. In fact, only 3% is white, but that's no great loss. Even to my unsophisticated palate – I can happily quaff that sixty-cents-a-litre tetrapak stuff they sell in Spanish supermarkets – today's Moroccan white was ropey at best. The burnt cherry red, however, was rich and velvety and tumbled down my throat as though quenching some primordial fire.

After an evening's entertainment by the hotel's in-house cabaret in an amusing if Butlins Training College sort of way, we retired. Well-sauced though I was, there was no amount of alcohol in the world that could knock me out when Mally fell asleep and opened up his nasal passages. Why am I telling you? I mean, you probably heard him yourself. So I collected my sleeping bag and ground mat and slept a contented night under the stars on the balcony. For such an expensive hotel, my experience was remarkably similar to camping.

*

"I can't believe you slept out here," said Gary, sticking his head out of the terrace door.

"I couldn't do it," I replied. "It was like trying to nod off at a Led Zeppelin gig."

Today wasn't going to be spent in an alcoholic haze. At least not the entire day. No, we took the hotel bus back to the centre of Marrakesh. Old Dave was in no state for athletics and, wilting slightly in today's 30°C heat, not far from Jemaa el-Fna, he requested a café break.

"You've got to try the mint tea," I said. "It's great."

A few minutes later, five glasses of hot sweetness arrived. Dave took a sip and wrinkled his face.

"Ach, that's fuckin' 'orrible. It's like drinkin' toothpaste."

As we sat there, a Moroccan customer approached the table beside us, one that contained a pile of msemen pancakes for sale. He leafed through them, one by one, before deciding not to buy anything. The guys looked on, mouth agape.

"And that's why the coronavirus is going to love it here," I said.

Suitably refreshed, and with minty breath and pearly whites, we hit the main square. So as not to get set upon by aggressive salesmen, my approach in Morocco has always been to show as little interest as possible in their products. Clearly, that wasn't going to be our technique today.

"How much is this then?" said Phil, fingering a black silk djellaba.

"Try it on, my friend," said the stall owner, smelling cash. "Try it on!"

The gown was thrown over his head. Phil examined himself in the mirror.

"Look, it's Florence of Arabia!" said Gary.

"No," Phil replied seriously, patting himself down. "I like it. How much?"

"For you, my friend, it is just 700 dirham."

"How much is that?" asked Phil to anyone listening.

"Seventy quid."

A sharp intake of breath or two later, he'd haggled the guy down.

"OK, my friend. You drive a hard bargain. Four hundred and fifty!"

Phil shook his hand.

"Who else wants one?" said the stallholder.

"Gary does," piped up Dave.

"Do I?"

Apparently, he did. Using negotiating skills that had clearly been wasted during his Navy career, Dave got the price down to 150. Gary received his goodies and Phil was mightily annoyed at paying three times the amount he needed to. Perhaps to average out his losses, Phil bought a second one at the new price.

"Anyone else?"

"Yeah, I'd quite like one of these," said Mally, feeling up a thicker, black-and-white striped winter djellaba, the sort I'd seen blokes wearing in the chilly Rif Mountain fog back in January. There was a lot more material to this style, and they did look wonderfully warm, and so when Mally got the price down to 350 and Gary confirmed he'd take it back to Spain for me, I decided I'd have one too. In ten minutes, the stall had shifted five djellabas and raked in almost £150. Meanwhile, having played the key role in negotiations, Dave disappeared and returned almost immediately sporting a fez.

"And now he's back, just like that."

"If you're wearing that, I'm gonna wear mine now too," said Phil after seeing Dave's headgear, taking the djellaba from his carrier bag and sliding it over his noggin.

"Me too," said Mally.

"Are you nuts?" I said. "Yours is a *winter* djellaba. It's boiling. And you're already fully dressed. You'll melt."

He sniffed dismissively and pulled his frock over his head.

"Nice, Dopey-Wan Kenobi."

But Mally was bullet-proof.

"Where did you get your fez, Dave," he said. "I wanna hat too."

The five of us, including two fancy dress Moroccans and one Tommy Cooper, trotted around the corner. When we emerged, Mally now also sported a neatly fitted skullcap. With his swarthy skin tone and slim grey beard, this Hertfordshire bloke, as English as possible, could easily pass as any nationality from here to Delhi.

We wandered the market a while longer, but it was clearly visible we were gullible chumps who'd buy anything and we felt the full force of the Marrakesh sales machine descend upon us.

"Look! You like?" came often.

"Please, my friend. My shop!" did too.

"Ali Baba! Ali Baba!" was another frequent if less comprehensible cry.

"We need to get out of here."

Finding a second café on the edge of the main square didn't relieve the sales pitch. In fact, now we were sitting still, we were an even easier target. Drunk on his haggling prowess, Dave did his best to encourage the onslaught, buying a 200-box of cigarettes and a fake Diesel watch.

The bus wasn't due to return for another three hours, but they'd had enough. Besides, there was nothing left to buy. We jumped into a taxi and were treated to fifteen minutes in the life of a rally car driver. We weaved backwards and forwards, slamming on or accelerating with a force that pinned back our cheeks like astronauts blasting into space. I'm not sure at one stage we didn't pass clean under a juggernaut. The lads enjoyed the ride a lot more than the cyclist we nearly totalled.

Back at the hotel, and after an alcoholic catch-up session, a re-animated Michael Jackson entertained us that night. His moonwalk was excellent and his crotch grabs legendary. He did a great job emulating the superstar. It was just as well there were no kids in the audience.

*

After the excitement of yesterday's excursion, today would be spent around the pool. I can't do that for long and so was thankful to spy a table tennis table. This was my chance for revenge. Whenever I play tennis with Gary, he beats me every single time and so comprehensively – 6-0 6-0 6-0 isn't uncommon – that I wonder what he gets out of it. I'm no table tennis expert, but I knew I was better than I was at tennis. I couldn't be worse.

"I like table tennis," said Gary, as he batted the first ball to me. "I had trials for Derbyshire."

My heart sank. No, I didn't win.

One of Michael Jackson's backing dancers, Adilah, came to play with us, a 23-year-old half-Moroccan half-Algerian woman. Joining her was Farida, a nineteen-year-old Moroccan, although she looked five years younger. She was in charge of the hotel's kids club, but, with none around at the moment, was at a loose end.

"This place is a lot quieter than normal," Farida said.

"Is that because of..."

"Yes, coronavirus. It worries me."

She told us Marrakesh had just announced its first case. The disease was hunting me down. More worryingly, the country had also suffered its first fatality.

We chatted for a while and the women were surprisingly open. Farida was particularly well educated, speaking Arabic and French, but also English, Spanish and Amazigh, one of the Berber languages. In fact, perhaps Adilah was a little *too* open. She wasn't keen on Moroccan men and told us about her Turkish boyfriend.

"But I'm still a virgin, you know," she said.

"That's nice," I replied, not really knowing what the correct response was. In your mid-twenties, is it a good thing not to have ever enjoyed sex? Conversation lagged for a moment. It was time for a new direction. "Do you like working here?"

They both nodded.

"Yes, it's great," said Adilah. "And the team is cool. It's hard work though. We do sixteen-hour days, six days a week, but we get 200 dirham a day."

"And you get a room and all your food?"

"Oh yes."

Board and lodging aside, she was earning three times what Marco the silver miner was making. That is, if he ever bothered to show up for work.

"Yes, it's fantastic. My friends are jealous of me."

Her phone buzzed. She looked at it and cheered.

"Good news?"

"Yes! I've got a new job!"

"Wow, that was quick."

*

I awoke on the terrace for the third morning in a row,

though this time encased in my lovely djellaba. It really was comfortable and warm, an outfit and a hug all rolled into one.

After breakfast, we packed up, carried our bags to the car and said our goodbyes. They had an overnight stay in Fes before catching the ferry back to Spain the day after.

"Thanks for coming to see me," I said. "I still can't believe you came, Dave."

I strapped my panniers to the bike and noticed he was watching me.

"You've got some big balls to do this, all by yourself," he said, shaking his head.

"No, I haven't. It's just a bike ride."

It's odd how many people believe this to be dangerous. It wasn't like I was cycling through a war zone, not this time. That said, the oncoming plague was adding a frisson of danger.

"When I'm back in Cómpeta, we need to go to the Tet," I said, talking about a local Moroccan restaurant, "all in our djellabas, Dave in his fez."

"Good idea!"

"Definitely!"

I looked at the old fella.

"Don't die, Dave," I said. "Not before then."

He chuckled.

"I'll try my best."

Unfortunately, his best wouldn't be enough.

Chapter 15: No Way Out

Demnate, Azilal and Beni-Mellal

It's always strange to cycle away from friends. Usually this happens at the beginning of a journey, when anticipation of what's ahead counters any sadness. Tempering the melancholy today was knowing I'd see them all again in just three weeks. At least that's what I thought.

To begin with the cycling was flat, trundling along Marrakesh's huge plain. There were forests of palms and distant mountains, the ones I'd traversed a few days earlier. Not long after setting off, I stopped for a drink of water. A young fella on an old moped pulled up beside me.

"Can I help you?" he asked.

"No, thank you," I replied. "I'm good."

"Where are you going?"

"Demnate."

His eyes widened.

"That is my town!" he shrieked.

"Is it nice?"

But he ignored that.

"Four hours on motor," he said, patting his machine. "You go on bicycle?"

"Yes."

He shook his head.

"No."

"Yes, I am."

"No," he said again. "Bye bye."

And off he went, put-putting up the road.

I was viewed with more suspicion today. My usual near

100% "Bonjour!" return rate was reduced to less than 50%. More people looked at me like I was an alien. Maybe it was simply because there were fewer tourists around here, or fewer people *benefiting* from tourists. Marrakesh sucks in those Moroccan villagers happy and able to deal with foreigners. Maybe the ones left behind would rather not have us here at all.

The scenery changed, from plateau to low hills to steep slopes. Three days off the bike shouldn't have affected my fitness, but perhaps alcohol-related dehydration was making this all seem like harder work than normal. Finally, I climbed the hill to Demnate and was more than happy to stop. I found a ten euro hotel. I didn't need the luxury of the last few days, enjoyable though it was. This'd do.

I walked around town and again received the odd looks. I saw only one other non-Moroccan, a guy with a large rucksack. What if this sudden unfriendliness was worry over Covid? After all, every case in the country so far – we were now up to five – had been imported. They didn't know I'd been here since this thing kicked off in China. I was as unlikely to have it as they were.

I wandered the streets and visited the market, enjoying the old odours of Morocco, those of caged birds and fish guts. There were a lot of people around, but in an area with so few tourists, I felt safer than I'd done in Marrakesh. Maybe I shouldn't have though. The town's Wiki page included this strange detail about the locals: "People are aware of E. coli and that all meat must be cooked thoroughly. Hand washing happens but not regularly or correctly."

I went for a tea and sat on the café's terrace. A table of lads next to me were discussing the virus while, at the same time, coughing roughly all over each other, as Moroccan men had always done. Now though, like yodellers or someone playing *Anarchy In The UK* on the bagpipes, they weren't something I wanted to be anywhere near.

I left and went to a snack bar to have a kefta sandwich. Before bringing my dinner, a kitchen assistant took himself out on to the street with a plastic washing-up bowl full of water. On the pavement he soaped his hands and feet in readiness for prayer. That sort of implied the snack bar had no facility to wash inside. Maybe this was what Wikipedia was on about.

And then, in a week of worrying news, I read some more. Should the virus reach Nador, that first fume-clogged town I'd cycled through on my entry into the country, then the Spanish authorities in Melilla, my exit port, would close its border with Morocco to protect itself. If that happened, what would I do? Live on a campsite until it was all over? Even on the Mediterranean coast, it'd soon be too hot for comfort in a tent. A spring morning could make it stifling inside. In summer, it'd melt my tent poles.

There was no point worrying about things I'd no control over, but maybe there was something I could do. I looked at the map and calculated that, cycling high mountains as well as distances longer than I'd ever done before, I could probably reach Melilla in six horrible days. But given the rapid progress of this virus, six days might still be too late. And then there was the danger that physical over-exertion negatively impacts your immune system. My escape attempt could itself bring me down. And besides, where would I be running to? Spain now had over 4,000 cases and had already suffered 86 deaths. It might be like cycling into a leper colony. I'd no home to go to in Cómpeta. Maybe I was safer in Morocco.

It was difficult to know what was the best option. Here in Morocco, with every bugger touching your bread, eating out anywhere or even buying anything that wasn't prepackaged could be dangerous. Maybe my food challenge needed to change. Rather than finding every dish Morocco had to offer, including my elusive quail pie, perhaps I should live without eating any food that had been exposed to air. Would it really be Snickers bars and Bonio biscuits all the way from now on?

*

Thoughts of the virus coloured everything. Last night, in a nearby room, someone was coughing up his guts. It wasn't like this didn't happen before in Morocco. It did, often, but it was just written off as some bloke with a cold. Now, whoever he was, he *definitely* had the virus and was a mortal threat.

Maybe, I thought, Morocco would change its ways, becoming more hygienic out of necessity overnight. But no. I bought some bread for breakfast. The shopkeeper picked up the loaf with his bare fingers, as they always did, and handed it to me, serving me a death sandwich and a smile.

Oh, the irony! On my previous rides, I'd always purchased travel insurance, even with its inflated price for my pre-existing high blood pressure. Insurance is like any form of gambling. Given enough time, and generally not very much time, the house always wins. Over those journeys I'd paid nearly £2,000 and hadn't claimed so much as an aspirin. For this trip I'd thought, "Bollocks to it!" I was going commando, so to speak, without the underpants of medical provision. But this had to be the occasion when a plague showed up! If I contracted Covid-19 over here, would I be left to wander the streets, infecting everyone I interacted with? Or would I be treated for free for the sake of public interest? Maybe I'd just be quietly shot.

The road climbed all day, first through forests, before the scenery became reminiscent of Andalusia's juicier green bits. The asphalt was narrow and, being on the way to the popular Ouzoud waterfalls, had plentiful fast traffic. Some of those cars came at me in the middle of the road. Maybe there was a price on the head of every disease-riddled European. The roadside unfriendliness continued too. You could see it in their eyes. Ey up, here comes Plague Boy! Although maybe not with that accent.

The hills only got bigger as the day went on, but they weren't anything like the size of those I'd done last week and yet I felt weary. Had I already picked up the virus in Marrakesh? As I approached Azilal, today's destination, a lad cycling in the opposite direction offered me a swig on his bottle of Coke. At least one person in Morocco wasn't worried about Covid.

There was a massive souk on the edge of town, covered in canvas. This only happened on Thursdays and had apparently been so located to enable those from surrounding villages to get to it as easily as possible. Of course, this now meant it could more rapidly transmit Covid around the region than other less well-thought out markets. Under normal circumstances, I'd probably have gone for a look, but I didn't because, well, people. Besides, I doubted I was missing much. Morocco had exhausted all it could show me in these small-town markets. There are only so many huge piles of olives you need in your life.

None of the hotels in Azilal looked great, but I picked the best of a bad bunch, a five-euro room with a shared bathroom. It was crummy but cheap and, under the circumstances, I'd have preferred my own facilities, but that wasn't an option.

As the grey clouds of the coronavirus passed over Morocco, so did *actual* grey clouds. The weather was taking a turn for the worse. It was a shame Gary had taken my toasty djellaba back to Spain.

I went out for a tea. With the colder weather I sat inside. On the café's television Manchester United were playing a Turkish team in an entirely empty stadium, which didn't help the creeping sense of apocalypse. A bloke sat down, oddly close to me. A little later I cleared my throat and he stood up and moved a few seats away. I felt better for that.

Walking back to my hotel I noticed a huge statue I hadn't seen earlier, something like a Brontosaurus, an entire skeleton of which had been found in the region. It was a measure of how preoccupied I'd become that on this small town's main street I could miss an actual life-sized dinosaur.

Nearby, a crowd gathered around a man making a speech in a language I didn't recognise, possibly the unique version of Tamazight for which the locals are famous.

"Plague Boy is amongst us. And he must be hunted down!" was obviously his message.

Avoiding any vigilantism, I returned to my room and looked at the news. One benefit of an authoritarian leader is that decisions can be made quickly. There's no fannying about getting things through a democratically elected parliament. And today a decision had been made: All Moroccan ferry ports were now closed until further notice. Although this ruling limited my options, I'd still be able to cross the Mediterranean just as long as the Melilla-Morocco border remained open. But would it?

*

I could hear another guy retching the next morning, this time in the shared bathroom. Wonderful. But five minutes into today – Friday the thirteenth – this still wasn't the worst thing that had happened. I'd woken up to news that all flights and ferries to Spain were cancelled and the borders with Ceuta and Melilla were now closed. In the distance, I imagined I heard a lone bugler.

The borders had actually been sealed yesterday afternoon. Gary and his carful of djellaba-wearing buffoons had been one of the last to squeeze into Ceuta before the drawbridge was raised. They'd made it back to Spain, just. But having arrived home, life was about to change for them all. Today,

Pedro Sanchez, the Spanish Prime Minister, announced a State of Alarm, which I believe is one level below a State of Emergency and one above a State of It'll Be Alright, Put The Kettle On. Tomorrow, the entire country would go into lockdown.

Whatever happened now, my plans had changed. Spain was only an option if I were prepared to wait this thing out, as well as handle the risk of being beaten to death here for the perceived danger I posed. But who knew how long that would take?

Alternatively, I could fly to the UK and the temporary shelter of my parents' place on the Isle of Man. But I'd never flown with my bike before and lacked the tools required to get it into a state an airline would demand to put it on board. It looked like I'd be taking my chances in Morocco.

And then came a ray of sunshine. I received a Facebook lifeline. After explaining my plight to the lovely folk who follow my *Europe by Bicycle* page, a guy called James kindly offered my bike a safe haven in Fes, the city I'd reach a few days from now, while I escaped Morocco. I suddenly had a new option.

But this presented another potential problem. At the rate the world was shutting down, a strong likelihood was that, between my booking a flight to Britain and landing there, all planes and ferries to the Isle of Man would be cancelled too. And then I'd be in the worst of all possible situations, homeless in the UK and with only the clothes I was carrying. Did I want to chance it?

I made a decision: I'd pretend none of this was happening. Things were moving too rapidly and no choice I made right now, especially regarding a flight out of Fes, counted for anything when it'd take me several days to get there. I'd continue as I'd originally planned, visiting the places I'd always intended to, and keep enjoying my time in Morocco, if that was possible under the circumstances. Maybe the whole thing would blow over. Perhaps someone would discover that rubbing seaweed on your gums and shouting "Expelliarmus!" cured even the most serious case of Covid. It was difficult to build my rescue rocket when its launchpad was constructed on shifting sands. By Moroccan immigration rules, I still had nearly three weeks allowable time here. Let's see how things were in a fortnight, I thought.

I left the hotel and pointed my bike in the direction of Beni-Mellal, a city of nearly 200,000. On the way out of Azilal I hunted for sustenance. This nation of once-friendly shopkeepers had changed. They wanted me out of their stores. One guy almost batted my bread request away. Eventually I found a patisserie with a girl behind the counter who served me sweetly. But yes, she still mauled my loaf.

Yesterday, there'd been cloud on the High Atlas Mountains. This morning, they wore a white cloak of snow. I wasn't sure how low it came, but it seemed a good covering. Even though it felt like months ago, it was only a week since I'd come over the Tizi n'Tichka pass. Maybe that wouldn't have been possible today.

I escaped the town and was happy to wallow in the rurality of the parts of Morocco in which few humans lived. When I did interact, it wasn't always mood-enhancing. The suspicious looks increased, and, at one point, a bloke on the side of the road yelled and gestured aggressively, a mime for me to clear out. Gladly.

For most people, though, disease aside, it was business as usual. A little boy stood at the roadside on one of the more remote stretches, offering a handful of herbs and miming a cigarette. Was he really a seven-year-old dealer?

And then I remembered why I was doing all this. An endless downhill slowly uncovered the stunning Bin El-Ouidane reservoir. It was probably all the more attractive for this year's lack of rain. Its water level was low, revealing islands and other features that would otherwise have been submerged. It had been constructed in 1953 by the same company responsible for the Malpasset Dam disaster in the south of France that killed 423 people six years later. That one had been breached due to excess water. The locals here were probably glad Bin El-Ouidane's levels were low.

And then excitement. At the bottom of the hill, by the lake's edge, was a sign banning photography. Why was that? Was this Morocco's Area 51? Did aliens visit the site after first studying the country's culture for decades? Unlike the E.T.s that landed in America, these ones wouldn't probe your bottom, but, having watched the locals, they'd almost certainly fondle your muffins.

Then came a dark tunnel, about 200 metres long, and, when I popped out the other side, I was confronted with Bin El-Ouidane's own enormous dam. Maybe this was why photos were banned. It probably wasn't the alien thing. The prohibition was a bit daft really. Snaps might be verboten but I could click on Google Earth and see it there instead.

Having reached the bottom of one side of the valley, I suffered a climb up its other, though I was handsomely rewarded with beautiful views as the ascending road followed a turquoise river far below. Eventually I reached today's highest point and knew it was all easy from now on. Rolling downwards, I saw a bloke pushing a car up the hill. Someone sat in the driver's seat, presumably trying to jump-start its engine. Why didn't they just turn it around and get it going downhill? And this was where the virus inhibited international relations. Normally, I'd have offered to help, but maybe they were a bit plaguey.

I turned a corner and saw an even greater view. From up high, I could see the town of Afourar 800 metres beneath me, sitting on the edge of Marrakesh's colossal plain. And it wasn't just the scenery. The local wildlife put in an appearance. I saw a snake, admittedly squashed on the road, but much better than that was my first tree-climbing goat. I'd given up on seeing one once I'd turned inland from Agadir, but here he was, halfway up its branches and nibbling on argan nuts.

Continuing downwards, I stopped at a panorama beside a twenty-something Moroccan couple.

"Nice view," the young fella said in excellent English.

We got talking. He lived in Tangier with his girlfriend. That seemed very modern for Morocco, but so did everything about this guy, including the way he dressed. He'd also recently showered in aftershave.

The conversation took an inevitable turn.

"The world's gone crazy," he said. "They announced the seventh case today, a tourist from Spain. By the way, what's your name?"

I told him and, caught up in my first pleasant Moroccan interaction since leaving the fancy hotel, we automatically shook hands. I screamed internally. I rode downhill towards Afourar afterwards as though I had a diseased paw.

But still my mindset wasn't prepared for avoiding danger. Cycling into Beni-Mellal, a guy on his scooter dropped his phone on to the road. Without thinking, I stopped and picked it up, handing it back. More stupid contact! Why didn't I just ask the locals to form an orderly queue and have them all spit into my mouth?

I eventually reached my target. The bloke on my hotel's reception coughed theatrically, but at least had the good grace to bend comically behind his counter and do it there.

I showered away today's potentially fatal encounters and headed to the hotel's café for a tea. The waiter stood way too close for comfort, nearer than anyone needs to stand to another human, unless they're actually having sex with them.

I suspect that, once this thing is over, those old-fashioned personal space abusers, the ones who used to be merely annoying rather than life-threateningly dangerous, will be cured of their affliction, either through repeated social admonishment or by being beaten to death.

I went out to look for food. Beni-Mellal was a strange town. Marrakesh aside, it was larger than anywhere I'd seen since Agadir, its streets full of cars but light on dining options. I walked about three miles before doubling back on myself and jumping into a place right next to the hotel that I'd originally dismissed. The only other eatery I'd seen was a McDonald's, but things hadn't got that bad yet.

Tonight's feeder was called Holy Food. I ordered the house special, the Holy Food pizza and chips. It contained every possible topping including something that looked like bacon, but in an Islamic country that wouldn't have been very holy. My dinner was accompanied by the joyous melody of another customer sitting close by and suffering what sounded like a life-ending coughing fit.

Let's face it. I was going to die.

Chapter 16: Run For Your Life

Khenifra, Azrou and Fes

Spain had closed down and Morocco was starting to. Events were moving quickly. The authorities understood the impact the virus could have on the country. It might be the fifth wealthiest out of Africa's 56 nations, but it was still poorer than Ukraine. With both cities and slums packing people tightly together and only a basic healthcare system, the situation looked dicey. Add to this cocktail the fact that every human within a two mile radius was legally obliged to finger your breakfast each morning, an apocalypse loomed.

Yesterday there was an announcement: All schools would close. The Moroccan ban on travel to and from Spain and Italy had also been increased to cover Germany, France and almost everywhere else that had registered a significant number of cases. The UK still wasn't on that list. I had a window of opportunity, a tiny window, high on a slippery wall without a ladder, but a window nevertheless.

Britain might already have had a higher number of casualties than Morocco, but hygiene standards were higher there. And surely a wealthier country would handle this better than a poorer one. So far here, the magic number, or really the *tragic* number, was just eight, and these were all foreigners importing Covid from abroad. If they were quickly isolated, if by some lucky break they hadn't yet passed it to anyone else, perhaps a tight lid could be put on this thing. Morocco could be safe. Should I stay or should I go?

Overnight, the statistics came in. The number of cases had jumped to eighteen, more than double, and, for the first time, this included Moroccan-to-Moroccan transmission. There wasn't going to be any lucky natural resistance or Allah-flavoured miracle. This was going to happen, and quickly.

There were other issues that influenced whether I should stay. I'd been in Morocco for seventy days. As a Brit, I could remain here for a maximum of ninety without any pre-arranged visa. If I wanted to stay longer, I could ask, but a yes wasn't a given. The normal practice was not to bother. Instead, travellers usually jumped across to Spain for a few days or popped into Ceuta or Melilla and then re-entered Morocco for the ninety day allowance to begin all over again. With the borders closed, these options weren't available to me.

There were *other* borders, but they were far from ideal. The closest to me, Algeria's, had been tightly sealed since 1994. Western Sahara, the land immediately to Morocco's south, was disputed territory. As it was de facto controlled by Morocco, this wouldn't count as leaving. Instead, I'd have to go all the way to Mauritania, on notoriously wind-battered desert roads, 1,500 miles away, to turn around and come back again. But would *that* border still be open by the time I got there?

Surely, if you were trapped here, Morocco's authorities would grant a visa extension? I thought so too. One Mexican had asked for one and been ordered out of the country by any means possible or else face arrest. Prison was a Moroccan adventure I'd rather have avoided.

With the plague rapidly spreading through a land unable to handle it and with visa extensions severely limited, returning to the UK was my only option. I replied to James, that kind fella who'd offered to house my bike in Fes. Yes, please, I wrote.

After another breakfast of omelette and choking fellow diners, I left behind the city of Beni-Mellal. Today's road – the main highway from Marrakech to Fes – was eerily quiet. Sometimes there was no traffic visible in either direction, and I could see for miles. Moroccans were being sensible. People weren't travelling unless they had to.

On this long, straight road, all that kept me occupied were some blue faded mountains in the distance. To relieve the tedium as much as my hunger pangs, I stopped at a garage for food, its restaurant completely empty.

"Is it open?" I asked a friendly petrol attendant.

"Yes," he smiled. "You want something to eat? I'll speak to the chef."

The cook appeared, a more sullen man. He grunted at me.

"Do you have food?" I said.

"You want a burger?" asked the petrol attendant.

This sparked an argument between them. The chef couldn't be arsed to make me such a hellishly complicated meal.

"How about breakfast?" the attendant said to me.

It didn't matter that it was half past one.

"Yes, whatever."

Tea appeared, along with a broken baguette and some oil to dip it in. It filled a hole. The food was accompanied by a small bottle of water. I twisted the lid and didn't hear its seal crack. They'd obviously refilled an old one with tap water. Whatever your view on Moroccan tap water, this was an especially bad crime in the light of Covid. Whose lips had already sucked this bottle?

Today's destination, Zaouiat Cheikh, was in a different league to yesterday's. Unfortunately, it was the Huddersfield and District Association Football League Division Four. The town clung mostly to a single road, with scruffy houses and a few businesses along it and then hovels further back. As always, there was an unfeasibly large number of people wandering about. I went for a tea and, yet again, the man on the table behind me sounded close to death.

Under the current circumstances, I wasn't sure about the wisdom of eating something made in the street, but I put things into perspective. Eighteen people had been taken ill in the whole of Morocco. Even if they represented only 1% of actual cases, this would still mean it was *highly* unlikely that anyone in this little village had it. Besides, that grilled meat sure did smell delicious.

The risk assessment was complete, won over by a rumbling stomach. I pointed to whatever was on the barbecue and received a scrumptious kidney, onion and harissa sandwich, sprinkled copiously with cumin and salt. It was so tasty I ordered a second. It was a shame I was being chased out of Morocco. I'd miss its street food.

I walked along the main road and was surprised to see a party of four Europeans. We eyed each other suspiciously. No wonder the Moroccans were giving me the cold shoulder if a bunch of middle-aged whities made me feel like grabbing a shotgun and loading it with silver bullets.

There were also Europeans in my basic six-euro hotel. A young, depressed-looking French couple were in the room next to mine. The only other room was taken by Germans, possibly the group I'd avoided in the street. I never saw them, but I *did* hear them. A lot. The hotel's tiled hallway rang out with angry Germanic shouting as well as weeping and wailing. Mixed with this were frequent bouts of heavy coughing, possibly from the Frenchies' room. Both these groups had, as of this morning, learnt they were stuck in Morocco, maybe even here in this shit town's shit hotel. At least I wasn't in their position.

While the sobs echoed around the building, and we all shared the single bathroom, I counted my own blessings. It was still possible to fly to the UK. At least for now. Could I get to Fes more quickly? Jump on a bus perhaps, if they'd allow bicycles, and get there in hours rather than days? But I'd be sharing its airspace with dozens of possibly infected zombies. The attempt to accelerate an escape could be my undoing. No, I'd stick with the bike. The social distancing it provided made it feel designed for happy plague-time travels. Besides, maybe Morocco wouldn't cancel all flights to the UK.

*

I put my head down and sped to Khenifra. The day passed with pleasant enough green scenery and a brain full of thoughts. The highlight of my day was passing a village called El Kebab, but I was preoccupied and nearly ran over a tortoise. It was on the road, obviously. I hadn't absent-mindedly ridden through a pet shop or anything. He retracted his wrinkly brown head just in time. This was hardly the stuff of Russian dashcam thrillers.

I got to where I was going and found a hotel. The woman on reception told me a room cost 280 dirham. After the single-figure euro bargains of the last few days, I said it was a bit expensive. The virus was turning Moroccan tourism into a buyer's market. She dropped the price to 230 and, before I had time to accept, it fell again to 200. Disease is the budget traveller's friend.

I greeted the internet with a smile and it blew a raspberry in my face. There'd been another ten cases of the virus in Morocco and the World Health Organisation had finally decided our little flu thing was officially a pandemic. The press had been calling it this for ages, because terrifying language sells newspapers. But at least we now had it from a credible source rather than Richard feckin' Littlejohn.

But in other news I learnt that Morocco *hadn't* cancelled flights to the UK, well, not specifically. They'd cancelled *all* flights, to everywhere and beyond. The country's borders were now sealed as tightly as the lips of the Vatican

Paedophile Investigation Squad, and I was on the wrong side of that barrier.

Still, they could hardly throw me in prison for requesting a visa extension now, could they? *Could they?* As we've already seen, this wasn't somewhere too hot on human rights.

"Could I extend my visa, please, officer?"

"No."

"B..but you've sealed me into your country!"

"Sorry. Say ciao to your new cell-mate. He's called Giuseppe. Don't worry about his little cough."

A wave of resignation washed over me. I was utterly powerless. Morocco was Simon Cowell, swaggering about confidently with his fulsome moobs tucked into his too-high belt strap, and I was little Louis Walsh, squeaking ineffectually in the background. But rather than cry about my new situation, or scream my head off – the response of last night's Germans – I'd take a more British approach: I'd celebrate my latest emigration. I now lived in a new country. Sod it. Let's get drunk! At the precise instant I made this decision, a huge thunderclap exploded outside my window. That's what you get for drinking in a Muslim country.

Luckily, Khenifra was a sizeable town, home to nearly 120,000, and one of the few locations in Morocco you can find a Carrefour supermarket. And, as we've already established, this company was one of the few reliable sources of alcohol here. There couldn't be a better part of the country to be stuck for the rest of my life.

The supermarket was a bit of a schlep away and I kicked through freshly formed puddles to get there. Something about this town appealed to me. It reminded me of Ukraine, and, although I may be in a minority, for me that's always a good thing. It even had a quirky side. A terrible roundabout statue consisted of three differently-coloured, really rubbish horses. And then I watched a baby stork floating down a slow-moving river on a small lump of polystyrene, doing an impression of a polar bear on a badly chosen iceberg. And once I entered the supermarket, it was full of sparrows. More of this kind of thing!

I made my purchases, which, for tonight's party, consisted exclusively of items a doctor would forcibly remove from your trolley – in alphabetical order – chocolate, crap sausages, crisps, fizzy pop and, most importantly, whisky. Any doctor, that is, except Doctor Feelgood.

"To a new life! Morocco!" I said, once back in my room, raising my plastic travel teacup, full of Scottish joy and fizzy apple juice, a cocktail I named Rabat-Arsed.

I went online to see how difficult it is to learn Arabic. Its alphabet has 28 or 29 letters, depending on who you ask, and that just represents the consonants. Each character looks different, often substantially different, whether it appears at the beginning, the middle or the end of a word and when it stands alone. And then, depending where you are, there are between six and eleven vowel characters. So that's a minimum of 118 symbols to learn before you can even start with words like "cat". That was a job for another day. Now was the time to get happily leathered. A thunderclap crashed outside.

*

The heat was off, the race to an airport over. I lay in bed lazily and went for breakfast as late as I was allowed to. The hotel restaurant was empty, which wasn't really a surprise, but it was more fully explained when I later read that, from today, all Morocco's restaurants, bars and cafés were closed. No one could accuse the King of treating this thing lightly.

Spain was taking Covid even more seriously. I saw a photo of Cómpeta, my cutesy, white-washed village of sugar cube houses, occupied by the army. It was a jarring image, feeling more like a promotion for an episode of *Black Mirror* than my friends' reality.

Lethargic, I stayed another night. I returned to Carrefour, not for alcohol this time – the party was over – but for food. Everyone looked at me nervously. Women especially went out of their way to avoid me, but there was nothing new about that.

Back at the hotel I sent an email to the British Consulate. Under considerable pressure from the thousands of holidaymakers trapped here, no response came back. If the borders were indeed sealed, there wasn't much they could do in any case. Maybe they'd lend us all a spade and we'd dig our way back to Britain.

And then came some better news. James, my Fes-based bicycle host, told me I could stay at his place. It turned out he wasn't in Morocco. He was mostly UK-based, but living in his home in Fes was a young Moroccan bloke called Amine, who'd be happy for me to stay as long as I needed. This level of generosity blew me away. It's one thing to store a bike for a month or three but a different thing entirely to let a complete stranger into your home. I enthusiastically accepted his offer. My future in Morocco was taking shape.

The day passed slowly, contemplating what lay ahead. My French-speaking cousin Sarah said she'd read Morocco was closing down completely at 6pm tomorrow. It was still two full days' cycle to Fes. Maybe taking this day off had been a mistake, but it was too late to beat myself up about it now.

As night fell, I lay on my bed in a daze, reading more and more news of a world slowly being eaten by the plague. A car travelled the dark streets outside, from its roof a loudspeaker barking incomprehensible instructions, well, at least to me. Maybe it was telling everyone to stay indoors, or perhaps he was just selling watermelons.

It felt dystopian. For the first time on my trip, I was scared. Is this how coronalife would be in Morocco, uninformed and cut off by language just when facts were at their most life-savingly valuable? Inadvertently breaking the rules in Britain would result in a smile and probably a small gift from the policeman who caught you – I don't know, it's been a long time since I've lived there – but not in Morocco. And a prison cell was no place for a cyclist's bottom.

*

The world into which I emerged this morning felt a very different one. I'd read all public transport was being carefully monitored, but a bus pulled up outside my hotel and people got on unchecked. But all cafés were now closed, and it was only once they'd gone that I realised how many there were in a typical Moroccan town.

Just up the road was a police check point, but as always they showed no interest in me. I'd see them regularly over the course of the day, even more than usual.

I needed bread and found a patisserie. Visible panic broke out as I entered the shop, fearful glances shared between staff members. Without even applying scary make-up, I'd become Freddy Krueger.

And then later, in a forest a long way from town, I had the same effect on someone else. A young, mask-wearing lad on a scooter was stopped at the side of the road, playing with his phone. He looked at me like I was there to collect his soul.

But not everyone was terrified. A little later, resting against a roadside tree, a bloke was slurping from a cup and called over to me.

"Coffee?" he shouted.

This was a strange day to receive such an invitation. Didn't he watch the news? Maybe he had a death wish. Or perhaps he planned to tempt me over and then end my plague-carrying ways.

And there were other kindnesses too. An old black BMW passed me and then stopped ahead. The driver got out and rooted through his boot for something. I feared he was looking for weaponry, but he presented me with two oranges and two apples. I cycled past, chanting my gratitude repeatedly, but I didn't want to touch anything I didn't need to. He looked sad and I felt awful. It was a lovely gesture but one with terrible timing.

In the small town of Had Oued Ifrane, people forlornly wandered the streets in search of cafés that no longer existed. And then a white European appeared in their midst, riding a bicycle. He was one of them! His kind had brought this disease and its inevitable economic destruction. They came over here all those centuries ago, sold us into slavery and raped our mineral wealth, and when we finally got shut of 'em, claimed our independence, and were struggling to find our feet – and succeeding! – they came back again with a new disease to finish us off. To be honest, even I'd have killed me.

And it wouldn't have been difficult. As I barrelled down one of their steeper streets, all it needed was for one malcontent to rush out and give me a nudge. I'd have been nothing but pavement paté.

Back into the woods, I stopped for lunch. I looked at the trees around me. If I had food and water, I could pitch my tent here and live out the plague away from other people. It'd be easy. Except for the not having any food and water part.

The roads got steeper and the scenery more Scottish, minus all the cacti obviously. Perhaps it was the weather. The sky was overcast. This was particularly annoying as reports had suggested Covid might be killed more quickly with heat. Just when we needed it to be plague-meltingly hot, Allah drew storm clouds over the country and sent the temperatures plummeting. Get your act together, man!

Sidi Addi was another small town, indistinguishable from all the others today. Its residents did their best to make me remember the place though. On approach, a man on a bicycle sneezed explosively into his hand, wiped it on his jumper and then gave me a big thumbs up. And passing through the village itself, two teenagers at the roadside softly chanted "Corona! Corona! Corona!" as I passed. There was something of a low-budget horror movie about their incantation. I was a ghoul they were exorcising.

Eventually I arrived in Azrou. If this morning's departure point had felt strangely Ukrainian, tonight's had a touch of Switzerland about it. I'm not sure whether it was the high green hills and the architecture, or maybe all the people walking about yodelling and eating fondue. I could've been mistaken about some of that. I still had a lot on my mind.

The hotel I'd read about here was also part-restaurant, and I'd worried perhaps, given the recent restrictions, it'd be closed. I found it and my fears were realised. As far as I knew, it was the only hotel in town, but a seedy-looking character, wearing a flasher's long, grey mac, came over and told me there was somewhere else.

I followed him to a little guest house, but the owner was taking advantage of the lack of tourists and having a clear-out, sending torrents of water cascading down her hotel's narrow stone staircase. She wasn't interested in re-infecting the place with someone like me.

Undeterred, I followed my guide into a much more expensive-looking establishment. Money didn't really matter right now. Barring severe mishap tomorrow, this'd be my last night in a hotel. At least it was open. The receptionist apologised when she put on gloves to handle my passport.

My opportunistic flasher was standing around, like a child waiting for a biscuit but without the confidence to ask for one. I put my hand in my pocket and extracted some coins. This woke him up.

"Twenty dirham," he said.

I gave him ten and he left without argument.

The room was great, with a bed so large I could've squeezed a female volleyball team into it. And the bathroom was perfectly adequate, but, as my DIY-loving mate Phil had said in Marrakesh of even our deluxe hotel, "it's the finishing that lets 'em down." The window only remained shut because it was wedged that way with a screwed up piece of toilet paper, one of the taps was broken and a tiled section above my head looked to be on the verge of collapse. And, remember, this was one of the more expensive places I stayed.

I searched online for a local supermarket or a convenience store in town and found nothing, but I did locate a patisserie. I went out to find it and have a look around. A lot of people saw me coming and moved out of my way. This must be what it's like to be Piers Morgan.

Azrou was an attractive little town, but it'd had its guts kicked out of it with all the restaurant and café closures. The locals looked lost. I found the patisserie and bought two French-style pastries that turned out to be excellent, on this, my last town before Fes. Why had it taken so long to find a decent cake?

On my way back to the hotel, some bloke shouted at me.

"Italiano?" he enquired.

With international stereotypes in mind, it felt a complimentary mistake for him to make. Clearly in his eyes I looked sufficiently sexy, tanned and well-dressed. It was only later I realised he was just accusing me of being a plague-carrying scumbag.

Tomorrow was Fes, hopefully. With things closing down more quickly than a BA in Childcare led by professor Josef Fritzl, nothing was a given. In any case, was this really a wise time to be heading into a large city, one with a famously labyrinthine medina and 1.4 million individuals, each with the ability to infect me full of plague juice? Hugely grateful though I was for James's kind offer of a home, I wasn't entirely comfortable with this arrangement. There were too many variables. In fact, I didn't know what all the variables were or how many existed. There was a variable number of variables and you can't get more variable than that. It'd be fair to say that, yes, there were nerves needing to be steadied.

*

Today I had a 16:30 appointment. In the centre of Fes, I was meeting Amine, James's housemate. His home in the medina was, by his own admission, difficult to find. Amine would show me the way. Now that hotels were closing down, missing this meeting might mean a rough night's sleep on the corona-coated alleyways of Fes's medina.

The route calculated by MAPS.ME told me I needed seven hours to get there, and so I was cutting it fine when, after a filling breakfast, I was on the road for half nine.

My mind was whirling. I was so focussed on the task at hand, I barely registered the scenery. I knew the day was going to start with a hill, but I breezed up that as though I were riding a 1200cc superbike. The weariness of the last few days had evaporated. A prediction to reach El Hajeb in two hours, today's first notable town, was smashed, arriving in 45 minutes. I was flying along.

I was helped by the weather, which remained overcast and cool. That was until halfway into the day, when the route bent eastwards and I was suddenly slammed by a fierce headwind, the strongest Morocco had thrown at me. Cycling into it was painful, especially when gusts picked up sand and dust and aimed them at my eyeballs. I put on a pair of sunglasses I'd brought for this purpose and had never yet used.

I hadn't received a "Bonjour!" all day. It was clear no one wanted me, or any other European, in Morocco. This didn't bode well for starting a new, if temporary, life here. I felt as welcome as Josef Mengele at a bar mitzvah.

As I approached Fes, battling the wind, the streets became grimier, the traffic heavier. Marrakesh aside, all the other large cities I'd visited in Morocco had been on the coast, lending them a sense of space. And my relatively quick entry into Marrakesh meant it hadn't felt like somewhere with close to a million inhabitants. But the seeming endlessness of penetrating the miserable outer regions of Fes made it feel like a mega-city.

Eventually, I reached its centre and headed towards our meeting point. I passed a small street market, a few dozen people milling about, buying fruit. They looked at me with disdain, like I'd sexually abused their favourite animal.

And then timing was everything. Here, just when I had an unhappy band of people within lynching distance, a piece of grit, launched by the breeze, stuck in my throat. I needed to cough, desperately, and yet this really wasn't a good time or place for a pale bugger like me to be expectorating all over town, visibly and contemptuously shedding his virus in the faces of the noble folk of Fes. I pulled to the side of the road and tried to clear my throat as subtly as possible, taking a swig of water. It really needed one huge heave to dislodge it, but it wouldn't be now. I chugged another half litre, but it wouldn't move.

I kept rolling through the streets. There was something intimidating about the place, a feeling I hadn't experienced elsewhere in Morocco since my first visit to Tangier all those years ago. Was Fes always like this or was it just that my mind was currently in a darker place?

There was a lumpy woman ahead of me. She was acting oddly. From a distance she looked like a drunk English tourist, dressed as she was in a red pixie outfit and a strange matching hat. Maybe she wasn't sozzled. Something about her movements suggested insanity. I stopped before I reached her for another drink of water, finally clearing away the grit.

She saw me by the side of the road and came over. Standing next to me, she mimed a spliff and then licked her palm with a fat, pink tongue, offering her hand in greeting. Even when there wasn't a plague, I didn't want that.

Finally, I found the Batha fountain, my meeting place with Amine, but, despite the wind, my adrenaline-filled legs had carried me here an hour and a half early. My map told me the old medina was just around the corner. With time to kill, I'd dip my head inside.

Aside from any apprehension I had, the alleyways here felt different to those of other medinas. They were narrower and less uniform, defying internal logic, feeling more ancient and cobbled together. And the effects of the virus were shocking. Having seen the bustle of Marrakesh, Rabat and Tetouan, the medina in Fes was broken. Almost everything was closed, shutters pulled tightly over people's dreams. Men sat slumped at the edges of the lanes and scowled, their livelihoods in tatters with the disappearance of tourism.

In one alley, just a few sweet pastry shops remained in operation, selling what they had while it was still fresh. I saw one with a mountain of chebakia in its window and went inside to buy some. I paid fifty dirham for a tiny bag worth a fifth of that. Either Fes was expensive or I was paying a Last Remaining Tourist surcharge. I'd cycled all day without food and so I also visited another stall and bought a couple of flatbreads. Both stallholders had looked utterly pissed off.

Being the only tourist left in Fes made me a target for every tout in the city.

"You want a hotel?"

"No."

"Something to eat?"

"No."

"You want hash?"

"No."

"What do you want?"

"Nothing."

"He wants corona," someone nearby said, which raised a chuckle from the djellaba-clad mob who sat around him. "Corona, corona, corona!" they chanted. I'd never felt more welcome, here in my new home town.

I kept moving, wanting out of there. Besides, I was due to meet Amine soon. I trusted my navigational instincts, but that was never a wise move, and while looking for my route back to the fountain, I got myself properly lost. I took out my tablet to peruse my map. An annoying kid wanted to give me directions for a price. I set off again.

"You don't know where you're going," he called after me. "Something bad will happen to you down there."

Christ, this was a much more full-on experience than any of Morocco's other medinas. A dozen or so seemingly random turns later, the fountain reappeared. I felt instant relief to be out of the oppressive lanes.

I waited and, earlier than expected, Amine arrived, a slim young fella. I was just about to say hello.

"It's this way," he said, pointing out another route into the medina and setting off at speed. I scurried to keep up. He wasn't taking into account I had a heavy bike to push, one that needed to negotiate large kerbs. He went around a corner and was in danger of disappearing. This was hardly the friendly introduction I'd hoped for. Great house-share this'll be! We came to a little downhill and I jumped on to my bike and caught him up. He stopped and looked at me.

"Ah, you didn't get the message," he said with a smile.

"No, what message?"

"Faux guides can be arrested. If the police see a Moroccan with a..." – he gestured towards me, looking for a word – "...a foreigner, it's a problem. Whenever I walk around Fes with James, I always walk several metres in front of him for this reason."

James had sent me a text to tell me this would happen, but I hadn't seen it. I'd just thought Amine was a bit rude. After too many twists and turns to remember, down dark and eerie passageways, we arrived at the nicest door I'd seen in the medina, a solid-looking wooden one with shiny metal studs. This looked promising. Amine opened it up and I walked inside. It was a TARDIS. The claustrophobic lanes outside became an inner courtyard with bright, white walls, three stories high, the space tiled with beautiful mosaics, classily furnished and finished with Moroccan paintings and statues. And this was my new home.

Amine gave me a quick tour of the house, which ended on the roof terrace. It looked out over the city and to the mountains beyond. Fes wasn't at its best right now, on this grey and blustery day. I assumed it'd look better when I eventually saw it in sunshine.

The loveliness of the house had calmed me slightly, but I was still a little freaked out by what I'd experienced in the medina. I was about to have a shower to wash away the dust and stress of the day, but before I could, I received a call from James.

"I've some good news," he said. "There's one last flight out of Fes. It isn't showing up on the airline's website, but I've a friend who knows about these things."

"If it's not on the website, how can I book it?"

"You can't. Just turn up at the airport and buy a ticket."

I was a maelstrom of emotions. I loved the house, and James and Amine both seemed like great guys, but in its current state I hated Fes. It felt evil, dangerous. I'd spent the last few days mentally preparing myself for my immediate future, one in Fes, but the house aside, the reality had been less appealing. I *could* make a go of it. I'd get through it. There hadn't been any alternative. But now a lifeline had appeared, an escape route. I could leave.

I took a few minutes to calm down, to think things through. It'd be sad, after all these miles, not to have seen more of Fes. I was particularly annoyed I'd miss out on one of the gastronomic highlights of this trip. Yes, the holy quail pie was the star quest, but like the Holy Grail, it'd always seemed unlikely to be found. But Fes was home to something that definitely existed, the meal I'd been looking forward to since the start, a dish all friends to whom I'd mentioned it had turned up their noses. Here was the stuffed camel spleen.

"I was in the medina today," I said to Amine, "and I didn't see any stalls selling freshly cooked food."

"No, they're open," he replied. "At least I think they are."

He described where they were. It was close to where I'd looked, but I could easily have missed them. Tomorrow's mission was the flight, but this evening's, my first and final one in Fes, was the spleeny delicacy.

It was still light when I left the house, but the streets would soon be darkening. In the alleyway outside the front door, I ran into one of James's neighbours.

"Ah, is James here?" she said.

"No, he's still in England."

We chatted as we walked, the woman talking fondly of James. And then the subject of the virus came up.

"I don't know who's doing it," she said, "but I hope they catch him soon."

It was difficult to respond to that. Did she really think that Covid-19 was the work of a Bond villain, living in a volcano and laser-beaming death-coughs to the world?

We parted company and after several wrong turns I found a street of butchers, one of whom sold stuffed spleen. Unfortunately, it was lamb rather than camel, but, worst of all, it was raw and he'd no facility to cook it for me. In fact, food wasn't being cooked anywhere as a result of the prohibition on restaurants and cafés. My mission had ended in failure.

I now had to find my way back to the house. In my haste to score a spleen, I hadn't considered how difficult this might be. Returning to the fountain this afternoon hadn't been too tricky. I'd stuck to the main medina alleyways, the wider ones, where my tablet's GPS worked. And if I'd got lost, I could always have paid for directions to the well-known landmark. An unknown house on an unknown lane among alleyways too narrow for my tablet to locate enough GPS satellites was a different story. Adding into the mix that it was now dark and the ancient tunnels of Fes were badly lit, usually by spooky sodium lights, things unravelled.

My house was marked on MAPS.ME with a bookmark pin. I found my way to within three streets of it, but the lane I needed on-screen didn't exist in reality. I looked around the alleyways at my various options, trying to remember if anything was familiar. It wasn't.

A lad of about eighteen approached me, asking what I was looking for. I showed the bookmark on my tablet. He thought for a moment and asked a passer-by for confirmation.

"Follow me!" I was reluctant to go. "It's OK," he said. "I'm not a guide. I'm a student."

Cycling around Europe had taught me to trust strangers. I'd received help in places as far apart as France and Russia, Greece and Norway. Morocco, especially Morocco's cities, had instead trained me to be wary. But surely not everyone was out to scam me.

We walked and talked. I wasn't at my most settled, just wanting to get back to the sanctity of the house. My non-guide wasn't helping.

"You have to be careful here at night," he said. "Bad people come out." Then he waffled something about every street having five things, a mosque, a hammam, a bakery and, oh I don't know, because I'd tuned out by then. And it was a load of bollocks anyway. My inner turmoil levels rose, remembering that I'd read of faux-guides leading gullible tourists down dead-ends and then presenting them with your-money-or-your-life alternatives. Today, I was that gullible tourist.

We were walking way too far, down alleys and back up others. There was no way this journey was the distance it'd indicated on my tablet. And when we went through a junction I was sure we'd seen before, I smelled a rat and stopped.

"We've walked too far," I said.

"No, it's this way. We are nearly there."

After several more turns, he came to an abrupt halt.

"It's just up there," he said, pointing uphill. "Go right and then left and that's your street."

"Really?"

"Yes. How about a little tip for my time?"

Ah, so he was a chancer.

"Come with me," I said. "If that's my street, I'll give you some money."

"It's up there," he repeated insistently.

"Come with me then. Why walk all these streets and not do the last two? Come with me if you want some money."

I set off walking. He tagged along.

"You don't believe me. You're calling me a liar."

"Yes, I am. Prove me wrong."

We came to a tiny square. The student started to talk to a woman sitting in it. There was enough sky visible for my tablet to work out where I was, information that, it has to be said, disappointed me. Before I could relay what I'd learnt, he piped up.

"Oh," he said. "I made a mistake. This isn't your street."

"No, it's not. In fact, I'm farther away now than when I

started. A lot farther."

"How about a little..."

"WHAT?" I exploded. In the whole of Morocco I'd been annoyed, vexed and agitated by idiot scammers, but I'd never been less than civil towards any of them. This time was going to be different. "You've got me lost. You said you weren't a guide. You *are* a guide. You're the *shittest* guide in Fes. Go away!"

"How about a..."

I bared my teeth. Anyone who knows me realises how ridiculous that sounds. I'm as aggressive as candy floss. Fortunately, this little tosser didn't know that.

"Go on. Go away!"

My tablet had given me a direction to aim for. I marched off. It looked like he was about to follow me, but wisely chose not to. I was livid, and a bit terrified, although I think the expression on my face might have made me look scarier than I was as I stamped around the dark medina. Pausing at one corner, another young lad approached.

"You can't help me," I said. "Go away."

"What, I..."

"Go away!"

It really was labyrinthine. While having more atmosphere than any other medina I'd seen, it was also scarier. It seemed designed to disorientate. Perhaps, under normal circumstances, when the place is full of visitors, I'd have had the option of following the crowds. But there *were* no crowds, just the occasional Moroccan shuffling through the gloom or a pair of shifty gits hanging around the shadows.

With intermittent help from my tablet, I hit a busier lane that I recognised, but I wasn't home yet. Street by street, I got closer and closer. A couple of dead ends and wrong turns later, finally, thankfully, there it was, my front door, only recognisable by its shiny studs.

I entered the house and slumped into a chair. Thank Christ I was leaving. Would this have gotten any easier? Presumably, with time. But how long would it take to confidently navigate the place? The medina contained over 10,000 businesses, none of which was a useful landmark when they were all closed.

"You alright?" asked Amine.

I told him what had happened and what I'd said to my idiot guide. He laughed.

"More people should treat them like that," he said. "I have someone for you to meet." A young woman was standing in the main room. "This is Sofia." I don't think Amine ever told me she was his girlfriend, but it looked that way. "She can take you to the airport tomorrow."

"That's great, thanks. I'll give you the taxi money of course."

"No," she said. "That's not the deal."

"Yeah."

"No!"

"OK, at least the petrol money."

"No, out of the question."

She was petite with longish hair framing her pretty face. Like Amine, she was a vet, mainly dealing with abused medina donkeys, but her surgery was all the way over in Casablanca.

Unknown to me, Amine was cooking food while I took another phone call from James.

"Dinner is ready!" Amine announced.

"OK, I'll just finish this call."

I didn't know who should get priority, the man cooking me a dinner I hadn't been expecting or the one who'd been kind enough to let me live in his house.

Amine had made a chicken tagine. By the time I sat down, Sofia had already eaten her share, but it didn't look like she'd had much. It did, however, taste great. Why couldn't your typical Moroccan restaurant make it as well as this?

We had a free-flowing conversation that frequently found its way back to corona, although we kept promising to change the subject.

Sofia was Arab while Amine was Berber.

"Is that a problem?" I asked.

"It can be," Amine replied, though his smile demonstrated it wasn't a problem for them.

He explained that Berbers were in the country long before the Arabs but have since been repressed by them. Amine held up a three-finger salute à la Ted Rodgers.

"What's that?"

"It means I'm Berber."

"Do Arabs have a signal?" I asked Sofia.

She shook her head.

I don't suppose there's a need for an Arab salute, a similar symbol of identity, when they're the ones with all the power.

"Berbers are not allowed to have Berber names," Amine said. "Amine isn't Berber. All names must come from a list, and on that list are only Arab ones."

Amine teased Sofia because she had a surname which implied a powerful connection, maybe something like Rothschild or Goldsmith might have for us, except that her link was to the King. Sofia played this down.

"No," said Amine to her, "remember when we were pulled over by the police that time." He looked at me. "As soon as they saw her name, one of them told the other that we had to be treated carefully."

I asked if they liked the King. They both did, especially Sofia.

"I like the King but not the government," said Amine.

"Who makes the decisions?" I asked.

"The King."

He wanted to know how popular the royals were in Britain.

"Some people like them. Some don't. But they've no power at all."

"Then that's pointless. I wouldn't like them if they were powerless and just spent your money," he said.

"And I heard your King is related to Mohammed."

Amine smiled.

"Yes, but I don't believe that. All the Arab kings claim to be related to Mohammed. How is that possible? And Mohammed only had daughters. The real line couldn't have been passed down."

This dismissal of female power was followed with a further explanation that included the phrase "only women".

"Oops," he said, as Sofia glared at him in mock-anger. "I shouldn't say that. Sofia doesn't like it. It's sexist."

Eventually though, our talk returned to the virus. Sofia said something that echoed what my conman guide had muttered earlier this evening as he was getting me lost in the medina.

"We are not scared of corona."

"Yes," added Amine. "We are good with death. Allah will protect us."

"You wouldn't think that from the way people have avoided me," I said. "I worry for Morocco." I mentioned the national sport of bread groping.

"If people followed the Koran, they would wash before every prayer, five times a day, and so they would be clean."

The two colds I'd had during this trip suggested that perhaps everyone didn't keep themselves so tidy, or maybe they didn't pray five times a day. In any case, you could be as clean as you liked but contagion would still seep out of your face.

"Science is useful and religion is useful," Amine said, "but we need to find a balance."

I wasn't going to start a religious argument. He was a nice guy and he'd cooked my dinner, but I'd prefer no balance at all. Let's calculate which side has defeated the most diseases and focus on that one. Let religion stick to what it's good at – making people feel better – but let's not think for a second it's going to provide any solution to Covid.

It was time for bed. We had an early start tomorrow. Amine and Sofia were both kind, intelligent people. It would've been nice to get to know them better. In this respect, it was a shame to leave tomorrow, but I needed to get home.

*

I didn't sleep a wink. Would I be able to get a seat on the plane? The prospect of escaping was exciting. The alternative, of being trapped in a nation where faith in Allah was the only defence against plague, was terrifying. I felt odd, stressed. When my alarm rang at six, I hadn't slept at all.

I got dressed, hoping Amine and Sofia wouldn't oversleep. A light flickered on somewhere else in the house. Excellent, they'd woken up.

"Steven?" came a disembodied Amine.

"Yes?"

"Didn't you get the message?"

When I'd packed my bag I'd put my phone in Flight Mode to save the battery for a long day. James had apparently texted me.

"No."

"Your flight has been cancelled."

A cannonball plunged in my stomach. I was staying after all.

Chapter 17: A New Home

Fes

So that was it, my final chance to leave.

I got undressed again and climbed back into bed. I felt deeply uneasy. I dozed, but never slept, feeling morose. I wondered what was happening to the other travellers I'd met on this journey. I knew my friend Juan from Murcia had already reached Senegal and returned to Spain just in time, but what of young Canadian Jackson I'd met on the ferry, Falkirk Steve and his motorbike, John and Nicole on their tandem, and that carful of dreamers taking a knackered old Renault 4 down to South Africa? At eleven, I opened the wooden shutters on the bedroom window to let in the light of a new day, my first as a reluctant resident of Fes.

I had a single job to do today and that was shopping. Even if I'd wanted to stockpile, this wasn't an option. I could only buy what I could fit into my rucksack, but the items had to be chosen carefully to last as long as possible. As the virus spread, going outside to shop would become less and less appealing. I walked the two miles to the Fes branch of Carrefour, a large one. Fortunately, there were no empty shelves as I'd seen reported elsewhere. Trucks were outside, delivering fresh supplies. Other shoppers once again gave me a wide berth, which suited me fine.

I filled my rucksack so entirely I also had to carry a few items in my arms. I lugged the heavy bag through the alleyways again. I'd memorised a foolproof way to get back to the house from the fountain. Doing it in the other direction was still tricky. Down a medina passageway a little girl strayed too close to this poisoned foreigner and she got a proper whop around the head from her granny. It would've seen Tyson Fury on the canvas.

Despite feeling more confident in my navigational skills, I realised I was vulnerable. If the businesses here stayed closed for much longer, people would get hungry. A non-local walking by himself and hauling a heavy rucksack, presumably full of food, wasn't going to have a great time of it. But there wasn't much option. Even in its wider alleyways, cars aren't allowed in the medina, let alone supermarket delivery vans.

Once at the house I climbed back under my cloud, drank tea and read for a bit. I got a strange, almost accusatory text from Nina, my girlfriend, that suggested I'd created this mess on purpose, or perhaps through my own incompetence. She was probably just aggrieved she was now under Spain's particularly tough lockdown. It wasn't like I should've been there to keep her company. We'd long ago realised we couldn't live together. And then my mum sent a message that broke my heart. She said she thought she'd never see me again.

I lay on my bed, still unable to sleep. Amine came home from work, coughing frequently. I hadn't noticed this yesterday and it made me feel even more vulnerable. I wasn't safe in my own, albeit borrowed, house. I could hide away as much as I wanted and Amine might still bring it home, like Tiddles dragging in what it thinks is a pigeon but which turns out to be one of those facehuggers off Alien.

My friend Elli in Switzerland messaged me, mentioning the UK Consulate services here in Morocco. I don't really do Twitter, but I was following the embassy's account. Elli's reminder meant I had a quick look to see if there was any new advice for the stranded.

Oh my word! Yes, there was. An updated list of flights had

been posted just a few minutes earlier. Actually, it was the same list as yesterday's, those which it had been impossible for me to reach in time, but with a single change, the addition of a Ryanair flight from Fes tagged on to the end. The tweet said there'd definitely be no more air services after these. This Ryanair flight would be the last one out of Morocco.

It wasn't all good news. The Embassy said there were definitely tickets available for all flights except mine. Maybe I could snap one up online. I raced to Ryanair's website and searched for the flight, but there was nothing at all going from Fes, not for today or the next six weeks at least. We were back to this morning's plan. I'd have to try to buy a ticket at the airport.

The flight was due to depart at 21:15. It was now 17:00. I raced around in a blind panic, unpacking my shopping and filling my rucksack with the things I needed to take with me. This really would be it, my last chance.

Unfortunately, Sofia had returned to Casablanca. I asked Amine how best to get to the airport. He said he had a taxi-driving friend and phoned him up. He wasn't in and we waited for a return call to find out if he was available. It took an age, every second reduced my chance of getting a ticket, if any existed at all. Amine's phone eventually rang. He looked at me and sadly shook his head.

"No," he said. "He's out of town."

"So how do I get a taxi?" I asked. "From Batha roundabout?"

And then I learnt about the needlessly complicated taxi system in Fes.

"You can only get a little taxi from there. That can take you to the train station. You can get a taxi for the airport there."

I said goodbye, not knowing whether or not I'd be back in an hour, and thanked him for his help. I legged it through the alleyways of the medina, aiming for the roundabout.

Obviously I got lost on my way there. I asked a few people for directions and they pointed me onwards. One old woman refused to answer this sweaty, plague-ridden idiot.

I popped out at the roundabout and saw a *petit taxi* was already waiting. There were two young women sitting in the back, but in Morocco taxis are to be shared. I ran to the driver's window.

"How much to the station?"

"It's on the meter," he replied.

"No, how much?"

"Twenty."

I yanked open the door and jumped into the passenger seat. With immaculate comedy timing, the two women threw wide their respective doors and fled with a shriek, a flurry of black gowns and dark fears. I was so focussed on reaching my flight, I didn't even feel guilty that I'd nicked their cab. Sorry, ladies.

The car shot out into the streets of Fes.

"The coronavirus is from China, is it?" asked the gravel-voiced driver, a man in his early sixties.

"Yes."

"They eat horrible things there." I thought he was going to list the country's dodgier dishes, like dogs and insects. "Rice," he continued. "Bleurgh! And chop suey."

I laughed.

"You don't like rice?"

He ignored me.

"And they eat pork!" Ah, the old Islamic fear. "Pork is dangerous," he added.

"Not any more," I said. "It was when the Bible and Koran were written. But it's safe now."

"Do you eat pork?"

"Yes."

He pulled a face.

"You should stop. What is corona from?"

"I heard it came from bats."

He wrinkled his brow.

"Bats? What are bats?"

His English was so good I'd forgotten he was speaking in a foreign language. I did a little mime.

"Ah, a bird mouse!" he said, which I thought a perfect description. In retrospect, he probably said "bald mouse", a literal translation of the less comprehensible French word for bat, *chauve-souris*.

I hadn't told him the purpose of my trip but he sensed my rush. He tore through the streets of Fes, both overtaking and undertaking.

"Where are you going?" he asked.

"Back to England."

"Married?"

"No."

"What is in England?"

"My mum and dad."

He liked this and put his foot down. Our masses neared infinity as we approached light speed.

We arrived at the station. I reached into my wallet and had nothing smaller than a fifty dirham note. He'd been quick, and entertaining. Besides, I needed to jump into another car.

"Keep the change," I said, handing him the money, feeling like I was in a Hollywood movie.

He'd liked that I was going home to my parents, but with the cash injection he was now *really* on my side. He yelled at the drivers of the larger taxis, trying to organise one for me.

"*Mata! Mata!*" he cried.

I assumed this was Arabic or Berber and meant something like "Quickly! Quickly!" rather than Spanish, in which it means "Kill! Kill!"

One driver lazily invited me into his cab. I climbed in the

back, but he wasn't going anywhere.

"Please leave," I said. "I'm in a hurry."

He sat there, not moving. After speaking English to the other driver, I'd forgotten where I was.

"*Vite! Vite!*"

He got the message. Sort of. We pulled out of the station, but he was perhaps the slowest, most cautious taxi driver in the whole of Fes. After what felt a lifetime, we arrived at Fes airport, a weird building that looked like an alien lair from a 1970s episode of *Doctor Who*. I almost threw my money at him and tore inside. It was six o'clock.

In the far corner of the airport hall was the ticket office. There was already a queue in front of its window. I joined it, realised it wasn't moving and so went directly to the front.

"We cannot sell any tickets until all the other passengers have arrived," said the woman inside.

"And when will that be?"

"Eight o'clock," she said, shrugging her shoulders. "Perhaps nine."

And breathe.

Suddenly all the urgency evaporated, but the uncertainty remained. My haste might not have been directly rewarded, but at least I was now in the queue. About ten people were ahead of me. As long as this flight had eleven spare seats, I'd be out of here.

But the situation wasn't ideal. As more joined the back of the queue, it started to bunch up. We were all standing way too close. I pulled the collar of my fleece over my mouth but had no idea how effective that might be. Things got worse. I could feel people, possibly infected zombies, brushing past me. I put my rucksack on my back and feigned interest in the airport's architecture, swinging it behind me to clear a space as I gawped at the ceiling.

An airport official, a man in his forties wearing a suit that may have once fitted him, started shouting at us to keep our distance. But there was no way to hold a position in this queue and make a space unless the people at the back moved first. What was the best course of action? To keep away from the crowd but then fail to get a ticket home?

The group's reluctance to disperse, as well as his too-tight belt, was increasing his anger. He was for disbanding the queue entirely. He looked like he was about to burst.

Luckily, a Canadian couple, the only two other white faces in the airport, were waiting for the same flight, and they had a helper, a young Moroccan woman who'd been driving them through the country. She was one of life's natural organisers and spoke to the manager, asking him to take our names in the order we'd queued, to ensure those who'd arrived earliest could buy tickets first. We'd then move away and maintain our space. He liked this idea. She'd defused a potential bomb.

Elsewhere, bombs had been allowed to explode. I later learnt the reason this flight existed at all was because, during a similar ticket grab in Rabat, a massive brawl had broken out among the wannabe passengers. In response, the authorities had closed the airport. Ryanair rescheduled that flight to leave from Fes instead, handing me a lifeline.

But this wasn't all good news. There weren't many passengers waiting for the flight here in Fes, but loads were being bussed in from Rabat, the ones who'd brawled for tickets. And they were running late. Maybe they'd stopped at a service station for another punch-up.

None of us knew whether the airport manager could be trusted. Flapping around in his crumpled outfit, he carried our list in his sweaty palm, but would he even use it? He'd got us all to stand a safe distance from one another, which was what he'd really wanted, but when it later came to selling tickets, perhaps he'd just do that in whichever way was easiest for him, maybe blowing a whistle and then throwing a handful of them into the air or have us compete in a *Hunger Games* style event in the airport lobby.

And he wasn't the only unknown. Two flights were leaving tonight, mine to Stansted and another to Charleroi in Belgium. Buses were arriving for that one too. How many of those waiting wanted tickets for that one instead? Maybe all of them. Perhaps none.

The clock ticked. Seven o'clock. Eight o'clock. Groups of people arrived and checked in to either flight, but we never knew if they were one of the busloads. Rumours spread among the passengers. We were still waiting for more people. Nine o'clock. Ten o'clock. One last bus was still due to arrive. Eleven o'clock.

The desk for the Charleroi flight closed. The odd passenger was still checking in to my Stansted flight two hours after it was due to have departed. I was ninth on the list of people waiting for tickets, but it counted for nothing if all the seats had already been sold, or if the manager "accidentally" lost the list.

Finally, at half eleven, we were told we could start to buy tickets. And what's more, they were using our lists. They decided to process the Charleroi flight first. More waiting followed.

And then it was our turn. We formed a line, nervously anticipating whether we'd actually be able to leave. As if there wasn't enough tension, a shriek came from the front of the queue as a man scurried off and away towards security, a man who wasn't on the original list.

"He's just bribed them!" someone yelled near the front.

Too far down the pecking order, the bloke had used his cash and Morocco's corruption to score himself a seat, possibly mine. He was now safely on his way to the plane.

The queue shortened. There were seven in front of me, then five. Still, the woman kept selling tickets. They would run out at some stage, but when?

And then it all came to a crashing halt. The stress of dealing with such nervy passengers for the last several hours had broken the poor saleswoman. She left the office to get some fresh air and a coffee. She was visibly shaking, her make-up running.

We waited and watched the clock. It was ten to midnight. The Moroccan authorities had said absolutely no more flights of any kind, repatriation or otherwise, would leave after today. Even if I bought a ticket now, my plane wouldn't be leaving before twelve.

The saleswoman eventually returned, still looking shaken, but got back to selling. There were four passengers ahead of me, then two. Finally, it was my turn.

"Just one bag for the hold," I said.

I was carrying my tent and sleeping bag. If all boats to the Isle of Man had been cancelled by the time I reached the ferry terminal and I was stuck in the UK for months on end, I'd rather be homeless with a tent than without. But its bag contained metal poles, not dangerous in themselves, but certainly enough to be rejected by security.

"No, there is only hand luggage tonight," she replied.

At five past midnight, I was finally handed a boarding card, tired and relieved, but the ordeal wasn't over yet. I still had to clear security with the dodgy contents of my bag and show my passport, the one with the missing gold on its front.

The last passengers were coming through. The only people behind me were an American couple and a bloke travelling by himself. Security didn't care about my metal poles, but the passport check took ages. By the time he let me past, only one person was behind me.

I scurried through the airport to my gate, down the passageway, across the tarmac and to the front steps of the aircraft. I'd be the penultimate passenger on the last flight out of Morocco. I climbed the staircase and entered the plane. An ocean of faces stared at me, most of them wearing masks.

It suddenly dawned on me why I was there. The nervous excitement of the last seven hours, the anticipation of waiting for a ticket had diminished the fear of proximity to people. All that mattered was to get out. But the terrified eyes, their faces hidden behind masks, brought it all back. And many of these had been sitting here for hours, breathing. If one of them arrived with Covid, they probably all had it now.

I found my seat, one by the window and next to two bemasked women, and squeezed in, stuffing my too-large rucksack under the seat in front. Ryanair flights are cramped at the best of times. With nowhere to put my feet, I felt like a battery chicken.

The plane waited. This wasn't over until the wheels left the tarmac. Another ten minutes passed. It was now half past twelve, well into the day on which there'd be no more flights. I willed the wheels to move using all the Jedi powers I could muster.

Slowly, they started to turn. We manoeuvred around the airfield. We were leaving, actually leaving. The plane stopped and then thundered down the tarmac, its nose tilting upwards, and we climbed into the sky. In the darkness outside my window, the lights of Fes twinkled beneath me. I was going home.

Thank you to every man and woman involved in that stupid fight at Rabat airport. I wouldn't have been here without you.

*

We weren't finished. What would I find in the UK? There was talk of a Spanish-style lockdown. That wouldn't help my chances of making it all the way to Heysham, the ferry terminal to the Isle of Man on England's north-west coast.

The plane was too tightly packed. With my rucksack

filling the space where my feet should have gone, sleep was impossible. This was the second night in a row without any.

I arrived at Stansted at four in the morning and was surprised how many people I found there and how casually they milled around. The mood was very different to the one I'd left in Morocco. In fact, had I not known about the virus, I wouldn't have guessed anything was the matter. Of course, Britain would pay for this complacency later.

I looked at my options. My original plan had been to catch a National Express coach from Stansted via central London to Preston, find a hotel to overnight there and then jump on the train to Heysham the following afternoon. But who knew when the country would lock down or the ferries would stop? Time was everything. And this arrangement involved a lot of public transport, which didn't fill me with joy.

Then an online friend suggested I hire a car at Stansted and leave it at another location. That sounded expensive, but when I calculated the cost of the coach, the hotel and the train, there was hardly anything in it. It'd be much quicker *and* keep me safely away from everyone else, for their good as well as mine. This wasn't the time to penny-pinch.

The car hire companies didn't open until six and so I'd a couple of hours to kill. As I might already have contracted the virus on the plane, I did my best not to murder any fellow travellers. I bought a coffee and took it outside, sitting on a bench away from the warmth of the huddled masses indoors. The frozen air made the world out here feel sterile and safe.

I was lucky to get a car. With so many people fleeing international locations on any available flight, landing at an airport hundreds of miles from where they'd parked their vehicles, everyone's plan was the same as mine. Only a handful of rentable cars remained at Stansted.

The roads weren't as empty as I'd expected. I crawled across the country, the radio on loud to keep me awake, but, after no sleep for nearly 48 hours, I was fighting a losing battle. The window was down to blow refreshingly cold air into my face, but it wasn't doing the job. Just before I hit the M6, I saw a car at the roadside on its roof and realised I'd be joining it if I kept this up.

I pulled into a service station, ready to sleep. My phone pinged. It was a message from Dave, my brother.

"What ferry are you on? Hope you get here today. There's talk of shutting down travel to the island."

It wasn't just a case of reaching Morecambe, where the car drop-off point was. From there, if I wanted to avoid public transport – and I did – I needed to walk four or so miles to the ferry terminal. If I kept driving and didn't end up in a ditch, I might just have made it in time for this afternoon's ferry. But it would've been tight, and that ditch was looking more and more likely. No, I needed to sleep, even if it was just for an hour. I couldn't find any official news to say the island was about to close and so I'd risk missing this ferry and catch the one at two in the morning instead. I wound my seat back, closed my eyes and within seconds was skipping through an orchard and being chased by machine gun-toting grannies.

An hour later I woke up, feeling much better. I made it to Morecambe without incident and wandered for ninety minutes through industrial estates and along dual carriageways to the ferry terminal. It's not a route I recommend.

By the time I got there, evening had fallen and the temperature with it. The boat wasn't for another six hours, if it was leaving at all. I tried one entrance to the terminal building, but it was locked, as was the second. I walked around the site and finally found an open door. I later learnt this had been left unlocked by mistake. Whoever's fault it was I thank you, as once inside, even though the terminal was supposedly closed, the heating was on. I found a comfy sofa and tried, and failed again, to catch up on a little sleep.

The terminal slowly came back to life. Yes, there was a ferry, but there wouldn't be many more. Two o'clock in the morning came and I was joined on the boat by a scattering of other passengers. I'd never seen it so empty.

Only the day before, the Isle of Man government had introduced a mandatory quarantine rule. Everyone arriving on the island had to self-isolate immediately for fourteen days. That had been my plan in any case. The last thing I wanted to do was to import the plague into my mum and dad's. The old fella in particular had a history of lung problems, having emerged from the womb with a cigarette in his mouth. Corona would finish him off.

On the boat we were all given forms to fill in, about where we'd come from and how we could be contacted. I handed the completed paperwork to the plague officer.

"I have a question," I said. "Is it allowed for me to walk from the ferry terminal to where I'm staying?"

"I don't see why not," he replied. "Where's that?"

"Port Saint Mary."

His eyes widened and he sucked in a breath.

"It's a long way, fella."

I knew that, but if it meant I'd avoid public transport and my folks didn't have to pick me up, it was a sensible, if slightly knackering option. So what if I only had my cycling sandals to walk in and I'd had just an hour's kip in the last 72. I'd survive.

After the calmest of crossings, at around six in the morning, the ferry arrived in the island's capital, Douglas, just as daylight emerged. I stepped out into the day's cool air and began a sixteen-mile trudge to the southern end of Manxland.

I only saw a handful of people, one man walking to work, a couple of runners and a cyclist. Four and a half hours later, after numerous bouts of dancing to remove the gravel that had sneaked into my sandals along the way, I arrived home with tender feet.

"Come into the house," my mum said, as I stood in the garden.

"No chance. Keep yourself away from me."

"I want to give you a hug."

"You can't. You'll have to wait a fortnight."

She shook her head.

"What are you going to do?"

"Just go inside and I'll set up my tent here in the garden."

"A tent? That's mental."

"No, it's not. It'll be fine. Camping's what I do."

"You can't do that. What are you going to do for a toilet?"

"Have you got a bucket?"

Luckily, she did.

*

The time in the tent, my new home, passed painlessly. Continuing the run of good weather I'd had throughout Morocco, it only rained once. Temperatures though were low, but each afternoon about three, as the sun finally made its way into the back garden, my tent was filled with a warmth that always sent me off to a happy dreamworld. I had a lot to catch up on.

All day long I read, listened to the radio and played on my tablet. On the fifth day, for something to do and after all that cajoling from those Moroccan barbers, I shaved my head and cut off my now jihadi beard. My new minimalist Dachau Look matched the current mood of the world.

I reflected upon my trip and my lucky escape. I learnt that, in my absence, Morocco had closed down even more tightly than Spain. Just to go shopping for food involved downloading a form, filling it out and presenting it to an official before being granted permission. Worst of all, that paperwork was only available in Arabic. Lockdown in Fes would have been a very hungry one.

I'd really enjoyed the bike ride. I'd seen some great places and sampled plenty of wonderful food, even if a lot of it might not have been to everyone's taste. But I hadn't got to try my stuffed camel spleen, let alone my special quail. There was unfinished business. One day, when the plague was over, I'd return to Morocco, pick up my bike and see the places I didn't get a chance to, like Meknes, Moulay Idriss, Volubilis, Oujda and Fes itself. I'd eat that stuffed camel spleen. Who knows, maybe I'd find the Holy Quail.

It was that time of day again, the one which had recently here become known as Howard O'Clock, after the first name of the island's Chief Minister, its numero uno. This was the hour at which he gave a daily update on the current virus situation, the number of new cases and the government's plans for the future. It was also the time that drinking could respectably commence.

The Chief Minister and his deputy were impressive guys, talking in a way that inspired confidence. How did a tiny island of just eighty-odd thousand have a couple of leaders like this when neither England nor the US could manage one between them?

And then I heard Howard's surname. After all my hunting in Moroccan bazaars and souks, perhaps I'd finally found what I was looking for. The spelling may have been different, and there may have been no holy connection, but in these plague-filled times we all have to make compromises. My quest was complete. Ta very much, Howard. Sorry, I should show more respect. Thank you, Mr Quayle.

THE END

Epilogue

At the time of writing, early July 2020, the Isle of Man has been clear of the virus for several weeks. Through solid leadership and well-disciplined community spirit, life has returned more or less to normal. In order to provide residents with somewhere to travel, an air bridge has been created to Guernsey, another island free of Covid. The Isle of Man isn't known as the most exciting of destinations, but at least now we can travel to one place even worse.

Meanwhile in the UK, Boris Johnson dithers. For a prime minister who famously wanted to be another Churchill, the only similarity is the tens of thousands of countrymen killed through choices he made, or didn't make, and, in Johnson's case, without the Second World War as a good excuse. The death will continue. The UK is still struggling with the virus even as lockdown restrictions are eased.

Morocco closed down entirely the day I left. Keeping people indoors and away from each other's bread, they got a hold of Covid and, three months later, by June 18th, only 9,074 had caught it with just 213 deaths. However, although borders remain closed, Morocco then started to relax restrictions and, as tales in this book predicted, the numbers quickly shot up. In the nineteen days since, there have been another 5,533 cases. It looks like it'll be a while before I can pick up my bike.

Not long after my quarantine, old Dave, my fez-wearing mate who came to Marrakesh, was rushed to hospital. His planned cancer surgery had been cancelled while Spanish hospitals focussed on Covid. Sadly, he died a couple of days later, one more victim of a disease he didn't even contract.

Also from Steven Primrose-Smith

The No. 1 Amazon International Bestseller
NO PLACE LIKE HOME, THANK GOD
A 22,000 Mile Bicycle Ride around Europe

After a near fatal illness, Steven Primrose-Smith decides that life is too short to hang around. Inspired, he jumps on his bicycle to travel a road that stretches 22,000 miles across the whole of Europe.

During his ride through 53 countries, climbing the equivalent of 20 Everests, he dodges forest fires, packs of wild dogs and stray bulls, is twice mistaken for a tramp, meets a man in Bulgaria who lives under a table, discovers if ambassadors really do dish out pyramids of Ferrero Rocher at parties, transforms into a superhero after being savaged by radioactive mosquitoes near Chernobyl and comes close to death in France, Norway, Ukraine and Russia.

Such a massive challenge requires calories and Steven gets his from the more unsavoury elements of European savouries: brains, testicles, lung and spleen stew, intestine sandwiches, sausages famous for smelling of poo, a handful of maggots and even a marmot. Nobody eats marmots.

But the distance and his culinary adventures are only a part of the mission. His real objective is much more difficult. Will he be able to confirm something he has long suspected or will he, after all his searching, eventually find somewhere in Europe worse than his home town of Blackburn?

"There are many books about cycle touring but few are as entertaining, informative and engaging as this one...The result is a funny and informative account of his travels to some of the Continent's well-known and more undiscovered corners. The writing is excellent..." – **CYCLE Magazine**

The No. 1 Amazon UK Bestseller
BIKING BROKEN EUROPE
6,000 Miles through an Unstable Continent

Europe is not what you think it is. Nestled within the stability of a continent that has changed remarkably little in nearly a hundred years, there are many pockets of discontent, unstable regions that want out of their current host nation.

Some of these movements are long-running jokes or the dreams of idle fantasists, but many are supported by millions and, in a few cases, thousands of people are dying for their cause.

After his bestseller *No Place Like Home, Thank God*, Steven Primrose-Smith wants to see a different side of Europe. Here, he cycles over 6,000 miles through thirty-nine of these wannabe nations, often through substantial regions of Europe you may never even have heard of.

Various governments warn you not to travel to Transnistria, Abkhazia and Nagorno-Karabakh, three of Steven's wannabes, frozen and not-so-frozen bloody conflicts. This time he's wearing a cycling helmet.

Amazon reviews for *Biking Broken Europe*:

"A great story, very well told. This book will appeal to non-cyclists every bit as much as cycling fans. The humour is sharp. The observations of the tough life in Eastern Europe bring the situation to life without being judgemental."

"I've read all of this fella's travelogues so far and really enjoyed them. This was certainly no exception. Witty and engaging, but interspersed with some profound insights as to the nature of nationalism and the conflicts it causes. Also, this fella will eat anything!"

HUNGRY FOR MILES

Cycling across Europe on £1 a Day

After blowing all his cash on his previous long-distance bike ride (*No Place Like Home, Thank God*), Steven Primrose-Smith wants to go cycling again. Without the necessary funds, he decides to see if it's possible to travel thousands of miles on a budget of just £1 a day.

Against advice, he puts together a team of complete strangers, including a fresh-faced student, a Hungarian chef, and a man with the world's worst bike, the beard of a goblin and a fetish for goats.

While cycling from Liverpool to Gibraltar through England, Wales, France, Spain and Portugal, they plan to supplement their cash-strapped diet by fishing and foraging. It's just a pity no one knows anything about either.

People quit, nerves are strained, and faces and bikes are both smashed. Will anyone make it to Gibraltar?

Amazon reviews for *Hungry for Miles*:

"A very humorous and frank account of an extremely difficult challenge and I really enjoyed reading it."

"Another great book from this author, easily as good as No Place Like Home. You know you are reading a good book when you can't put it down and are sad when it comes to an end...good fun and highly entertaining."

"He's obviously one of life's top blokes. He can strike the balance between fact, fiction, humour, sadness and in this case famine...Thank you for sharing your intelligent wit and passion for all things good..."

The No. 1 Amazon UK Bestseller
ROUTE BRITANNIA
A Spontaneous Bicycle Ride through
Every County in Britain
Part 1, The Journey South and **Part 2, The Journey North**

Tired of seeing Britain continually attacked by the media, politicians and the British themselves, Steven Primrose-Smith wants to see it for himself. All 97 counties of it! Surely it can't be as bad as everyone tells him.

After twenty years living abroad, he thinks the time is right to search his homeland for the best of British using new eyes, those of a foreign tourist, and in the only way he knows how – by bicycle. Armed with a list of recommendations gathered from friends and strangers alike and the most spontaneous of routes, he pedals 5,000 miles through damp English country lanes, soggy Welsh moorland and windswept Scottish mountains. He gets wet quite often.

Following on from the success and irreverent style of both *No Place Like Home, Thank God* and *Hungry for Miles*, Steven seeks out the quirky in the people he meets, the places he visits and the food he eats.

Can his initial store of positivity survive the journey, or will it be ground down by the traffic, the weather and his British, vegetable-free diet of beer, pies and pork scratchings?

Amazon reviews for *Route Britannia*:

"Steve's done it again; he's written another enjoyable cycle tour book. It was another page turner."

"Have really enjoyed Steven's other two cycling books...This was no exception."

The No. 1 Amazon UK Bestseller
GEORGE PEARLY IS A MISERABLE OLD SOD

Seventy-year-old British ex-pat miserymonger George Pearly lives on the Costa del Sol, all alone except for his ancient, three-legged dog, Ambrose. George hates his life and everybody in it. These feelings are mutual. Everyone hates George too.

From this unhappy equilibrium the situation quickly deteriorates. First, George discovers he is dying of a mystery illness. Then his 35-year-old ape-child nephew, Kevin, moves into George's tiny and once tranquil home with a passion for Vimto, Coco Pops and slobbing around in his greying underpants. Worst of all, George's neighbours start to disappear and all accusing fingers point towards George.

Pull up a sun lounger, grab yourself a piña colada and enjoy a murder-mystery romp on Spain's sunny southern coast.

Amazon reviews for *George Pearly Is A Miserable Old Sod*:

"A bit like Tom Sharpe on speed – ridiculous plot, outlandish characters, unbelievable situations – great. Whizzes along and is great escapist stuff and light reading."

"Loved this – George Pearly is indeed a Miserable Old Sod and very funny with it – couldn't put it down."

"This book made me laugh out loud, much to the embarrassment of my son. Original and quirky."

LOVE AND OTHER COMPLETE WASTES OF TIME

It's 1986 and Adam is Evie's mysterious high school crush. On the night that she's determined to take it to the next level, Adam suddenly disappears, presumed murdered.

After pining over his memory for twenty-nine years, Evie accidentally stumbles upon Adam in a supermarket, now inexplicably disguised as a pineapple and claiming to have just been released from prison. But something doesn't appear to be quite right about him. In fact, nothing seems quite right. He's stuck in the 1980s in more ways than one.

Evie is torn. Despite being the doting mother of her eight-year-old son and happily married to a successful lawyer, she finds herself unable to resist this blast from the past. But when she eventually learns Adam's amazing secret, Evie makes a rash decision that threatens to destroy everything she holds dear and leave her little son howling motherless throughout eternity.

Amazon reviews for *Love and Other Complete Wastes of Time*:

"Really funny and slightly mad...I enjoyed every single minute of it."

"An enjoyable little book that kept me hooked to the end. The little revelation at the end came as a bit of a surprise to me; I didn't see it coming."

"Just read this and read it in one go. A bit of time travel, space travel, the eighties, life long regrets and some action. It's brilliant."

HOW NOT TO BE A UNICORN

Mothers just want their children to be happy. That's why, when five-year-old Gary says he wants to be a unicorn, his New Age mum does everything in her power to make it happen. One night, while he is sleeping, she superglues a horn to his head. His life will never be the same again.

Follow the ups but mostly downs throughout forty years of Gary's unicorn life, as he struggles with his mum and her army of lovers, one sister who thinks she's a mermaid, another who's a personality-morphing nutjob and little brother, Mikey, a perpetually two-foot tall, fur-covered troll. Along the way are unicorn hunters, religious sects, rubbish superheros, crucifixions, duels, escaped lions, cannibals, immaculate conceptions and Nazis but mostly lots and lots of ridicule.

Like Gary, you can be whatever you want to be, but be careful what you wish for.

Amazon reviews for *How Not To Be a Unicorn*:

"Steve's done it again; he's written a thoroughly entertaining good book that's a real page turner. I enjoyed following the story of Gary the Unicorn through his sad pathetic life; a bit of a loser he may be but he's a loveable loser unicorn :)"

"What a great, entertaining and quirky book, but I've always loved this author, so I expected no less!"

"Another fun and entertaining read from this quirky writer! Loved it. Just glad I didn't grow up as one of the Jacksons!"

Printed in Great Britain
by Amazon